D1564828

NATIONAL
GEOGRAPHIC

EXTREME
WEATHER
SURVIVAL GUIDE

Firefighters escape
a burning blaze in
eastern Oregon.

EXTREME
WEATHER
SURVIVAL GUIDE
Understand · Prepare · Survive · Recover

THOMAS M. KOSTIGEN

NATIONAL GEOGRAPHIC

A mile-wide tornado kicks through north-central Kansas.

CONTENTS

HOW TO USE THIS BOOK

WE INVITE YOU to use this book many times and in many ways: casual browsing, focused reading, and for reference when you need it. Because much of its advice and information pertains to times when reading is difficult—time is of the essence, power is down, other demands are more pressing—the best approach would be to roam and absorb the chapters on weather extremes you are most likely to face, so you know the basics and the organization of this book if and when catastrophe hits. Here is a guide to the features you will find in every chapter.

All content and information published in this book is provided to the reader "as is" and without any warranties. The situations and activities described in the book carry inherent risks and hazards. The reader must evaluate and bear all risks associated with use of the information provided in this book, including those risks associated with reliance on the accuracy, thoroughness, utility, or appropriateness of the information for any particular situation. The authors and publisher specifically disclaim any responsibility for any liability, loss, or risk, personal or otherwise, which is incurred as a consequence of the use and application of any of the contents in this book.

CHAPTERS each focus on a weather extreme and begin by providing a general overview.

BEST PRACTICE boxes collect advice from the experts and agencies most experienced in handling these emergencies.

EXTREME WEATHER BASICS boxes explain the meteorology and estimate how timely and accurate today's forecasting methods can be.

EXTRA FEATURES include "Good Idea," "Did You Know?," and "Gear and Gadgets," all ways of sharpening your emergency responses.

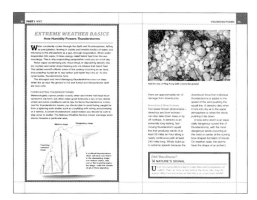

FIRST-PERSON stories share lessons learned from disaster survivors and others who have handled weather extremes.

EXPERT Q&As in every chapter include observations of scientists and other professionals in weather extremes present and future.

HOW TO sections conclude each chapter with two pages each on how to prepare, survive, and recover from each weather extreme.

DOS AND DON'TS are divided into "Indoors" and "Outdoors," creating organized checklists for before, during, and after.

Flooding from the Souris River breaches a highway in North Dakota.

GET READY

A hurricane is coming. Do you have a plan? Should you leave home or stay put? Do you know how to access local alerts? At home, are you better off upstairs or downstairs? Is your yard in order? Where would you go if you had to leave home? Do you have what you need to make it through a power outage? What about family members? What about pets? Perhaps you've faced such an emergency. Were you ready? Did you even know what to do to be sure you were ready? Many face those questions in the heat of the moment, but it's best to think the answers through carefully, long before the storm begins. This book tells you how. It will help you understand, prepare, survive, and recover.

We seem to be getting slammed harder and more frequently by extreme weather—with record-breaking temperatures, storm intensities, property destruction, and even fatalities. The news is filled with catastrophic events—Hurricane Sandy brought epic destruction to New York and New Jersey in 2012; monster Typhoon Haiyan wrought havoc in the Philippines in 2013; and a dip in the polar vortex in 2014 made Chicago colder than the South Pole's summer temperature. In many places, summers are hotter, winters are colder, and new weather records seem to be set all the time.

What's causing all this destructive phenomena? Why do they appear to be happening more frequently than they used to? Is climate change to blame? If so, how and in what instances? We'll discover the answers to these questions and more in the pages that follow. What seems to be certain:

Did You Know?
⬎ YOUR EMERGENCY KIT

Here is a basic checklist of contents for a household emergency kit, useful no matter what the weather throws your way. Keep it in a safe, accessible place where everyone in your family can find it.

Also, make sure to tailor your emergency kit to meet your needs. There may be need for additional medical supplies or senior, baby, or pet care products. Customize according to where you live as well. Include rain gear or winter gear depending on your locale. Think hard about what you might need under the worst conditions.

Your kit should contain:
• Water for every person in your household. That means one gallon per person per day. Keep a three-day supply in case of evacuation and a two-week supply in case you get confined to your home.
• Food that won't spoil and is easy to prepare. Canned goods or ready-made dry food products that have long shelf lives and are made specifically for emergencies are good choices. Also keep a three-day supply on hand in case of evacuation and a two-week supply in case of home confinement.
• At least one flashlight and an extra supply of batteries
• A battery-powered radio or one that can be powered by a hand crank. If possible, a NOAA Weather Radio is ideal as it provides a steady stream of weather reports and alerts.
• A first aid kit. A ready-made kit is ideal as it contains different types of bandages, antibiotics, tapes, and medical tools as well as an instruction booklet.
• Any medications that you or your family require. A seven-day supply is recommended, and these should be updated to account for any possible expiration dates.
• A multipurpose tool such as a Swiss Army knife or Leatherman
• A whistle or other shrill noisemaker and a brightly colored bandanna to use as signals
• Matches or butane lighters
• A two-week supply of personal hygiene items such as toilet paper, soap, and those for feminine hygiene
• Copies of important papers and personal documents such as birth certificates, passports, and insurance policies
• A mobile phone fully charged with a backup battery and charger
• "In case of emergency" contact information
• Some cash or currency
• An extra blanket
• A map of your location and surrounding area

Abnormal is the new normal—we need to learn to expect the unexpected.

The general mantra for an emergency is to plan and prepare in order to survive and recover. In fact, everyone can take three actions to remain safe during any extreme weather event. The first is to get informed. The second is to make an emergency kit. And the third is to have a plan.

The information in this book goes a long way toward helping you achieve these three steps. Here, you'll learn how to prepare, survive, and recover for and from just about every kind of extreme weather event—from driving in blizzards and whiteouts to preparing to take shelter from a tornado; from beating the heat to battening down for a hurricane; from building a seawall against floods to following nature's signals to determine if a storm has passed.

Steps to Safety

First, you and your family need to agree on a basic action plan. An agreed-upon plan will keep you safe in times of trouble. It will also give you peace of mind knowing you can lean on it to help yourself or others in need. Set up a meeting with all members of your household. Talk about how best to prepare and respond to emergency situations. Alert everyone to the types of problems that may arise. Identify tasks for each member of the household, and discuss how you can work together when an emergency arises.

For example, if there is a flood, who's in charge of moving furniture to a higher, drier place? Turning off the power? Or getting the sump pump going? If a tornado is reported, who's responsible for making sure everyone is accounted for? What about pets—who is minding them? If a heat wave hits, can elderly family members care for themselves? If not, who will look in on them? Assigning responsibilities such as these ahead of time makes for a well-organized, swift, and safe response to disasters.

Also, it's important to plan what to do in case you are separated during an emergency. Meeting places need to be chosen—one nearby in case of, say, a fire. And one in a different area in case you need to evacuate your home.

It's also wise as part of your emergency plan to have

emergency contacts saved on your mobile phones and identified as ICE, or "in case of emergency." Emergency responders are trained to look for these labels on mobile phones.

More tactically, agree on an evacuation plan, and make sure everyone understands what to do. This means knowing what route to take and how to get to your agreed-upon meeting place. Have different options in case you cannot leave in a vehicle, and choose different locations to meet. If you know of a local shelter, you may want to identify that. Then practice your evacuation procedures twice a year. Don't wait. Start planning and preparing—now.

Don't forget that technology can be extremely helpful during emergency situations. There are apps that provide weather updates directly to your smartphone or tablet. You can also text to find local shelters. You can use websites (such as the American Red Cross Safe and Well website) to let your family know that you are okay.

Good solid preparation will allow you to maintain control over your emotions when a disaster hits. Staying calm and focused are critical practices that every emergency responder knows can make the difference between life and death. Knowing that you need to stop, drop, and roll if you catch fire, or that you should never take refuge under an overpass during a tornado—these are lifesaving lessons, and having them at hand to follow will muster courage and emotional control when most needed.

Of course, you cannot experience the extreme weather event until it happens, but you can prepare for it by doing drills, talking through plans, and keeping well informed. And you can take steps to mitigate dangers. Many people, for example, don't check or change their smoke and fire alarms frequently enough—every month is recommended. Nor do people realize that hard objects left loose outside—such as outdoor furniture—can become flying weapons during a storm. Little facts like these could save lives.

With more extreme weather events occurring now than in the past, we have to brace for a new kind of survival. Learning how to prepare, survive, and recover from extreme weather events is—like it or not—an integral part of life in the 21st century.

Lake beds are drying up due to increased droughts.

PART 1

W

"AND THE WATERS EXCEEDINGLY UPON

RAINFALL It is refreshing. Part of Earth's life-enhancing cycle, rainfall distributes fresh water and replenishes our drinking supply, allows crops to grow and livestock to feed, helps our rivers to run, and fills our lakes and reservoirs. But extreme rains can wreak havoc on human life and on nature. Including the storms that accompany it or the floods that come, too much rain can mean disaster.

Average annual rainfall on the planet is 39 inches—a little more than 3 inches a month. If only rain fell in accord. Rather, it comes in patches, sometimes violently. Some regions receive an annual deluge while others thirst for rain year-round. Mount Waialeale on Kauai, Hawaii, can receive more than 450 inches of rain a year, while Puako, on the northwestern coast of Hawaii's Big Island, receives less than 10 inches.

The likelihood of lightning, hurricanes, or tornadoes accompanying precipitation varies tremendously as well. Regions near warm bodies of water, especially the oceans, and high mountains see more lightning strikes than anywhere else, because combined heat and moisture bumping up against land create perfect storm conditions.

Hurricanes and typhoons form over warm ocean waters and begin to weaken once over land, so coastal regions feel the brunt of their force, but regions inland can still see wind and flooding downpours.

Tornadoes form out of supercell thunderstorms, given certain conditions—conditions best provided by the configuration of the North American continent. Worldwide, 80 percent of all tornadoes happen in the United States and on the Canadian plains.

PREVAILED
THE EARTH" — GENESIS 7:19

Is there more rain coming? More severe storms and more flooding after? No one can answer that question for sure, although data indicate that Earth's precipitation rate has increased slightly over the last century, with the continental United States on average receiving 5 percent more precipitation than in 1901.

But more rain does not necessarily mean worse disasters. The intensity of a storm, its path, its duration, and its unpredictability often mean more in terms of natural and human impact than the amount of rain the storm brings. And your preparedness will make all the difference in how wetter weather impacts your home and family.

A thunderstorm crosses a highway in the Nevada desert.

Lightning
strikes
high in the
mountains.

CHAPTER 1

THUNDERSTORMS

It's a warm spring evening at an outdoor festival. Families are eating, playing games, and listening to live music when suddenly the mirth descends into mayhem as the weather takes a turn. The skies open up, unleashing a volley of grapefruit-size balls of ice propelled by winds reaching 70 miles an hour. Parents huddling over their children are pummeled with the enormous hailstones, people run to cars seeking shelter only to be showered with shattered windshields, and families become separated in the chaos.

Such was the scenario when a supercell thunderstorm ripped across Fort Worth, Texas, on May 5, 1995, during the annual Mayfest; 400 people were injured, 60 were hospitalized, 4 critically. Remarkably, nobody attending Mayfest was killed. But as the storm moved into Dallas County, it was engulfed by a squall line that had been following it, and together the storms merged into something entirely different. In 30 minutes, three inches of rain fell; in some portions of northern Dallas, rain fell at rates approaching nine inches an hour. Massive flash flooding ensued, and hundreds of homes, businesses, and vehicles were damaged by hail and winds. The roof of an industrial plant in Dallas County collapsed, a boy was struck by lightning at a birthday party, and high water forced two area hospitals to close their emergency rooms.

In all, 20 people died and hundreds more were injured. Most of the victims drowned; two died from lightning strikes. The

---

FEMA BEST PRACTICES SEVERE DOWNPOUR

If you are driving and find yourself caught in a severe downpour, leave the roadway as soon as possible and park. Turn on emergency flashers and remain in the car until the storm passes. Make sure to avoid touching metal or other surfaces that conduct electricity inside and outside the vehicle.

National Weather Service (NWS) calls this 1995 storm "the most damaging non-tornadic severe thunderstorm in the United States, and perhaps world history." It racked up economic losses approaching $2 billion.

Compared with other extreme weather events, thunderstorms are often small in dimension and short in duration. Think of a thunderstorm as a cluster of traffic congestion on a weather map:

An average thunderstorm measures 15 miles in diameter and typically takes only 30 minutes to travel through an area and then move on or dissipate.

But in spite of their diminutive size and brief existence, thunderstorms can pack a devastating punch. Of the estimated 100,000 thunderstorms that occur each year in the United States, about 10 percent are strong enough to cause serious damage. And

FEMA BEST PRACTICES TO AVOID INJURY

Be aware that lightning, hail, flash flooding, and tornadoes can accompany a severe downpour. To avoid injury from lightning, find protection in a secure building, but refrain from seeking shelter in open structures such as picnic shelters and sheds. If you cannot find shelter, avoid high ground, water, tall trees, and metal objects that can become electricity conductors.

Drivers should use caution when crossing flooded roads.

Severe weather, such as this storm, can appear without much notice.

the dangers they inflict—from injurious hail and tornadoes to flash floods, bursts of lightning, and wicked winds—demand our attention.

What Is a Thunderstorm?

What makes a thunderstorm so dangerous? At its most basic, a thunderstorm is a rain shower accompanied by thunder and lightning. It transforms the energy of the atmosphere into a powerful engine, at times violent. Thunderstorms have three stages in their life cycle.

In its developing stage, a cumulus cloud grows upward as a rising column of warm, humid air called an updraft feeds the growing cloud. The cumulus cloud becomes a "towering cumulus" when it takes the shape of a tall column as the updraft continues to develop. At this point, things are relatively mild; there may be occasional lightning, but little, if any, rain.

The storm enters the next phase, the mature stage, as the updraft continues to push the storm up. If you are in a setting where you can see the entire cloud, you will see the anvil-shaped thunderhead building atop the cumulus tower. Eventually precipitation begins to fall out of the storm, creating a downdraft of air cooled by the rain. When the downdrafts hit the ground and spread, they produce a line of gusty winds—a gust front. This mature stage is associated with most thunderstorm

The Midwest and central United States often produce the right thunderstorm ingredients.

activity, signaled by lightning and its thunder, hail, heavy rain, strong winds, and possibly tornadoes.

Eventually, the dissipating stage begins when enough precipitation is produced that the downdraft overpowers the updraft. Meanwhile, at ground level, the gust front extends far from the storm and cuts off the warm, moist air that was fueling the thunderstorm. Although lightning may continue, rain declines and the storm eventually dissipates entirely.

Thunderstorms vary in strength; they are classified as "severe" when they contain one or more of the following: hail an inch or greater in diameter, winds gusting in excess of 50 knots (57.5 miles an hour), or a tornado.

Know Your Thunderstorms

Thunderstorms come in a variety of configurations; learn the types of storms to know what to expect when you hear alerts or observe storm clouds building.

Ordinary Cell: A cell storm contains a single updraft and downdraft. These thunderstorms are generally short-lived. They may produce hail and gusty wind, but they are usually mild.

Multicell Cluster: Thunderstorms often group in clusters with numerous cells in various stages of development merging together. The cells in a cluster act individually, but they form a kind of chain reaction, with one

---

Did You Know?
⬊ THUNDER WARNINGS

Thunder is the sound made by lightning. As lightning passes through the air, it heats the air quickly, up to an astonishing 50,000°F—five times hotter than the surface of the sun. The air expands from the heat, then quickly cools, creating vibrations and a sound wave that we hear as thunder.

You can figure out how far you are from a flash of lightning by counting the seconds between when you see the lightning and when you hear the thunder. Take the number of seconds and divide it by five; the answer is the distance between you and lightning in miles. So, for instance, if you count 20 seconds between lightning and thunder, it means the lightning struck roughly four miles away (20 ÷ 5 = 4).

Normally, you can hear thunder about ten miles from a lightning strike—which means you are within reach of dangerous lightning and should seek shelter immediately.

cell maturing and moving downwind as another cell forms above it, over and over.

You can tell how many individual cells are in a cluster by listening to the thunder. Note which direction the first thunder you hear comes from; the sound will increase in volume as it nears, then decrease as it passes. Each successive round of nearing-receding thunder coming from the initial direction will indicate how many cells there are.

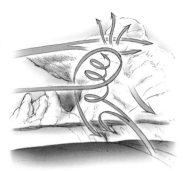

Supercell thunderstorms create massive winds and can last for hours.

Multicell or Squall Line: At times, thunderstorms form side to side and create lines that can extend laterally for hundreds of miles. Called squall lines, they can be long-lived because they essentially feed themselves, with new cells reforming at the leading edge of the line. Updrafts and downdrafts can become quite powerful, resulting in episodes of large hail and strong gust fronts. Tornadoes can form here, but the leading edge of a squall line more often creates "straight-line" wind damage.

Supercell Thunderstorms: A supercell thunderstorm is an intense, long-lasting, self-perpetuating single-cell thunderstorm. Winds in its updraft can surpass 100 miles an hour, and the storm can create massive

---

Did You Know?
⬊ SHELF AND ROLL CLOUDS

Few cloud formations are as ominous as shelf clouds, which are often found along the leading edge of a squall line. The imposing wall of wedge-shaped cloud is a result of warm, moist air at the front edge of the storm being lifted by rain-cooled air behind it, produced by the storm. When the warm air condenses, the shelf, attached to the thunderstorm, forms.

A rare cousin of the shelf cloud is a roll cloud, which looks like a giant tube of clouds rolling along the sky. Roll clouds may begin as shelf clouds, but they detach completely from a thunderstorm.

An ominous squall line sweeps in from the Timor Sea, north of Australia.

hailstones and strong tornadoes; similarly powerful downdrafts threaten property and lives. Most of the tornadoes in the United States—and most hail larger than golf balls—are produced by supercells.

Supercells occur when the winds are veering or turning clockwise with height, producing a change in wind speed and direction that causes the storm's updraft to begin rotating as a "mesocyclone," corkscrewing from near the ground high into the storm. Although all supercells are the product of this dynamic, they are divided into three groups based on visual characteristics. There are "rear-flank" supercells, which result in little precipitation, and there are "classic" and "front-flank" supercells, which are high-precipitation events.

Most supercells are the classic type, with expansive, flat bases, usually with rain or hail falling from part of the base. They often have a wall cloud extending down from the base. A wall cloud can be a precursor to a tornado, because supercell tornadoes usually occur within wall clouds.

Will Thunderstorms Get Worse? There is not yet consensus among experts as to whether we will see more or stronger thunderstorms in a warmer world, although there are reasons to believe that might occur. As the atmosphere warms, it can hold more water vapor than a cooler

An umbrella provides little protection in heavy rain.

atmosphere. Because heat and humidity supply the energy that drives thunderstorms, the extra energy could make thunderstorms stronger, and the extra water vapor could create heavier rain.

Is our world in for heavier rains? Probably so, says the Intergovernmental Panel on Climate Change in its 2013 report, judging by recent history: "It is likely that since about 1950 the number of heavy precipitation events over land has increased in more regions than it has decreased. Confidence is highest for central North America with very likely trends towards heavier precipitation events."

Heavier rains do not necessarily turn ordinary thunderstorms into destructive supercells, however. It takes winds that are veering or turning clockwise with height—called "vertical wind shear"—to supply the spin that creates a supercell's mesocyclone, the ingredient that makes a thunderstorm a supercell.

Some models of future climate show vertical wind shear decreasing in a warming world, which would reduce the number of supercells, while ordinary thunderstorms would grow stronger and produce more rain. One 2013 climate model study, however, found that most of the decrease in vertical wind shear over North America east of the Rocky Mountains should occur on days when the atmosphere lacks the energy needed for supercells. Days with enough energy for supercells should also have the needed wind shear, the study found. If this study is correct, we could be in for more thunderstorms, including supercells.

Lightning Hazards

Lightning occurs in every thunderstorm, even when it is not visible. And although we know it well for its dramatic display and the damage it can inflict, the physics behind it aren't completely understood. For instance, we are still not sure how a thunderstorm cloud initially gains its charge. By some process, the movement of air, cloud droplets, and

Continued on page 30

NATIONAL STORM DAMAGE CENTER
BEST PRACTICES DERECHO ALERT

You may never hear a specific derecho warning but rather a severe thunderstorm and high wind warning. Derechos can hurl debris at high speeds, so take cover inside, away from doors and windows, if possible in a basement or storm cellar. After the storm passes, use caution as wind and flying debris could uproot trees, dislodge roofs, damage gutters, and destabilize building structures.

Caution tape alerts residents that an electrical wire is down.

People evacuate
a flooded area in
Bangkok, Thailand.

EXTREMES
STORM FLOODING

• Severe thunderstorms in December 2012, in Melbourne, Australia, caused flash flooding, with waters rising 6.5 feet in just a few hours.

• In September 2009, days of storms brought as much as 20 inches of rain to parts of Georgia, Alabama, and Tennessee. Eleven people lost their lives.

• An outbreak of thunderstorms and high winds in the summer of 2012 caused nearly $3 billion worth of damage across 11 states.

ice particles manage to separate positive from negative charge at the molecular level. It's thought that possibly the ice particles gather electrical charge as they bump into one another, with smaller ice particles tending to become positively charged while larger ones become negatively charged.

The small particles move up with the updraft, the large ones sink, and their charges become separated. With the top of the cloud positively charged and the bottom negatively, the cloud becomes like a capacitor, storing electrons that are ultimately discharged as lightning. When the attraction between the positive and negative charges becomes strong enough to overcome the air's resistance to electrical flow, lightning flashes between the two areas. Although we see plenty of cloud-to-ground lightning, the most common type of lightning happens up high and inside the clouds.

Gear and Gadgets
↘ LIGHTNING PROTECTION SYSTEM

If you live in a thunderstorm-prone area, consider installing a lightning protection system. These systems typically consist of lightning rods affixed to the high point of your roof, which will be more likely to attract lightning than other parts of your home, and divert the strike through cables connected to a low-resistance earth-grounding system. The "ground," or earth, is considered to have zero voltage, or potential, and therefore acts as an electricity sponge, pulling it away from other things that might attract it. Surge protectors for your home's electrical system are often included with a lightning protection system.

Lightning protection systems have to be properly planned and dimensioned depending on the size and shape of your home, among other factors, and there are many standards and protocols to which to adhere. That's why it's important to involve an experienced contractor or your local fire department. Installed correctly, lightning protection systems can protect your home from damage, including fire, and you and your family from electrocution.

A lightning rod tops a Victorian turret.

A microburst looms above the rocks of the Grand Canyon.

A monstrous derecho, with winds exceeding 100 mph, roars through Kansas.

The energy from one lightning flash could light a 100-watt incandescent lightbulb for more than three months. Lightning strikes account for an average of 53 fatalities and some 300 injuries each year in the United States, usually when people are caught outside on summer afternoons and evenings. Relying on latent heat to get their power, thunderstorms most often occur toward the end of the day, the warmest time in most 24-hour cycles.

Downbursts Versus Tornadoes
Severe thunderstorms spawn tornadoes (so devastating they get a chapter of their own), but a storm's ferocity also creates downbursts, wind events that can become incredibly violent as they pass over an area.

A downburst is severe localized wind that blasts down from a thunderstorm. It occurs when cold air drops from the middle and upper levels of a thunderstorm and strikes the Earth; as it expands out laterally, it is compressed, causing winds to increase significantly. Meteorologists classify these severe downdrafts in two ways: as microbursts or as macrobursts.

When the downburst covers an area less than 2.5 miles in diameter and lasts 5 to 15 minutes, it's called a microburst. Although they are small, microbursts can cause damaging winds that have been measured as high as 168 miles an hour. When the downburst covers an area of at least 2.5 miles in diameter and lasts 5 to 30 minutes, it's called a macroburst. Macrobursts can cause damaging winds that have been measured as high as 134 miles an hour.

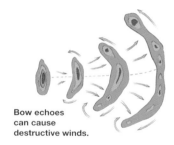

Bow echoes can cause destructive winds.

Downbursts can be just as destructive as tornadoes and are often confused with them. The difference is that in a tornado, all wind spirals into it; you can see this in the aftermath as all debris rests at angles because of the curve of inflow winds. With downbursts, the winds flow out of it; the debris afterward is more often found in straight lines because of the straight line of outward wind flow. For this reason, they are also called straight-line winds.

Despite the fact that tornadoes receive more media attention, downbursts are much more frequent than tornadoes; for every report of tornado damage,

---

Did You Know?

◥ WORST PLACES FOR LIGHTNING

Central Florida attracts more lightning than almost anywhere else on Earth. This happens because the state gets two sea breezes—from its east coast and its west coast. When the breezes converge, thunderstorms develop. Hence, more people die from lightning strikes in Florida than any other place in the United States. The month of July (when school is out) counts the most deaths, especially the Fourth of July holiday when people are outside.

In the United States, lightning strikes the ground an estimated 22 million times a year. Around the globe, lightning, including cloud-to-cloud bolts, can strike more than 3 million times a day.

The country of Rwanda is known as the lightning capital of the world, and receives about two and a half times as many strikes as Florida. The least likely places in the world for lightning are the polar regions. And in the continental United States, the least likely place you'll get struck by lightning is in Washington State, which receives the fewest number of strikes per square mile.

EXTREME WEATHER BASICS
How Humidity Powers Thunderstorms

Water constantly cycles through the Earth and its atmosphere, falling as precipitation, flowing in visible and invisible bodies of water, and returning to the atmosphere as a gas, through evaporation. When water evaporates into vapor, it takes energy called latent heat from the surroundings. This is why evaporating perspiration cools you on a hot day.

Water vapor condensing into cloud drops or depositing directly into ice crystals and water drops freezing into ice release that latent heat. This added warmth offsets some of the cooling occurring as air rises, thus enabling humid air to rise farther and faster than dry air. As this cycle builds, thunderstorms form.

The strongest and most damaging thunderstorms occur on days when the air near the ground is hot and humid and temperatures aloft are very cold.

FORECASTING THUNDERSTORMS
Meteorologists cannot predict exactly when and where individual thunderstorms will form, but often make good forecasts a day or two ahead where and when conditions will be ripe for fierce thunderstorms. A forecast for thunderstorms means you should plan to avoid being caught far from a lightning-safe shelter such as a building with wiring and plumbing or a vehicle. A severe thunderstorm watch means you should be sure to stay close to shelter. The National Weather Service issues warnings when storms threaten a particular area.

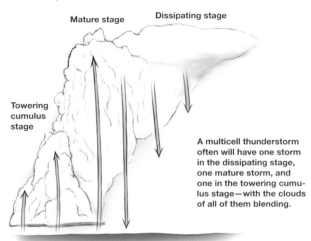

Mature stage

Dissipating stage

Towering cumulus stage

A multicell thunderstorm often will have one storm in the dissipating stage, one mature storm, and one in the towering cumulus stage—with the clouds of all of them blending.

Hail the size of Ping-Pong balls covers the ground.

there are approximately ten of damage from downbursts.

Derechos & Bow Echoes

Two lesser known phenomena—derechos and bow echoes—can also take down trees or rip off rooftops. A derecho is an extremely long-lasting, fast-moving thunderstorm squall line that produces winds of at least 58 miles an hour along a nearly continuous path at least 240 miles long. Winds build up to extreme speeds because the downburst force from individual thunderstorms is added to the speed of the wind pushing the squall line. A derecho dies when it runs into dry air in the upper atmosphere or when the winds pushing it die down.

A bow echo storm is an especially dangerous curved line of thunderstorms, with the most dangerous winds occurring at the crest or center of the curving bow-shaped formation of clouds. On weather radar, the storms have the shape of an archer's

Did You Know?
↘ NATURE'S SIGNAL

Up to 12 hours before a storm, black flies and mosquitoes will swarm. Then, an hour or two before the storm hits, they disappear. Why? Insects thrive on humidity but avoid direct rainfall.

Lightning strikes Woolsey Butte, along the north rim of the Grand Canyon.

bow, giving the phenomenon its name. Bow echoes are sometimes triggered by winds from isolated supercells but most come from squall lines, especially derecho squall lines. In fact, almost all derechos produce bow echoes, which often cause the derecho's most destructive winds.

Dodging Hail

The largest hailstone in the United States was recorded in South Dakota in 2010. It weighed 1.94 pounds and measured eight inches in diameter. Death by hail is rather rare, surprisingly enough, but crop damage isn't. In fact, hail damage to U.S. crops is estimated at $1.3 billion annually.

Hail is precipitation in the form of ice and is usually linked to multicell, supercell, and cold front–induced squall line thunderstorms. It is manufactured within the central part of a storm cloud, where it begins its life as tiny ice pellets that merge with water droplets. The water and ice merge and freeze as updraft winds push them upward into the colder regions of the cloud, and the pellets increase in size. Gravity and downdrafts then work in tandem to pull the pellets down, where they meet more water droplets and freeze once again as they are pushed back upward into the cloud by updrafts. The more times a hailstone makes this trip up and down, the larger it will become. Large hailstones are signs of very strong updraft and downdraft winds within a storm cloud, which is why large hail indicates a powerful thunderstorm.

Because mountain ranges quickly force air vertically, hailstorms are more frequent in mountain regions and in areas where thunderstorms migrate from these heights. Colorado, Nebraska, and Wyoming are known as "Hail Alley."

Protect Your Pets

The biggest threat to pets during a thunderstorm is their own fear. Astraphobia (see sidebar) not only makes many a pet cower, whimper, tremble, and try to hide during a storm, but also often makes them try to run away in a panic. Storm-destroyed fences can abet their desire to escape.

To comfort your pets and keep them safe and sound:

→ When a storm is approaching, bring pets in.

→ In case your pet escapes, you'll want to be sure that it has a collar or microchip, and you have a recent photo.

→ Create a safe haven. Most pets have favorite hiding locations. ■

Did You Know?
↘ AFRAID OF LIGHTNING?

Does the sound of an approaching thunderstorm strike such fear in your heart that you race to cram yourself into a cupboard? If so, you may suffer from astraphobia, the fear of thunder and lightning. The symptoms of astraphobia run the gamut from sweating, crying, and trembling to anxiety, panic attacks, and feelings of dread. Often, sufferers will try to smother the sound by burying their heads, or seek shelter in a place of comfort such as under the covers or in small confined spaces. Curiously, astraphobia is one of the few phobias seen in both humans and animals. Fortunately, it is curable in both.

Caught in a Thunderstorm

A bolt of lightning lights up the night sky.

DAVID SMITH was on his 19-foot motorboat off the coast of Florida when a thunderstorm hit. Smith knew the storm was coming. But he and his teenage son thought they could beat it; they were eager to get their boat in the water and drive it over to the dock—a 15-minute journey at most from the public ramp where they put in to the dock near their home.

"I had always prided myself as being a boater because from the age of ten years old, I have never really having been caught off guard in bad weather," Smith says. "The only time I was ever in bad weather was if I wanted to be."

That was until 2008, when a mad punch of thunderstorms followed tropical storm Fay from the Florida Keys north, all the way to the Florida Panhandle. Smith lives in Manasota Key, near Sarasota—which was almost directly in Fay's path.

"What we didn't calculate for was that the weather would arrive after we launched at what was a very low tide. We had to approach the intercoastal channel, where we have deep water, with the motor tilted up in shallow water. Also, we were in a no-wake zone. So even if we could level the motor, we couldn't go very fast, at least not legally."

Smith found himself in a pickle. "We saw this weather approaching and it was a nasty thunderstorm and we had heard that it was coming. We were just a little bit helpless because we were puttering along in shallow water. All I had to do was make it another 100 yards to the Intercoastal, where I could have dropped the motor down and then we literally could have just floored it and gotten back to our dock. What happened was the storm arrived very, very quickly with 55-mile-an-hour, or maybe

60-mile-an-hour winds. It just blew us right out of the shallow channel of about three feet onto a shoal."

Because Smith had landed on a shoal, or sandbar, he wasn't concerned about drowning. But he was worried he and his son might get struck by lightning.

"The scariest part was the lightning. I've never seen so much lightning. That was the part where I got frightened, because when you're in severe wind, you can power the boat and go with the waves, or you can go and dance with the wind if you want to, but when you're stuck up on a shoal and it's lightning coming down at you, it's a totally helpless feeling. It was about 45 minutes of just relentless lightning everywhere," Smith recalls. "The wind was so strong that even if we had wanted to get out and push the boat off the shore, I don't think we could have with that wind. We were just stuck up there as the storm came upon us. We were up against the shore, and the wind was blowing. The rain was horizontal at that point."

Even though drowning didn't seem likely, he and his son donned their life vests. "That life vest served as a bulletproof vest for us. The rain was

> **"When you're stuck up on a shoal and it's lightning coming down at you, it's a totally helpless feeling."**

coming down so hard it hurt. We couldn't have had the canopy up, because the wind was so strong it would have just lifted it right off the boat," he says.

There was nothing to do but wait out the storm, which they did, getting pelted for nearly an hour. Finally the wind died down and the storm passed. "Then we just pushed ourselves off the shoal and powered out to the Intercoastal and made it back to the dock."

Thinking about it, what worried him most wasn't so much the storm's wrath as his wife's: "If we had died out there, she would have killed us," he says, laughing.

Still, he now knows trying to time a thunderstorm is no joke. "I'll never cut things that close again."

Boats cluster in the waters off Miami, Florida.

EXPERT WITNESS: **Mary Ann Cooper**

How to Avoid Lightning Injuries

Lightning hit a tree, causing it to explode. Never seek shelter under a tree during a thunderstorm.

Mary Ann Cooper, M.D., *professor emerita of Emergency Medicine at the University of Illinois at Chicago and former director of the Lightning Injury Research Program*

→ How common are lightning injuries?

In recent years, there have been fewer than 30 deaths from lightning in the United States, a two-thirds reduction from a few decades ago. We've really come a long way in terms of public awareness—you know, "when thunder roars, go indoors."

→ Are the most hazardous situations still the ones we normally think of, like open fields, under trees, swimming, boating, golfing?

Not golfing. That makes up only 2 or 3 percent of the deaths. A lot of people killed today just aren't paying attention. They want to finish mowing the lawn or washing the car. Most are within 30 to 50 feet of a safe building. One person was in a shopping mall and couldn't get good cell phone service, so he stepped out of the building into the parking lot and was killed.

→ Do people often survive a lightning strike?

Ninety percent do. There are ten times as many injuries as deaths. The reason for that may be that only a very small percentage are direct hits by lightning strikes.

→ Most are injured by indirect strikes? Like when lightning hits a nearby tree and spreads across the ground?

Yes, it actually goes out in a hemisphere, down into the earth as well as out in waves, like when you throw a rock in a pond and see the ripples going out.

→ I was surprised to hear that lightning doesn't often cause burns.

When lightning contacts the body indirectly, the vast majority of the energy flashes over it. It's not in contact with the body long enough to cause significant burns. When it does cause burns, generally it's secondary. The sweat or rainwater on the surface of the body turns to steam. Or the metal necklace heats up and tattoos into the skin.

→ What are the most common medical injuries from lightning?

For the small percentage who dies, it's cardiac arrest. For everyone else, it's mostly a neurological injury. It causes injury to the brain similar to the symptoms you see in concussions: irritability, attention deficits, word-finding problems, and memory-coding problems. In addition, it can cause nerve injury, and as the nerves heal, they can become more irritable and it can cause a lot of misfires up to the brain, which then causes chronic pain.

→ It sounds like some aftereffects might be tricky.

Well, people who have had an injury may deny that anything has happened to them. They know they were hit by lightning, but they don't recognize the deficits. They don't know why they aren't understanding jokes, why they're so irritable, why their friends aren't coming around anymore. It can also be a question of teasing apart whether a person has the symptoms or something else is going on. If you have a teenager who has had a lightning injury and they're sleeping all the time, and they're irritable and forgetful and don't pick up after themselves, is that because of the brain injury or because they're a teenager?

→ There are support groups for lightning survivors, aren't there?

Yes, they've been around for nearly 25 years, and they have a lot of good material. For example, there is Lightning Strike and Electric Shock Survivors International (www.lightning-strike.org).

HOW TO: **PREPARE**

→ WHAT TO DO

Indoors

- ✓ Start to prepare for thunderstorm emergencies in early spring, before the period when most thunderstorms occur: May through September.

- ✓ Keep an emergency kit handy.

- ✓ Follow the 30/30 Lightning Safety Rule: When you see lightning, start counting. If you hear thunder before you count to 30, head indoors—and stay indoors for 30 minutes after you hear no more thunder.

- ✓ Run through storm safety techniques with all residents and/or family members of your house.

- ✓ Choose a gathering spot inside your home that is away from windows, skylights, and glass doors.

- ✓ Close all windows and doors. Also, close all shutters, blinds, shades, or curtains.

- ✓ Unplug sensitive or electrical equipment and appliances of which you are not in immediate need.

- ✓ Find out if your community has an emergency warning system for severe thunderstorms—and tune in.

- ✓ Consider getting certified in first aid in case of injuries.

Outdoors

- ✓ Tie down and/or fasten objects outside your home that might blow away and cause damage.

- ✓ Inspect outside barns or buildings that house pets or that animals use to make sure they are storm safe; have a plan to bring pets inside if needed.

- ✓ If you are hiking or camping, have a plan in case a storm comes. Find shelter options, and make sure every one in your party knows where to go.

A farmer watches a storm approach. Being prepared helps mitigate damage from bad weather.

→ WHAT *NOT* TO DO

Outdoors

⊠ Do not let loose items or trash pile up outside your home. Also, don't ignore dead or rotting trees. These can fall or blow in high storm winds and cause serious injury and/or property damage.

⊠ Do not plan outdoor activities if a storm watch is in effect.

⊠ Do not install lightning rods without first consulting your local fire department to ensure they abide by fire codes.

⊠ Do not slack on your landscaping. You can make trees more wind resistant if you keep them trimmed and healthy.

⊠ Do not wait until a storm approaches to discuss lightning safety with your children.

⊠ Do not ignore the signs of an approaching thunderstorm, such as darkening skies and winds picking up.

HOW TO: SURVIVE

→ **WHAT TO DO**

Indoors

☑ Evacuate mobile homes or other light shelters that can blow over in high winds. Get to sturdier buildings with stronger foundations.

☑ Keep monitoring the storm by listening to weather reports and updates from local officials.

☑ Stay indoors and away from windows and doors. Don't hang out on your porch area.

☑ Keep all windows and doors shut, as well as any shutters.

☑ Safely unplug appliances that you don't need, including computers and air conditioners.

Outdoors

☑ If you are driving in a vehicle, exit the road and park. Remain in your vehicle and turn on the emergency flashers until the storm ends.

☑ If you are on foot, seek shelter in the nearest and sturdiest building. Don't head for smaller structures in open areas.

☑ Be conscious of your surroundings; even though you may be in what seems like a safe location, tractors, farm equipment, motorcycles, golf carts, golf clubs, and bicycles can attract lightning.

☑ If you are camping, go for a valley, ravine, or other low-lying area (while remaining alert for flood possibilities). Tents do not offer protection from lightning, so seek sturdier structures if possible.

☑ Stay away from water and wet items. Water is an excellent conductor of electricity, and therefore a lightning strike far away can travel long distances via water.

☑ If you in a small boat, get to shore as quickly as possible. If that isn't an option, drop anchor and stay as low as possible. According to the National Oceanic and Atmospheric Administration (NOAA), the majority of lightning injuries and deaths on boats occur on smaller boats that do not have cabins. NOAA reports that large boats with cabins, especially those equipped with lightning protection systems, are relatively safe. Still, it advises people to stay inside the cabin and away from any metal surfaces, as well as to stay off the radio unless it is an emergency.

Mobile homes as shown in this aerial view are vulnerable to high winds.

→ WHAT *NOT* TO DO

Indoors

✗ Do not use corded phones and/or devices. Instead, operate cordless or wireless phones (devices not directly connected to wall outlets).

✗ Do not keep in contact with electrical equipment or cords. Power surges from lightning can cause serious damage.

✗ Do not touch plumbing. That means sinks, tubs, and showers. So don't wash your hands or take a shower, and don't wash dishes or do laundry. Plumbing and bathroom fixtures conduct electricity.

✗ Do not hold any metal objects.

Outdoors

✗ Do not head for high ground or isolated trees.

✗ Do not go to low places, such as picnic shelters, dugouts, and sheds.

✗ Do not stay out in the open at the beach or in fields.

✗ Do not touch metal or other surfaces that likely conduct electricity, especially inside or outside your vehicle.

✗ Do not wait for the storm to get too close. Get safe and take shelter immediately if you hear thunder.

HOW TO: **RECOVER**

→ **WHAT TO DO**

Indoors

- ☑ Keep listening to weather reports to be sure the storm has passed. And remember the rule to remain indoors until 30 minutes after the last clap of thunder.

- ☑ Check your home for damage, especially windows, doors, and chimneys.

- ☑ Check your basement for floods and your roof for possible lightning damage.

- ☑ Lightning strikes can manifest into home fires.

- ☑ Be alert for debris flows and flash floods that can ensue from thunderstorms.

- ☑ News reports will issue "flood watches" and "flood warnings." A "watch" means a flood is possible, whereas a "warning" means it's occurring.

Outdoors

- ☑ If lightning has struck someone, call for medical assistance as soon as possible. Meanwhile, if needed, administer CPR until help arrives, as lightning can cause heart attacks.

- ☑ If a lightning-strike victim has a heartbeat and is breathing, you need not apply CPR, but you should still check for broken bones, impaired eyesight or hearing, external wounds, or other health impacts.

- ☑ Keep away from storm-related damage areas.

- ☑ Assist people who have been put in danger without risking your own personal safety.

- ☑ Listen to news reports to find out about road closures, and plan alternative routes.

- ☑ Keep an eye on your pets. Thunder and lightning are especially frightening to animals.

- ☑ Let your family and friends know that you are safe.

Detail of a
water-damaged
basement

A fallen tree destroys a parked car.

→ WHAT *NOT* TO DO

Indoors

✖ Do not ignore minor leaks or stains indicating water damage in your walls or ceilings. They may signal more serious structural damage, and a speedy response will minimize necessary repair.

✖ Do not stop monitoring weather reports for your area just because one thunderstorm has subsided.

✖ Do not let pets go outside in the immediate aftermath of a heavy storm.

✖ Do not plug electrical appliances back in until you are sure the last of the storm has passed— 30 minutes after the last thunder is heard.

Outdoors

✖ Do not worry about touching a person who has been struck by lightning; no shock will occur.

✖ Do not drive through flooded areas; turn around instead.

✖ Do not go near storm-damaged areas to keep from putting yourself at risk from the effects of severe thunderstorms.

✖ Do not go near downed power lines. Always report them to your local utility company, fire department, or police.

✖ Do not think that once the storm has passed, so have the dangers. Debris flows and flash floods can occur. Get out of the storm-affected area immediately.

A thunderstorm creates flashes of lightning over the plains of New Mexico.

EXTREMES

DEVASTATING THUNDERSTORMS

• In May 1995, a costly and deadly thunderstorm in Fort Worth and Dallas County, Texas, produced softball-size hailstones; its 70-mph winds caused incredible destruction.

• In 2013, a supercell thunderstorm in the U.S. Midwest spawned tornadoes that whipped into speeds of nearly 300 mph.

• The top wind speed record for a tornado was in 1999, when a storm blew through Oklahoma and created wind speeds of 301 mph.

Use caution when traveling through flooded areas.

CHAPTER 2

FLOODS

The deluge began slowly. An inch of rain fell on Boulder, Colorado, on September 10, 2013. Another two inches fell the next day. But on the third day, it came down in buckets—more than nine inches in 24 hours, smashing the previous record twice over. Roads became impassible because of standing water. Basements were flooded. Schools were closed. Phone lines went down.

Communities nestled along the Rockies have seen their share of floods before; the natural architecture of the region, known for its towering peaks and picturesque canyons, is conducive to such. But it was the rain that was so extraordinary in this round of raging waters.

The largest rainfall amounts fell over the foothills of the Rockies. Some parts of the Denver metro area saw more than 14 inches of rain. Water gushed down the mountainsides into the major tributaries of the South Platte River. Boulder and St. Vrain Creeks, and Big Thompson and Cache la Poudre Rivers were

---

FEMA BEST PRACTICES PLAN FOR FLOOD INSURANCE

Flood insurers frequently require a 30-day waiting period between purchase and coverage. If you wait until flood damage occurs, it will be too late. Flood insurance policies vary, but they typically do not cover currency, precious metals, or valuable documents. Temporary living expenses due to flood damage are usually not covered, nor is any property outside of your house, such as pools or cars. The cost and recommended level of coverage depend on the flood zone and the date of construction of your home, among other factors.

Centralized into one online location—*hazards.fema.gov/fema portal/prelimdownload/*—are flood hazard data and flood maps, which you can access to determine your level of flood risk. Enter your location and get an early look at your home or community's projected risk for flood hazards. People are also advised to attend call-in webinars where they can listen to and ask questions of flood and insurance specialists. FEMA hosts these events regularly, and the webinars are free.

A Colorado house is torn apart by flooding along the James Creek.

altered beyond recognition. The Front Range and the foothills became conduits for cascading water that ripped through 24 counties, taking nine lives, mangling roads, rinsing away entire towns, and affecting, by some estimates, 4,500 square miles of the state of Colorado. Almost 2,000 homes were destroyed, and more than 26,000 households were affected; 120 bridges were destroyed or left in need of repair. The epic flooding caused some $2 billion in damages.

This dismal scenario was caused by an unfortunate confluence of weather events. It began when a strong, slow-moving storm got trapped to the south of an unusually strong ridge of high pressure that was parked over the Pacific Northwest and southwestern Canada. The circulation around the storm tapped a plume of extremely moist, monsoonal air from Mexico that pushed up against the mountains and grew colder as it pushed uphill, which converted a good share of the air's invisible water vapor into all-too-visible and abundant rain.

The 2013 Colorado flood was just one of many that occur every year in the United States; in fact, the Federal Emergency Management Agency (FEMA) notes that floods—one of the most common hazards in the

United States—come in a variety of forms. Some build slowly, giving people time to prepare, but others develop in a matter of minutes and without visible signs of rain. Either way they develop, floods are deceptively strong, dangerous, and destructive. For these reasons, knowing what to expect and how to prepare for a flood can prove invaluable.

What Is a Flood?

Floods are overflows of water that submerge dry land. They have beleaguered us forever, to the point that they've even deluged our collective conscious. Stories of great ancient floods are woven into the mythology of hundreds of cultures, from the Book of Genesis to folklore from the Americas, India, China, and southern Asia, to name just a few.

And with good reason: Floods are dramatic. Floodwater has immense destructive power. Beaches, riverbanks, and man-made barriers have proved no match for water's surges.

Good Idea
↘ HOW TO TURN OFF THE POWER

If it looks as if a major flood (or any other extreme weather event) is going to disrupt power coming to your home—and, under flood conditions, create a risk of electrocution—you should disconnect your power supply, even if you have already lost power, either by your utility provider deliberately turning off the power to your area or by accidental disconnection.

Here is how to manually turn off the power:
• Locate your fuse box.
• Find a dry spot to stand on.
• First, if possible, turn the entire fuse box off. Look for an ON/OFF handle on the outside of the box. Use a wooden stick or broom handle to push it into the OFF position.
• Use the stick to open the fuse box door and remove all the main fuses.
• Unscrew each circuit breaker.
• If your fuse box works strictly on switches, use the stick and push each breaker to the OFF position.
• After conditions dry, reinsert all your fuses and switch back on all your breakers.

The service panel of your fuse box

Springtime can bring flooding, which here covers train tracks.

Water can sweep away boulders, trees, cars, homes, and towns. It is an erosive force, able to seep beneath structures and erode foundations or race under vehicles and heavy machinery and carry them off.

Disaster experts and the media rank floods according to the probability of their occurring in a specific time frame. A "hundred-year flood," for example, is an event so severe it would be expected to happen only once every century. The 2013 Colorado flood was described by many as a thousand-year flood—meaning that the chances of one happening in any given year were one in a thousand. But disastrous floods like the one in Boulder seem to be happening more often now than they used to.

FEMA BEST PRACTICES FOLLOW POST-FLOOD PROTOCOL

It's important to follow correct protocol after a flood. Stay away from damaged areas and roads to allow emergency responders access. Listen to local alerts, and only return to your home when it is declared safe. Be careful when reentering buildings as flooding can cause structural damage. Also, keep in mind that floodwater is dangerous even after the flood is finished.

A cyclist rides through deep water. It's best not to travel during times like this.

What to Expect

In fact, around the world, the past decade has seen a marked increase in the annual number of record large floods as well as the annual number of extreme floods.

Our changing climate is likely to blame. According to the Fifth Assessment Report from the Intergovernmental Panel on Climate Change, changes in the water cycle will likely occur in a warming climate, and thus global-scale precipitation is projected to gradually increase in the 21st century. Changes of average precipitation will not be uniform; locally, rains may increase, but they also may decrease or change very little. The high latitudes are likely to experience greater amounts of precipitation due to the additional water-carrying capacity of the warmer troposphere.

In June 2013, President Obama told students

Did You Know?
↘ NATURE'S SIGNALS

Heavy rain isn't the only signal a flood may be on its way; rising creek or stream levels are signs, too. Water will turn cloudy or muddy. A roaring noise from upstream means a flash flood is on its way. On land, look for earthworms: They migrate upward, fleeing rising groundwater levels underground.

Cloudy or muddy water may indicate a flood is on its way.

The fast-paced water of the Little Colorado River reaches the cliffs of Grand Falls.

at Georgetown University, "Droughts and fires and floods, they go back to ancient times. But we also know that in a world that's warmer than it used to be, all weather events are affected by a warming planet."

Scientists agree that droughts and wildfires are probable with increasing frequency and severity as the planet warms with climate change, and both of those extremes can lead to more severe flooding. Drought parches and hardens the soil so that when rain does come, the ground absorbs less water. Fires strip the land of vegetation that would otherwise control and capture rainfall. Both result in the water of a hard rain streaming over the land rather than penetrating into it.

Know Your Floods

Overbank or Overland Floods: Overland flooding, the most common type of flooding event, typically occurs when waterways such as rivers or streams overflow their banks as a result of rainwater or melting snow. When the area flooded is broad and flat, water tends to spread out and be

Continued on page 61

North Dakota homes are inundated with floodwater from the Souris River.

EXTREMES
RECORD-BREAKING FLOODS

• A catastrophic flood occurred in 1927, along the Mississippi River, inundating parts of Arkansas, Illinois, Kentucky, Louisiana, Mississippi, Missouri, and Tennessee.

• The worst tidal surge in 60 years swamped the east coast of Great Britain in December 2013. More than 15,000 homes were evacuated.

• In September 2013, unprecedented floods in Colorado caused damage across nearly 2,000 square miles and destroyed some 2,000 homes.

EXTREME WEATHER BASICS
The Forces Behind Floods

Floods begin when rain falls faster than it can sink into the ground and flow away in streams, or when winter's snow melts too fast for the rivers it flows into to handle. Melting snow and spring rain or nearly constant, heavy rain falling on a region for days or weeks create widespread overbank flooding. Heavy, localized showers and thunderstorms are the biggest causes of flash floods. At times, such as when a dying hurricane carries heavy rain inland over mountains, local flash floods on small streams cause overbank flooding of rivers into which they flow.

FORECASTING FLOODS

The National Weather Service's Advanced Hydrologic Prediction Service (AHPS) is the core of U.S. flood and drought forecasts. It collects data such as precipitation amounts from weather stations and water levels from automated stream gauges operated by the U.S. Geological Survey and other organizations. AHPS makes the data available to NWS and other forecasters and others who need it, such as emergency managers.

The NWS operates 13 River Forecast Centers, which predict overbank flooding and issue watches and warnings along major rivers, while local NWS offices forecast flash floods and issue watches and warnings for their regions. Recently, the NWS upgraded its network of Doppler weather radars to improve their detection of precipitation in clouds, enabling forecasters to issue flash flood warnings before flooding starts.

Radio transmitters use microwaves to detect precipitation intensity and locations.

slow-moving. In more mountainous areas, the water funnels through narrow, steep canyons and crevices, moving more quickly and creating floods that tend to be of shorter duration.

Flash Floods: A flash flood, like its name suggests, is a short-lived event of rapidly rising water. Flash floods are caused by heavy rainfall in a short period of time and can occur within a few minutes or a few hours after rain. Although they are usually associated with riverbeds, urban streets, or mountain canyons where water capacity is maxed out from heavy rain, they can also happen without rain, for instance, following the failure of a levee or dam or the rushing release of water after an ice jam has dislodged.

Flash floods are deceptively powerful. Six inches of fast-moving water will knock over a person; flowing water with a depth of one foot will cause most vehicles to float. And, in

Gear and Gadgets
↘ SUMP PUMPS

There are two basic types of sump pumps to help you bail floodwater:

1 A pedestal pump is the old-school standard. This type is positioned out of water and above the sump basin.

2 Submersible sump pumps are put under water directly into your sump pump basin. These latter pumps have become the most widely used.

No matter which type of pump is in use, new switch technology and electronic sensors should be used to replace tethered and vertical float triggers.

Older-style mechanical floats can get obstructed by debris, resulting in motors being overworked, pumping needlessly, and breaking down. Electronic sensors are smaller and more sensitive and can connect to smartphones, smart home signal systems, or security systems, letting you know when there is a problem. Some new pumps feature permanent-split capacitor (PSC) motors, which eject water faster and use less electricity.

And it's always a good idea to have a power source backup such as a battery pack or generator, just in case you lose power during a flood.

fact, flash floods are the leading cause of death associated with thunderstorms, with more than 140 fatalities in the United States each year.

More than half of all flood deaths are people in vehicles who get caught up in a flood. Water over a road can look deceptively shallow. Consider these warnings from the NOAA "Turn Around Don't Drown" campaign:

→ Six inches of water will reach the bottom of most passenger cars, causing loss of control and possible stalling.

→ One foot of water will float many vehicles.

→ Two feet of rushing water can carry away most vehicles, including sport-utility vehicles (SUVs) and pickups.

Many fatalities also happen in areas adjacent to a stream or river. A sudden strong

Good Idea
↘ DIVERTING FLOODWATERS AROUND YOUR HOUSE

Floods don't have to be biblical in size to do serious damage to property and structures. Diverting floodwater—even from a neighbor's slope—is a smart precautionary tactic to preserve your landscape and perhaps your basement.

Here are several ways to divert runoff:
• Create a berm—a small mound that you can build with soil, grass, and other plants. Berms can direct runoff flow before it builds up.
• Dig a dry well to which you can direct water flow. Position dry wells near gutters and downspouts to prevent puddles and any ensuing flows.
• Grade smooth surfaces such as concrete and asphalt. Also consider replacing these surface materials with more permeable alternatives such as gravel, stones, or "permeable pavers," which allow water to drain through manufactured gaps.
• Make a shallow ditch, or swale, with sloped sides. Sometimes called a "French drain," these are man-made gravel-filled trenches. The gravel slows the water speed, and the trench directs flow.

Off-the-shelf drainage solutions such as pre-engineered tubes also exist. These are relatively easy to install and can help redirect and manage water flow. For bigger and more involved projects, it's best to hire a professional.

A car travels a flooded highway. One foot of water will float many vehicles.

thunderstorm can turn a six-inch-deep creek into a ten-foot-deep river in less than an hour, according to the National Weather Service.

Ice Jam Flooding: In cold weather, chunks of ice can join together on bodies of water to create a natural dam that can lead to ice jam flooding. Behind the ice blockage, water builds up and spills into flat areas nearby. But eventually, when the ice jam breaks, a flash flood happens; its dangers are compounded by the large chunks of ice that may be rushing along with the torrent of water, increasing damage to structures in its path.

Coastal Flooding: Hurricane Sandy focused the public's attention in 2012 on the dangers of coastal flooding. Such flooding normally happens along the ocean's shore and is created mostly by storm surges and wave damage from hurricanes, tsunamis, or tropical storms. It can also be caused by winter storms. Storm surge occurs when water is pushed toward the shore by the force of the winds moving cyclonically around a storm. The rise in water level can cause severe and devastating flooding in coastal areas, especially when it coincides with normal high tide, resulting in storm tides reaching up to 20 feet or more in some cases.

Coastal areas historically unaccustomed to flooding may find themselves in harm's way if sea levels continue to rise. FEMA and NOAA keep coastal flood maps accurate and up to date, determining hazard liability and developing evacuation plans.

Listen for these terms to identify flood hazards if any of these scenarios threatens your area:

Flood Watch: Flooding is possible.

Flash Flood Watch: Flash flooding is possible; be prepared to move quickly to higher ground.

Flood Warning: Flooding is occurring or will occur soon; if advised to evacuate, do so immediately.

Flash Flood Warning: A flash flood is occurring; seek higher ground on foot immediately.

Flood Advisory: Flooding is expected to occur but is not expected to be dangerous.

What Causes Floods?

Water levels rise and water stands in areas usually dry. But there are many causes for flooding. Some may threaten your area regularly; others may rarely or never occur.

Tropical Storms and Hurricanes: Hurricanes are a double whammy for floods. Their storm surges inundate coastal areas while their heavy rainfall can

---

Good Idea
↘ AVOIDING WELL WATER CONTAMINATION

O ne big danger associated with flooding is water contamination, caused from debris and organic matter floating or diffusing in flowing floodwater. Wells are especially at risk.

Protect your outside water well by these practices:
• Pile up sandbags to protect the area around the well.
• Check that the well has a tight-fitting, waterproof cap.
• Remove any livestock waste, fertilizers, and pesticides from the surrounding area.
• Turn off the electricity to your well pump if a flood occurs.
• Check for abandoned wells nearby and seal them, too, because contaminants could fill them and seep from them into your well.

Cap wells with a watertight lid during a flood.

A street sign is partially submerged by floodwaters in Missouri.

Cumulonimbus storm clouds can produce torrential rain and flash flooding.

cause flooding hundreds of miles inland. When they diminish and turn into tropical storms, they create especially damaging rainfall and flooding when the storm slows and the rain collects in one place. The 2001 tropical storm Allison, for example, brought more than 30 inches of rainfall to Houston in just a few days; over 70,000 houses were flooded, 2,744 homes were destroyed.

Spring Thaw: When the land is frozen, melting snow and spring's heavy rain are unable to soak into the soil. The result? Spring floods. Each cubic foot of compacted snow melts into gallons of water that runs off the surface and finds its way into lakes, streams, and rivers, often exceeding their capacity and causing spring floods. NOAA issues an annual Spring Flood Outlook. Look for it on their website during the third week of March each year (www.nws .noaa.gov/hic/nho/).

Heavy Rains: Different parts of the country are at increased risk of flooding due to that region's particular brand of rainfall. The Northwest, for example, is at high risk due to La Niña conditions, while the Northeast is at high risk due to rains produced from nor'easters.

Rain comes in different intensities. There is light rain, which is measured in millimeters per hour; moderate rain, which can see accumulations of nearly half an inch in an hour; heavy rain, which can rate as much as two inches an hour; and violent rain, when precipitation adds up to more than two inches in an hour.

Levees and Dams: Levees are dams are created to control water, but unexpected volumes of water can overpower them—with catastrophic results. Levees can weaken over time or be stressed by weather events, causing them to be overtopped or breached. Dangers are reduced but not eliminated, so if your home is near a levee or dam, it's important to inform yourself and your family about flood contingencies and emergency plans specific to the area.

What About Flood Insurance?

A homeowners' insurance policy does not automatically provide financial protection against damages incurred during floods. Flood insurance needs to be specifically added or acquired. The U.S. Congress oversees requirements and opportunities for homeowners' flood insurance based on the Flood Insurance Reform Act of 2012. As flood risks change, flood insurance policies change as well, so existing property owners as well as prospective ones do well to keep up with their neighborhoods. Use the resources FEMA offers *(www.floodsmart.gov/)* to

Levees in New Orleans after Hurricane Katrina

determine risk, cost, and protection. Insurance is also available for those who rent.

Flood insurance specialists recommend reviewing all flood zones in your area and their requirements. By assessing risks and knowing rates, homeowners can put into effect the best precautions for their homes.

Community Considerations

Flood risks are community challenges, so the more a neighborhood or larger community works together, the better the chances of a smooth and effective response and recovery when flood dangers arise. FloodSmart.gov, the FEMA website for the National Flood Insurance Program, has a comprehensive Community Resources section that offers a wide range of tools for helping your community become prepared and educated about floods. Flood Outreach Toolkits are available for particular community challenges, such as nearby levees or changing flood map assessments. As well, the Federal Emergency Management Agency (FEMA) links to "Addressing Your Community's Flood Problems," which targets elected officials, but was written to help citizens of a community as well. You can download it at

---

Did You Know?
↘ COMMUNICATING CLEARLY

Communicating essential messages—warning of impending dangers or notifying others that everything is safe and secure—is critical in times of crisis. Good communication can mean the difference between life and death. You may be in a panic, but you need to calm down your communication to a steady minimum.

Remember that in high-stress situations, people are able to process no more than three messages. They tend to remember only what they hear first and last. Keep messages brief and easy to understand. Mention actions to be taken first or last so they can be remembered and repeated easily.

Mental noise can reduce a person's ability to process information by more than 80 percent. That's why it's critical to be clear and concise in relaying messages during extreme weather.

A smartphone can be a lifesaving device. Learn local alerts to keep you informed.

www.fema.gov/media-library/ assets/documents/ 3112?id=1653.

Waterlogged telephones, mobile or landlines, won't let you get in touch with family members or first responders. That's why having a dedicated communication plan—and one that includes waterproof devices—is a good idea. Waterproof two-way radios (walkie-talkies) are durable and have a range up to 35 miles. Assign a radio to each family member and agree on a specific Family Radio Service (FRS) frequency that all will tune to, if necessary.

Hybrid devices allow you to also tune into the General Mobile Radio Service (GMRS), which puts you in touch with those outside your family or community network, including the Radio Emergency Associated Communication Teams (REACT) and the National SOS Radio Network. These organizations recommend channel one on the FRS as an emergency channel.

There's an App for That
Available for download from iTunes and/or Google Play, these apps may be helpful during flood threats:

→ **FloodWatch** uses data from the U.S. Geological Survey and NWS, to present recent and historical river heights, precipitation totals, and flood stage data.

Graphs are available to help you visualize the rise and fall of the river and, importantly, the app allows users to monitor the current status of rivers and streams throughout the United States, and especially in their zip code.

→ The **Flood Damage Assessment** app from iTunes turns your smartphone into an all-in-one tool designed to simplify and organize the process of making flood damage insurance claims.

→ For Android smartphones, the **Flood Warning** app provides around-the-clock information from the NWS for the 49 continental states in addition to national forecasts and severe weather alerts.

→ **FloodMap Mobile** for iPhones and iPads provides detailed maps and information about your particular location, including elevation data, flood hazard zones, stream gauge data, and other valuable information.

→ **Shelter View** is a flood shelter app developed by the American Red Cross. It lists the locations of shelters that have been opened to provide assistance

Gear and Gadgets
↘ SENSORS AND SIGNALS

Freeze and flood monitors connected to security systems can provide an extra measure of protection for your home and property. The latest breakthroughs in home security system technologies involve small and easily placed sensors that alert you when home temperatures have gotten too

Let technology—like this home control system—keep you prepared.

low and pipes are in danger of freezing (and possibly causing them to burst and flood your home), or when water has seeped into a basement or onto floors.

Signals from these sensors can be directed to a maintenance service or directly to your computer or smartphone. These monitors are part of what is now being called a "smart home." Smart, indeed, especially if you are away from your home and cannot check on things yourself.

Victims in the Midwest evacuate during a flood. Always follow evacuation routes.

for flood victims. Complete with screen shots and maps, the utility also automatically presents the latest, most relevant news for users.

Protect Your Pets

The best pet flood safety policy is one that the loving owner prepares beforehand:

→ Every pet disaster plan should include a carrier that will prove invaluable during evacuation, and you and your pet should be comfortable using it. A carrier can be picked up at almost any pet supply store or big-box store.

→ You can obtain stickers specifying how many pets you have, which you can post near your home's entrance. The American Society for the Prevention of Cruelty to Animals (ASPCA) offers free decals in its Pet Safety Pack available at *aspca.org/form/ free-pet-safety-pack.*

→ Do not leave your pet at home alone during a flood warning; although your home may not be threatened, roads may be closed, leaving you unable to return to your pet. And especially don't leave your pet home alone leashed or caged during a flood warning; if you are unable to return, your pet will be unable to reach safer ground on its own.

→ If your area is flooding, keep pets close at hand. Water that is shallow enough for an adult to walk through may be strong enough to whisk away a pet.

A cat is rescued through a window in California. Keep your pets safe in a flood.

→ Before letting your pet back inside after a flood, check for uninvited creatures that may have sought shelter inside your home; snakes, in particular, are prone to displacement.

→ After a flood, slowly reorient your pet when you return. Flooding often rinses away scents and may have destroyed landmarks your pet relies on to orient itself. Without those, getting lost is more likely. Walk your dog with a leash for a few days until he is reacclimatized.

Cleaning Up

Living through a flood event is bad enough; cleaning up afterward is worse, with the smells, the damage, the hard work—not to mention the unseen dangers like mold and mildew, bacteria, and disease.

Flood Safety, a nonprofit organization dedicated to spreading knowledge and sharing information, advises these important safeguards for those who have to dig out after floodwaters flowed through their homes:

1. Always wear a face mask when working through flood-infested materials.

2. Shovel out, then spray off all the mud you can from the house and possessions.

3. Clean and disinfect all surfaces. Use hot water and heavy-strength household cleanser, and then disinfect using a solution of ¼ cup chlorine bleach per 1 gallon water.

4. For rugs, furniture, clothing, and bedding, air outside as soon as possible.

5. Upholstered furniture, mattresses, stuffed animals, and other items that have absorbed floodwater may need to be discarded.

6. Rinse mud off papers and photographs, then freeze in plastic bags for slow and careful drying later.

7. Replace wallboard, plaster, and paneling at least up to water level.

8. Thoroughly dry out walls and wiring before testing and repairing electrical circuits.

9. Pump standing water out of the basement at a steady rate of about two to three feet a day. The reason: Increased water pressure that's greater outside the walls than inside can lead to cracks.

10. If your house has a private sewage system, check for standing water that is impeding flow through the system, which could cause backup of tainted water into your household drinking supply. ■

CDC BEST PRACTICES CLEAN PLAY AREAS AFTER A FLOOD

Keep children and pets out of the affected area until cleanup has been completed. Wear rubber boots, rubber gloves, and goggles. Wash all clothes worn during the cleanup in hot water and detergent. These clothes should be washed separately from uncontaminated clothes and linens. When you're done, wash your hands with soap and warm water. Use water that has been boiled for one minute (allow the water to cool before washing your hands). Seek immediate medical attention if you become injured or ill.

FIRST PERSON: Laura Bevan, southern regional director for the Humane Society of the United States

Rescuing Pets in Crisis

A couple dares the floodwaters of the Mississippi River to rescue a puppy.

LAURA BEVAN, who rescues pets for a living, recounts one particularly heavy flood that left pets stranded. "In 1994, tropical storm Alberto stalled south of Atlanta, Georgia, and in a 24-hour period dumped up to 24 inches of rain on a huge portion of the state," says Bevan.

This would turn out to be the event that sent Bevan into floodwaters for the first time to rescue pets. She says it was also the first time she began experiencing nightmares about her work.

Saving a pet can be physically challenging, Bevan says. "A local resident offered up his pontoon boat for rescues, and we used it to drag a canoe and johnboat through the raging Flint River into flooded neighborhoods. The canoe and johnboat were paddled and poled behind homes and alleyways to look for pets, while the larger boat waited in the flooded street with the animals already saved.

"When you are rescuing animals in floods, you quickly become hypervigilant. You start out thinking the dogs will bark when they see you—sensing you are there to help—but they don't. In the eerie quiet, you look for the slightest movement in a bush telling you that a dog or cat is perched precariously in its branches. What looks like a black rug caught in the current next to a house is actually a large black dog. The brown bump in the water on a porch actually belongs to a puppy tied to the post and standing with its paws on the railing with only its nose above water."

Not only is alertness necessary during a pet rescue, so too is expert pet handling. Bevan describes a scene: "We found one dog wedged around the steering wheel of an old VW van in an overgrown backyard. My partner saw him first and we maneuvered the canoe over. A chow mix, his coloring matched the van and the polluted flood-water, and from his loss of hair and infected skin, it was clear he wasn't cared for before the flood. He must have swum into the van when the water rose, but now was stuck. The doors were held shut by the water, so we tried to gently pull him out through the window. He felt safe and made it clear he wanted none of our help. Finally, my partner scruffed him and yanked quickly, almost

toppling the canoe, but achieving our goal."

The circumstances involving the pets you can see may be harrowing, but there is even more anxiety about the animals you cannot find, Bevan says. "The dogs on chains are the worst. Some manage to climb on a doghouse, but others swim in circles for as long as they can. As you canoe through back-yards, you see the doghouse, but don't know if its former occupant was evac-uated by the owner, broke off the chain itself, or is some-where underwater. You become acutely aware that for many of the ani-mals left behind, the difference between life and death is as simple as a collar loose enough to escape, or the extra inch of growth of a puppy leg. Those are the images of nightmares."

> **"When you are rescuing animals in floods, you quickly become hypervigilant."**

A cat and its owner are reunited.

EXPERT WITNESS: Jennifer Pipa

Sheltering People During a Flood

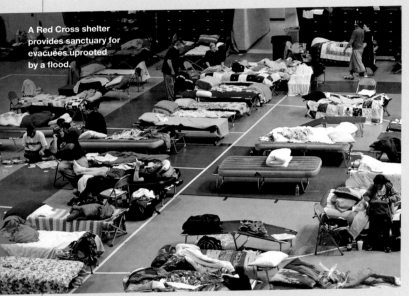

A Red Cross shelter provides sanctuary for evacuees uprooted by a flood.

Jennifer Pipa, *director of volunteer mobilization and support at the Red Cross. She is based in Washington, D.C.*

→ How quickly can you set up a shelter during a flood emergency?
We can usually open shelters within a couple of hours of the onset of a disaster. As soon as we identify where the affected populations are, we look for the closest locations for a shelter, because we want to keep people as close to their own neighborhoods as we can.

→ How do you know how many cots and blankets you're going to need?

A lot of times, for planning purposes, we estimate that 10 percent of the population may need our support. In practice, it tends to be less than that, but it gives us a nice safe margin. Our local Red Cross chapters each have a disaster plan, so they know their own community's demographics and exactly what they'll need at a shelter.

→ What do you offer people at shelters?
When people evacuate, they

may not have a lot with them. If they had to leave in the middle of the night in their pajamas, we might purchase clothing for them, shoes, those kinds of things. Our first concern is making sure they're in a safe location and that they can be fed. We usually have licensed nurses in the shelters in case anybody has medical needs. If they evacuated without their medicines, they may need replacements.

→ What special challenges do floods pose?

Well, until the rain is over, you don't know where the affected area will be. For a fast-moving flood, the challenge might be just getting in and cleaning it out quickly. When it's a slow-moving flood, things get a little more complicated.

→ How many shelters did you open up during the recent floods in Colorado?

We opened up or supported about 20 shelters in all in Colorado. A lot of times local churches or other community partners will open up shelters initially and then need some additional support or expertise in how to run a shelter.

→ Who came to the shelters?

Because the water rose so quickly, we saw whole families—multigenerational families who lived together—evacuate to the shelters. We also saw a lot of people who live up on the mountain and tend to be fairly independent and resilient. They came down to get some safe shelter and food and to be taken care of for a couple of days. And they ended up staying longer than they anticipated because of the damage to roads and bridges.

→ How long did the shelters stay open?

About 21 days. We had just over 5,000 overnight stays. We also used our Safe and Well website (safeandwell.communityos.org/cms/index.php). If someone had to evacuate quickly, and wasn't able to let family know that they were okay, they could register their location on Safe and Well to say, hey, I'm in a Red Cross shelter and I'm okay. I'll call when I get a chance.

→ How many volunteers did you need?

At peak deployment we had just over 800 volunteers. It started out with local volunteers. They opened up the first shelters the night it started to flood. And then, as they started to see that it was going to be a fairly significant event, they asked for additional help. We brought in people from as far away as Alaska and Hawaii to help with the flood response.

HOW TO: **PREPARE**

→ **WHAT TO DO**

Indoors

- ☑ Check flood hazard maps to evaluate the risk of flooding in your area.

- ☑ Determine what type of flood insurance you may need. The less the risk of flood to your home, the lower the cost of flood insurance.

- ☑ Get familiar with flood hazard issues and consider the vulnerability of your home and property. Use FEMA's website *(floodsmart.gov)* for information and resources.

- ☑ Have an emergency kit and family communication plan ready to use during and after a flood.

- ☑ Keep a battery-powered radio and your phone charged at all times.

- ☑ Put together an evacuation plan and share it with family members. Consider conducting flood drills.

- ☑ Ensure your furnace, water heater, and all electric panels are off the ground and located in areas of your home difficult for water to reach.

- ☑ Construct flood barriers; seal and waterproof basement walls and windows.

- ☑ Be aware of your proximity to streams, drainage channels, canyons, and other low-lying areas that are known to flood.

- ☑ Consider installing backflow valves to prevent water from backing up in your water system during a flood.

Outdoors

- ☑ Investigate your environs, and be aware of nearby flood zones before a storm watch threatens.

- ☑ Plan a flood escape route if you are expecting to be in a flood-prone zone, even if conditions are predicted to be dry.

- ☑ Study water flow patterns around your home during lighter rains to see if there are spots where water pools or drains toward your house.

- ☑ Hikers and campers should think through a flood escape plan, because they will endure longer outside exposure time.

- ☑ Monitor weather reports for heavy precipitation.

- ☑ Bring any outside furniture indoors or tie it down securely.

Residents build a barrier to protect their homes from the rising Mississippi River.

→ WHAT *NOT* TO DO

Indoors

☒ Do not ignore the risk of floods, even if you live in an area that is not predisposed to flooding; floods can happen almost anywhere.

☒ Do not build in a floodplain without taking precautions to elevate and reinforce your home.

☒ Do not put off cleaning out your drains. Inspect them regularly, keeping them clear of leaves, mud, and other debris.

Outdoors

☒ Do not plan to be in areas that have been scorched by fire if precipitation threatens; floods can occur more easily on burnt ground, which doesn't absorb water well.

☒ Do not ignore rising tide levels on rivers, lakes, or streams.

Levees can break and floods can ensue.

☒ If you are planning on camping or hiking, do not head for valleys or low-lying areas during wet seasons.

HOW TO: **SURVIVE**

→ **WHAT TO DO**

Indoors

- ☑ Stay tuned to weather and flood reports on the radio, television, or on your smartphone.

- ☑ Be on the alert for disaster sirens.

- ☑ Evacuate immediately if there is any possibility of flash floods occurring.

- ☑ Move important items to an upper floor, and secure your home before evacuating.

- ☑ Shut off your utilities, if advised.

- ☑ Turn off electricity at central switches and close off the gas at main valves.

- ☑ Disconnect all your electrical appliances.

- ☑ If water is already rising inside your home, go upstairs to a higher floor, to the attic, or even onto the roof.

- ☑ Clean your hands often with soap and disinfected water or with hand sanitizer, especially if you have come into contact with floodwater.

Outdoors

- ☑ If you are driving as floodwater rises around your car, stop the car and get out. Driving through just six inches of water can cause most vehicles to stall, and you can easily lose control of your vehicle.

- ☑ Use a stick or other nonconducting object to check that the ground in front of you is safe to walk on.

- ☑ Move to higher ground.

- ☑ Follow designated evacuation routes.

A portable digital radio

A man walks a flooded street. Be alert when walking through floodwater.

→ WHAT *NOT* TO DO

Indoors

☒ Do not wait. Evacuate immediately if floods threaten.

☒ If possible, do not walk through moving water. Just six inches of flowing water can force you to fall down. If there is no choice but to walk through water, walk where the water is not moving.

☒ Never touch or go near electrical wiring or equipment if you are standing in water or are wet.

☒ Do not attempt to save floating objects. Cuts during floods can be doubly dangerous. Not only the wound itself but also the risk of infection from contaminated water can be dangerous.

Outdoors

☒ Do not drive through flooded areas. Strong floods can sweep vehicles away.

☒ Do not camp or park near streams, rivers, creeks, or other waterways if floods threaten. Keep a safe distance—at least 200 feet or more—away from any body of water.

☒ Do not approach downed power lines or anything electrical. Water conducts electricity, which means you could be electrocuted even without touching a power line.

☒ Do not assume you can walk on familiar pathways after floodwaters have surged through.

HOW TO: **RECOVER**

→ **WHAT TO DO**

Indoors

☑ If you have evacuated, return to your home only after officials declare it safe.

☑ Before you reenter your home, check outside for loose or down power lines, broken gas lines, and any damage to your foundation.

☑ Approach entranceways carefully. Check porches, roofs, and overhangs.

☑ Look out for any wild animals, especially reptiles, that may have washed into your home.

☑ Sniff for natural or propane gas, and listen for any hissing noises. These signs may indicate a leak. If you sense a leak, leave the house immediately and call the fire department.

☑ Keep watch on children and pets, and make sure they stay away from any hazards.

☑ Check with local authorities to dispose of cleaning products, paint, batteries, fuel, and other hazardous items that may have become damaged and dangerous.

☑ Investigate and get instructions on water treatment to ensure it isn't contaminated.

☑ If you have a private well, drain it by running water through it for at least 15 minutes or until pressure is lost. Pour in a quart of liquid chlorine bleach and leave it for at least 4 hours. Then run water through each tap in the house until you smell the chlorine. Let this water sit in the pipes for up to 4 hours. Then flush thoroughly until the chlorine smell disappears.

☑ Wear protective clothing during cleanup efforts.

Outdoors

☑ Continue to listen for flood warnings even after a flood appears to have subsided.

☑ Avoid any moving water.

☑ Stay on firm ground and pay attention, even on familiar roads and walkways. Erosion can pose danger, and flood debris can hide animal carcasses, broken bottles, and other items.

☑ Use caution when traveling through areas where floodwaters have receded. Flooding often weakens road surfaces, causing collapse.

☑ Use extreme caution when entering any building or structure. Structural damage can be serious but hidden from view.

Disaster response groups pitch in to muck out homes after a flood.

→ WHAT *NOT* TO DO

Indoors

☒ Do not step in puddles or standing water if there are downed power lines in the area; there is risk of electrocution.

☒ Do not use tap water immediately after a flood except to flush the toilet. Don't use it to drink, to wash dishes or laundry, or to clean or bathe with.

☒ Do not drink anything but bottled water until your water supplier or health department indicates otherwise.

☒ Do not use any items that have come in contact with floodwater without first cleaning them.

☒ Do not eat any food items that were touched by floodwater, including even food in cans or in jars and bottles with screw-top lids.

Outdoors

☒ Do not enter flooded areas to assist others unless requested by police, fire, or professional responders.

☒ Do not travel unnecessarily; you can end up in the way of emergency workers.

☒ Do not enter any building that is or has been surrounded by floodwaters without necessary precautions.

Trucks surge through floodwater in North Dakota to work on reinforcing levees.

EXTREMES
THE DAMAGE LEFT BEHIND

• In 2005, Hurricane Katrina's 140 mph winds and 20-foot storm surge broke the levees around New Orleans, causing much of the city to flood.

• The Mississippi River breached its banks in 2012, and 130,000 acres of Missouri farmland were flooded.

• In 2012, Hurricane Sandy flooded coastal New York and New Jersey. In the aftermath, more than 23,000 people sought refuge in shelters, and more than 8.5 million customers lost power.

Satellite imagery reveals the eye of Hurricane Katrina, a devastating storm that hit in August 2005.

CHAPTER 3

HURRICANES

On August 23, 2005, a tropical depression formed over the Bahamas. Early morning the following day, its winds reached about 40 miles an hour, earning the storm the name tropical storm Katrina. By the time the storm made landfall in southern Florida on August 25, it was a moderate Category 1 hurricane—and while it caused some flooding and several deaths, it moved on to weaken, and it was reclassified as a tropical storm.

But by August 28, after stalling on the water underneath a large upper-level high-pressure area, Katrina gathered immense strength, growing to a Category 5 storm with winds raging at 175 miles an hour. The storm took a turn north toward the Louisiana coast and weakened

to Category 3 before hitting the Louisiana-Mississippi border on August 29.

Katrina plowed into Gulfport and Biloxi, Mississippi, ravaging both cities. Initially, New Orleans looked like it may have dodged the bullet, comparatively. By August 31, however, 80 percent of the city was under water—in some parts, in fact, the water was 20 feet deep.

New Orleans' extensive levee system—built to protect a city surrounded by water that sits on average six feet below sea level—was no match for what Katrina brought to town. Storm surges breached the levees in numerous places. Most of the levee failures were caused by water rising over the top and scouring out the base of the landward embankment

NOAA
BEST PRACTICES DON'T TAPE WINDOWS

Taping windows does not prevent hurricane damage. It only causes flying glass to stay in large chunks, which may do more harm than good. Make long-term plans to build shutters or, in a pinch, cover windows from the outside with sheets of plywood, metal, or polycarbonate.

Did You Know?
↘ HURRICANES BY CATEGORY

Hurricanes are categorized by sustained wind speed, as laid out in the Saffir-Simpson Scale. Here, word for word, are the definitions of hurricane categories as spelled out by the National Weather Service's National Hurricane Center *(www.nhc.noaa.gov/aboutsshws.php):*

Category 1: Sustained winds of 74 to 95 miles an hour
Very dangerous winds will produce some damage: Well-constructed frame homes could have damage to roof, shingles, vinyl siding, and gutters. Large branches of trees will snap, and shallowly rooted trees may be toppled. Extensive damage to power lines and poles likely will result in power outages that could last a few to several days.

Category 2: Sustained winds of 96 to 110 miles an hour
Extremely dangerous winds will cause extensive damage: Well-constructed frame homes could sustain major roof and siding damage. Many shallowly rooted trees will be snapped or uprooted and block numerous roads. Near-total power loss is expected with outages that could last from several days to weeks.

Category 3: Sustained winds of 111 to 129 miles an hour
Devastating damage will occur: Well-built framed homes may incur major damage or removal of roof decking and gable ends. Many trees will be snapped or uprooted, blocking numerous roads. Electricity and water will be unavailable for several days to weeks after the storm passes.

Category 4: Sustained winds of 130 to 156 miles an hour
Catastrophic damage will occur: Well-built framed homes can sustain severe damage with loss of most of the roof structure and/or some exterior walls. Most trees will be snapped or uprooted and power poles downed. Fallen trees and power poles will isolate residential areas. Power outages will last weeks to possibly months. Most of the area will be uninhabitable for weeks or months.

Category 5: Sustained winds of 157 miles an hour and higher
Catastrophic damage will occur: A high percentage of framed homes will be destroyed, with total roof failure and wall collapse. Fallen trees and power poles will isolate residential areas. Power outages will last for weeks to possibly months. Most of the area will be uninhabitable for weeks or months.

Winds more than 100 miles an hour from Hurricane Wilma blast palm trees in Miami, Florida.

or floodwall. The system was not designed for a storm of such strength.

More than a million people in the Gulf region were displaced by the storm. Officials at NOAA say that Katrina was the most destructive storm to hit the States. With an estimated $125 billion in damages, it significantly outranks the competition in terms of property damage. Superstorm Sandy of 2012, the second costliest storm for the United States, lags far behind with damages in the $65 billion range. Sandy had transformed from a hurricane into a post-tropical storm when it came ashore with damaging features of both a hurricane and a strong storm.

The East Coast of North America tells the story of extreme weather by recounting the hurricanes.

Predictably Unpredictable

Hurricanes fascinate and horrify us. They epitomize the extreme weather experience: fierce, long-lasting, merciless, leaving

Waves destroy an erosion-control fence on North Carolina's Outer Banks.

destruction in their wake. We know they are coming. We know the shape they will take: a great spinning vortex of counterclockwise winds, with a center of uncanny calm. These days, meteorologists can even predict with some accuracy where they will hit. And yet all we can do is prepare for the onslaught: We can do nothing to stop them.

It used to be that only those communities in the United States touched by hurricanes— primarily the Gulf Coast and the southeastern coastline, up through Virginia on the East—would pay attention, but today media weathermen track them vigilantly from the middle of the North Atlantic on, and even those people never likely to feel their winds are glued to the news.

The Atlantic hurricane region experiences an active season starting June 1 and stretching to the end of November. The Pacific hurricane region starts two weeks earlier, May 15. Scientists model global forces, both oceanic and atmospheric, to make long-term predictions about a coming hurricane season. But they never really

---

NOAA BEST PRACTICES PRUNE NEARBY BRANCHES

In spring, before hurricane season, look around your yard for trees and shrubs that may have grown precariously. Trim them so branches don't break and fall or fly into your home.

Big trees pose hazards to nearby houses when high winds prevail.

The streets of Brooklyn, New York, are flooded after Superstorm Sandy hit.

know until a hurricane takes shape what will happen when, especially when it comes to the question of landfall and property damage.

Hurricanes can bring with them an array of hazards to life and property: ripping and persistent winds, torrential rainfall, coastal storm surges, inland flooding, and even tornadoes.

Defining Terms

A hurricane is defined as a tropical cyclone with sustained winds that have reached speeds of 74 miles an hour or higher. A storm begins as a tropical depression, an area of low pressure circled by winds blowing counterclockwise at a speed under 39 mph. If the winds reach 39 mph, the storm gains the status of tropical storm and is given a name. If the winds increase to 74 mph, the storm becomes a hurricane. A tropical cyclone can last for days, some strengthening but many remaining tropical storms until they die.

Hurricanes are classified using the Saffir-Simpson Hurricane Wind Scale, which assigns a category between 1 and 5 based on a hurricane's sustained wind speed. The ratings offer an estimate of potential property damage;

thus a hurricane of Category 3 or higher is considered a major hurricane because of the potential for significant destruction and loss of lives.

Weather reporters and meteorologists use language carefully to describe the degree of danger presented by an oncoming storm. Listen for the distinction between "tropical storm" and "hurricane" and between a "watch" and a "warning":

Tropical Storm Watch: Tropical storm conditions—sustained winds, 39 to 73 mph—are possible within 48 hours.

Tropical Storm Warning: Tropical storm conditions—sustained winds, 39 to 73 mph—are likely within 36 hours.

Hurricane Watch: Hurricane conditions—sustained winds, 74 mph or higher—are possible within 48 hours.

Hurricane Warning: Hurricane conditions—sustained winds, 74 mph or higher—are likely within 36 hours.

What to Do
Most people who live in hurricane-prone areas already

Gear and Gadgets
↘ CLIPS AND STRAPS SECURE THE ROOF

Hurricanes can produce so much wind that the roof can literally be ripped off a home—through a combination of wind pressure against walls and upward lift. Hurricane clips or straps provide uplift protection. They come in a range of pressure protection designed to battle winds of 110 miles an hour or more. Typically made

Secure your house's rafters in case of high wind.

of galvanized steel, hurricane clips or straps strengthen the connection between your roof trusses or rafters and your walls. Best installed as a house is built, they can also be retrofitted during roof repairs or roof replacement.

recognize the dangers and plan ahead. Hurricane preparedness involves long-term, proactive planning as well as wise immediate response:

Planning ahead: Determine the best television, radio, and online sources for local weather and safety alerts. Inform yourself about evacuation procedures in your area. Recognize the hazards and vulnerabilities of your personal property, from gutters and drainage pipes to outdoor furniture. Keep things clean, clear, and ready to be brought inside or tied up for safety.

Responding wisely: Don't panic. Follow guidelines of public officials as well as you can. Keep informed about storm conditions, and keep loved ones informed of your safety as well. Help others if you can do so without endangering them or yourself. Don't risk life and limb to save physical property.

Storm Surges

The Saffir-Simpson Scale does a good job of alerting people to the wind dangers of hurricanes, but it does not necessarily describe storm surges and storm tides and the threats they pose.

Storm tides occur when the wind of an ocean-borne storm combines with existing tides to create an extremely high water level. Waves crash much higher on shore than they would otherwise. The undertow sucks down, under, and back out to sea with equally massive force. Recent hurricane devastation in the United States came as much from storm surge and

Continued on page 99

Did You Know?
↘ FINDING SHELTER

The Red Cross, local governments, and FEMA operate shelters for storm victims. Call your local city hall office, download the Red Cross shelter app, or text SHELTER plus your zip code to 43362 (4FEMA) to find a shelter near you. In addition, religious organizations are sometimes overlooked sources for help. Neighborhood places of worship can provide helping hands and places of comfort when you need them.

Gear and Gadgets
↘ PROTECT WINDOWS WITH STORM SHUTTERS

If you live in an area susceptible to hurricanes or other high-wind storms, your windows are at risk of breaking, either from the wind itself or, more likely, from debris hurled by the storm winds. Short of having storm-grade shutters professionally installed, a do-it-yourself option can suffice, as long as you follow key guidelines.

• Use at least ½-inch-thick plywood; some suggest ⅝-inch marine grade. Most building codes also allow Oriented Strand Board (OSB) to be used. Although it is lighter to mount, it does not provide equal impact resistance for the thickness. Metal and polycarbonate panels can also be used.

• Anchor shutters securely. Although nailing boards to the exterior wall can work once, refastening at the same place over and over will weaken your walls. Reusable bolts or other permanent anchors will allow you to install and remove panels every time a hurricane approaches.

The building codes in most hurricane-prone regions in the United States require a certain level of storm shutter, whether temporary or permanent, and whether operated manually or motor driven. FEMA, state emergency management agencies, and hardware manufacturers all provide extensive specifications for shutter materials and design.

Shutters are mandatory in some areas where storms occur frequently.

Water surrounds homes in New Orleans after Hurricane Katrina in 2005.

EXTREMES

HURRICANE IMPACT

• In 2005 Hurricane Wilma, a devastating storm in the North Atlantic, caused more than $16 billion in damage in Florida.

• That same year, Hurricane Katrina caused more than $100 billion in damages, primarily from storm surge and flooding.

• The deadliest hurricane to hit the United States occurred in 1900, when the Galveston Hurricane killed between 6,000 and 8,000 people.

EXTREME WEATHER BASICS
How Hurricanes Happen

Hurricanes begin as tropical disturbances in the open ocean and develop into more mature storm systems. As moisture evaporates, it rises high into the atmosphere where the water vapor condenses, releasing latent heat that forces the air to rise higher and faster. Air flowing in to replace the rising air creates the storm's winds, which increase in speed as rising air accelerates upward.

Earth's rotation causes the winds to curve, spiraling into storms counterclockwise in the Northern Hemisphere, clockwise in the Southern. Hurricanes assume a predictable shape: a spiral of winds circling around a center of calm. Imagining this shape can help you stay safe through a hurricane. Wind direction indicates what sector of the hurricane is passing over you. Remember that a calm does not mean the end of the storm: It is possible that the eye is passing over you and winds just as fierce but blowing the opposite direction are on their way.

Water above 79°F feeds these winds, and the storm grows; when it moves over land or cooler water, it weakens. But that can be a lingering death. The water vapor that rose into a cyclone condenses into thick clouds, with some falling as heavy rain. Even as a hurricane weakens, it can carry enough water vapor and condensed water to spread flooding rain far inland.

FORECASTING HURRICANES

Six days before Hurricane Sandy came ashore—it was over the Bahamas at the time—forecasters predicted it would hit the United States in New Jersey and New York on October 29, 2012, just as it did.

This success illustrates how hurricane path forecasts are improving, and yet strength predictions are not—in fact, they can be off by a whole category on the Saffir-Simpson scale. Predicting the global-scale winds that steer hurricanes is easier then understanding, measuring, and predicting the interactions among air moving up, down, and around, and water changing among its vapor, liquid, and ice phases that help control wind speeds. Satellites and airplanes that fly through hurricanes cannot capture all of the data needed to reliably predict when and by how much a storm will strengthen or weaken.

Steering current

Air leaving the storm's top

Low-level winds spiraling into the storm

Hurricanes feed on winds for strength.

Superstorm Sandy darkens Manhattan, which suffered a power outage as a result of the storm.

floodwaters surge as from the hurricane itself.

A hurricane's fastest wind speed is only one of the factors that determine surge height. A hurricane's size, its wind speeds, the configuration of the land including the coastal ocean floor, the tidal cycle, and even the weeks of weather preceding a hurricane all contribute to surge shape and strength. As the wind circulates around the eye of a hurricane, it blows on the ocean surface and piles up water under the storm. When this happens in deep water, some of the water just swirls away. But when it happens in shallow water, the ocean floor

IBHS
BEST PRACTICES AVOID USING GRAVEL

If you live in a hurricane-prone area, don't use gravel or pebbles as landscaping. Strong gusts can pick up these small stones and hurl them, causing property damage.

High winds blew sea foam onto North Carolina's Jennette's Pier, as Sandy moved into the area.

resists the swirling and the surge gets higher as it is forced toward shore. This explains why places where the water is relatively shallow far offshore, such as around much of the Gulf of Mexico, see higher storm surges than places with deeper water offshore. Storm surge can travel several miles inland and is sometimes higher when it's squeezed into the mouth of a bay.

Hurricane strength does not predict storm surge intensity. For example, Hurricane Charley (2004) was a Category 4 hurricane when it made landfall in southwest Florida in 2004, yet the storm surge it produced there maxed out at 3 or 4 feet.

In comparison, Hurricane Ike (2008) had weakened to a Category 2 storm when it scraped over Galveston Island, but its storm surge measured 15 to 20 feet above normal tide levels. Hurricane Katrina (2005) hit Mississippi and Louisiana as a 125-mph Category 3 hurricane but produced about 25 to 28 feet of surge in some places.

Storm surges, by definition, impact development along the coastline. According to statistics from NOAA, more than half of the U.S. economy depends on activity within coastal zones. As much as 67 percent of the nation's interstate miles, nearly 50 percent of the nation's railroad miles, 29 airports, and virtually all Gulf Coast ports lie low enough that a 23-foot storm surge could devastate them.

Because storm surges and storm tides can impact life and property dramatically, the U.S. National Hurricane Center is including information on them in its hurricane watches and warnings, hoping that those in the paths of storms become more aware of the surge dangers that come with them.

Build a Seawall of Sandbags
Technology these days gives us early warning and plenty of information about approaching hurricanes and even the accompanying danger of storm surges before, during, or after the time that the storm hits land. We can keep lines of communication open, both among family and friends and also with community representatives and weather experts.

But as important as advanced technology is to our knowledge and response to extreme weather, sometimes the best recourse for safety is a tried and true old-fashioned response, such as creating an artificial seawall to hold back water surging in vulnerable places.

If you live in an area known for storm surges, you should know

---

Gear and Gadgets
➘ HOW TO PURIFY WATER

Water contamination can be a hazard after a hurricane. If your local public health department has issued a boil-water order, you should be careful to do that or to use only prestored water.

To follow the boil-water order as you use water from the tap, do the following:
• Strain water through paper towels; alternatively, let the water settle for 24 hours and pour it out, leaving sediment behind.
• Keep at a rolling boil for at least 10 minutes.
• You may use chemical treatments such as iodine or chlorine. For iodine, use 2 percent tincture, 20 drops per gallon. For unscented liquid chlorine bleach, use 2 drops per gallon.
• Stir and let the water sit for 30 to 60 minutes.
• Mix between containers and add a pinch of salt per quart to improve the flat taste.

Outfitters also sell water purification kits for camping. These can come in handy during hurricane recovery as well.

ahead of time how to build a seawall of sandbags.

First, know where a supply of sand and sandbags will be available. Communities in surge zones usually stockpile for their citizens. You can also purchase empty sandbags at retail outlets and online, and if you do not live near a beach, where sand is abundant, you may need to buy some. Purchase coarse sand, the kind you would use in a sandbox or to rough up an icy road. Determine well ahead of hurricane season where you will get your supply.

Filling a sandbag is ideally done by two people: one to hold the bag open (feet shoulder width apart, bag slightly in front of feet) with a collar folded over, and the shoveler to fill it with sand (one-third to one-half of capacity). Partially filling allows the bags to be lifted more easily and leaves room for a good seal.

To build a barrier, first clear any debris from the area where the bags are to be placed. As you position each bag, fold the open end as if you were wrapping the end of a package, with each corner tucked down diagonally and the triangular point folded under.

Place bags one on top of the next lengthwise and parallel to

Did You Know?
↘ CONE OF UNCERTAINTY

The National Hurricane Center illustrates its track forecasts with a "cone of uncertainty." The black line shows the forecast path of the hurricane's eye, and black dots show its locations at specific times. Two-thirds of the time the eye should travel within the predicted area, but if the eye veers near the edge, hurricane winds will spread outside the cone.

Even if the projected lines suggest an approaching storm won't hit you, if you're urged to evacuate, do it. Emergency managers know how to apply forecasts to their communities. You're better off returning from an evacuation to find your house hardly damaged than being there when storm surge washes it away.

Neighborhoods and highways in New Orleans remain flooded after Hurricane Katrina.

A reserve pararescuer scans the ravaged Texas landscape after Hurricane Ike in 2008.

the water flow, with the open end tucked under and facing against the flow. Build up a solid wall, overlapping each bag's edge with the next one. Stomp them into place to form a strong joint. Think of your project as creating a wall—a sand castle if you will—built almost like one made of Lego blocks. It needs to be solid, orderly, and packed densely.

Sandbags stacked three high represent a seawall of approximately one foot high. If you need to build higher, the U.S. Army Corps of Engineers recommends using a pyramid placement method, carefully alternating the bags crosswise and lengthwise to form a pyramid. Taller sandbag sea walls are less sturdy, however. Where they are needed, it is best to have an expert on the scene. To form a barrier one foot above a levee that is 100 feet wide requires 600 sandbags, according to the Army Corps of Engineers.

There's an App for That
Available for download from iTunes and/or Google Play,

these apps may be helpful during hurricane season.

→ The iPhone app **Hurricane Tracker** provides detailed storm maps, National Hurricane Center info, threat-level maps, forecast updates, real-time feeds, and push alerts. It also works on iPads, Macs, and PCs.

→ **iHurricane** allows you to track hurricanes using satellite and radar data, set up email alerts, and calculate your distance from various points of the storm.

→ The **Hurricane American Red Cross** app helps monitor conditions but primarily provides information on preparing home and family, finding help and shelters, and alerting others of your status.

→ **Hurricane Pro** offers fairly comprehensive meteorological information, including tracking maps, satellite views, five-day forecasts, radar, and bulletins from the National Hurricane Center.

Avoiding Vacation Disappointments

Although the odds are relatively low that a hurricane will hit the Caribbean island, Gulf of Mexico coast, or Mexico's Pacific coast you're visiting, it could happen. And if it happens, the consequences could be serious, if not deadly.

Local authorities or the hotel management will likely help you get to safety, but even so, you could enter a world without power, running water, and people to cook food and clean your room. If you like adventure, this saturation of events will make for great stories when you get home. If you're the kind of

A man searches through debris in Galveston in the aftermath of Hurricane Ike.

person who calls the front desk to yell at the clerk if room service is late, the aftermath of a hurricane will be hell.

Thus, it's wise to keep the dates of hurricane season—June 1 to November 1—in mind when making plans to visit hurricane-prone locales. And if you do choose to travel then, today's forecasters usually can give at least two or three days warning that a storm will hit, so you should have time to evacuate.

But in some cases, this may not be possible. For example, Hurricane Wilma in 2005 went

Gear and Gadgets
⬊ HOME GENERATORS

When the power goes out, a home generator can keep the lights on, heat going, and food from spoiling. Many people opt for one that can be wheeled into place when it's needed, although *Consumer Reports*, the independent product reviewing and testing magazine, says that a stationary model with a built-in transfer switch is best. The switch connects the unit to your circuit box and eliminates the need for extension cords.

Most households will do fine with a generator that outputs 5,000 to 7,000 watts. A refrigerator, by example, needs about 600 watts to run; the average lightbulb, 60. A window air conditioner requires 1,000 watts, and a portable heater 1,500 watts, so if your goal is to operate one or more of those, in addition to other household lights and appliances, you should shop for a higher-power generator.

A big consideration is fuel. Stationary models operate on propane or natural gas, which offers extended run times and eliminates hazardous fuel spillage on the ground. Most portable generators run off gasoline or diesel fuel. Whichever yours uses, be sure to stock enough to last for several days. A gas or diesel generator running constantly can require more than 20 gallons of fuel a day.

Important: Never run gasoline generators in enclosed spaces, basements, or garages—even with the garage doors open, carbon monoxide can seep into a house. According to *Consumer Reports*, more than 80 people die each year in the United States from inhaling carbon monoxide fumes, although this doesn't necessarily occur from running generators.

A portable electric generator

A family seeks refuge during a hurricane at a temporary Red Cross shelter.

from a Category 1 or 2 to a strong Category 5 in less than a day in the Caribbean Sea. Fortunately, because it was about two days away from hitting near Cancun, Mexico, the authorities were able to get thousands of residents and tourists to safe places in time.

As for a Caribbean cruise in hurricane season, today's ships almost always have the information they need to avoid sailing into storms. Even so, if a hurricane is anywhere in the Caribbean, the waves and swells in the entire sea will be large, and that will be an adventure in itself.

Hurricanes in the Future

A rise in global temperatures and the resulting upsurge in extreme weather do not necessarily lead to more hurricanes each year. It may instead change the nature of the hurricanes we experience.

The National Center for Atmospheric Research notes that sea-surface temperatures across the tropics have gone up along with global temperature over the past century and are expected to continue to rise in the next century. All else being equal, it claims, warmer oceans can support stronger hurricanes. The organization reports that the additional water evaporating into the atmosphere because of warmer oceans can increase rainfall from hurricanes by as much as 8 percent for every 1.8°F of temperature rise.

Scientists at NOAA's Geophysical Fluid Dynamics Laboratory (GFDL) use computer models to envision changing patterns in climate caused by natural and human causes. They have concluded that it is too early to ascribe past changes in hurricane activity to a global warming, yet they note that simulated hurricanes tend to be more intense in a warmer climate. GFDL model projections for the late 21st century suggest that climate changes related to global warming, such as increases in vertical wind shear over the Caribbean, will actually result in fewer yet more intense hurricanes in the future. They conclude that warming by the end of the 21st century will likely cause hurricanes globally to be more intense on average by 2 to 11 percent. ∎

Good Idea
↘ HOW TO TURN OFF YOUR GAS SUPPLY

To prevent gas leaks that could be caused from a storm, sometimes it's necessary to turn off your gas supply.

To close off your natural gas:
• Use an adjustable wrench.
• Locate your gas meter (outside).
• Turn the valve handle on the pipe entering the meter so it is perpendicular to the pipe (one-quarter turn).

To close off your propane tank:
• Find the shutoff valve under the cap on top of the tank. For underground tanks, the cap should be sticking out of the ground.
• Turn the valve cap clockwise until it stops. In tanks manufactured before 1994, you may need to turn the valve counterclockwise to close it.

In both cases, when the danger is over, DO NOT attempt to relight your pilot lights. Contact your fuel provider or fire department to do this for you and to check for any leaks.

Cars clog the road as Galveston citizens scramble to get out of Hurricane Rita's path.

FIRST PERSON: Andy Pedersen, resident of Sea Bright, New Jersey

Riding Out Hurricane Sandy

A flooded New Jersey street is dimly lit during rains from Sandy in 2012.

WHEN HURRICANE Sandy came crashing into the East Coast on October 29, 2012, no one could have known just how much destruction it would cause: billions of dollars in damage, more than 100 people killed in the United States, and more than 23,000 people seeking refuge in shelters, according to FEMA. Some people stayed put in their homes, despite calls for evacuation. Andy Pedersen was one of them.

"To be honest about it, we weren't as prepared for it as we should have been," says Pedersen. He and his family had lived through a hurricane the year before, and he felt they overreacted. "It really wasn't severe at all," Pedersen says. This time, he underreacted.

Pedersen lives in Sea Bright, New Jersey, at the tip of a peninsula with an average width of only one-fourth of a mile. His wife and children left when news reports began predicting an epic storm, but Pedersen remained. As the storm hit, he realized there was nothing he could do to stop the flooding. He scrambled to the top floor of his house and braved it out.

"I was upstairs listening to ships and boats and different types of debris smashing into the side of the house throughout the night. The tide kind of came in and then went out. I had a little sailboat that was probably 15 or 18 feet long in my driveway on a trailer, and the water came so high it just picked that up, and I watched that boat go up and down the street a couple of times and then just disappear. Our wall in the back of the house was punctured and that's where the majority of the water had come rushing in through and then burst out through the windows downstairs."

> **"Watching the water rise and continue to rise is a helpless, scary feeling."**

Afterward, the damage was overwhelming. "Everyone was sort of walking around in a daze," he says. "Out in the river, there were sailboats that were upside down." The National Guard barricaded entry into the town, which was destroyed.

"Buildings that were there the day before were gone," says Pedersen. "It was like a war zone." No power, no heat, looting in the neighborhood. Slowly he realized that the damage was beyond anything he could fix alone, and Pedersen drove with his family to Vermont, where a daughter lived. With scant emergency supplies available in New Jersey, the Pedersens bought generators and loaded up with gasoline and dry goods in Vermont. Returning to Sea Bright,

they had to show identification to prove they owned property there.

Unlike hundreds of others, Pedersen's home wasn't lost to the storm, but rebuilding would come at a cost: "It was a slow, slow process, and actually I find it sometimes hard to believe that it was only a year ago. It seems much longer now, and we hope it never happens again."

Looking back, Pedersen admits he should have evacuated before the storm. "If the house had collapsed—and that happened to people—it would've been nothing I could have done. I was completely at the mercy of nature is the best way to put it. Watching the water rise and continue to rise and come so close to the community is a pretty helpless and scary feeling at the same time."

A destroyed home along the Jersey shore

EXPERT WITNESS: **Kerry Emanuel**

Global Trends in Hurricanes

A New Jersey pier devastated
by Hurricane Sandy

Kerry Emanuel, *professor of atmospheric science at Massachusetts Institute of Technology*

→ **Does the fact that there's more moisture in the atmosphere today mean we could see a rise in the destructiveness of hurricanes?**
Yes, because of the rainfall. For a given storm of a certain size and wind speed, it's going to rain more. Substantially more. That's one thing that all scientists agree on—hurricanes will rain more.

But there's another factor. Hurricanes are inhibited by the relative dryness of the atmosphere about two or three miles above the surface of the ocean. The relative dryness actually goes up with global warming. So the inhibition to hurricanes also goes up. And that generally is thought to result in fewer storms, even though they may get more intense.

→ **We're talking about global trends, right? You can't say whether we're going to have more hurricanes in Florida, say.**
No. The tracks that hurricanes take are also affected by climate change, because the large-scale

winds will change too. The problem is, models don't agree very well yet on exactly how they will change. It's conceivable that hurricanes will become more numerous in the North Atlantic and that they will hit the United States less often if the tracks were to change in the right way.

→ Why is climate change likely to increase the strength of hurricanes?

Well, you can think of a hurricane as a massive heat engine—a giant machine for converting heat energy into wind energy. And what determines how much wind energy it can produce is the rate at which you can shovel heat into the front end of the engine. In the case of a hurricane, you're putting it in at the ocean surface and taking it out way up ten miles or more in tropical atmosphere where the air flows out of the hurricane. There's a huge difference in temperature, because it's very cold up there. That makes a hurricane a relatively efficient engine.

→ How does climate change affect that?

When you put more greenhouse gases into the atmosphere, you block infrared radiation from leaving the surface of the ocean and going into space. But at the same time, the ocean is absorbing just as much sunlight

as ever. So it's got to get rid of the heat somehow. And the only way it can get rid of it is by evaporating water.

→ Have we seen any evidence during the past 50 years or so that climate change has already begun to affect hurricanes?

For the Atlantic as a whole, definitely yes. For the U.S. coastline, probably not. Over the last 30 years, hurricane power has doubled in the Atlantic.

→ Will rising sea levels also make the destructiveness of hurricanes worse?

People should understand that the storm surge is historically the single most lethal aspect of hurricanes. Having a storm surge is like having a tsunami in the middle of having a hurricane. It's essentially the same thing, except that it's excited by winds rather than by an earthquake.

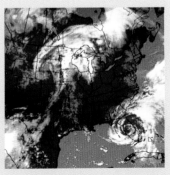

Map showing Hurricane Frances over Florida in 2004

HOW TO: **PREPARE**

→ **WHAT TO DO**

Indoors

- ☑ Keep an adequate supply of bottled water in a safe place. Water may not be available for days.

- ☑ Become aware of how prone to hurricane damage, including storm surge, your community is.

- ☑ Put together a plan on how to best secure your property, including how to cover windows and better fasten your roof to its frame.

- ☑ Find out if your area has community evacuation routes.

- ☑ Install a power generator, if possible, in case of outage.

- ☑ If you live in a high-rise building, determine a place to go on a lower floor—experts recommend below the tenth floor.

- ☑ If you live in a single-family dwelling, consider establishing a safe room where you can go during a storm. A reinforced basement is a good option because it already provides underground protection from winds and the dangers of flying debris.

- ☑ Prepare for possible outages by gathering as much water as possible. Fill sinks, tubs, and other large containers.

Outdoors

- ☑ Become aware of any bodies of water close by, including man-made dams and levees, that could be affected by a hurricane or its accompanying storm surge.

- ☑ Check trees and shrubs around your home to ensure they are well trimmed and wind resistant.

- ☑ Keep all gutters and drains clean and clear.

- ☑ Have a plan and a place to store outdoor furniture and loose items such as grills and garbage cans.

- ☑ If you have a boat, have the equipment, location, and plan to secure it well before a storm hits.

Boats may be safer in yards than in the water during a hurricane.

→ WHAT *NOT* TO DO

Indoors

☒ Do not ignore storm warnings. Listen closely to weather reports and respond accordingly to public warnings and announcements.

☒ Do not tempt timing. Trust public announcements and safety directions, even if they seem conservative. Better safe than sorry.

☒ Do not open and close your refrigerator as much as usual before a storm. This will keep things colder longer.

☒ Do not keep all appliances plugged in if a storm is approaching. Only leave necessary electronics plugged in.

Outdoors

☒ Do not let your vehicle's fuel tank dip too low. Keep a full tank in case you have to evacuate.

☒ Do not leave your windows exposed. If you don't have storm shutters, board windows with plywood.

☒ Do not leave the main valve to your propane tank on if you know a storm is coming.

☒ Do not forget to detach the propane tank for your barbecue grill before securing the grill or bringing it under cover.

HOW TO: **SURVIVE**

→ **WHAT TO DO**

Indoors

☑ Stay attuned to weather reports in case you are advised to evacuate.

☑ Make sure you close all your storm shutters.

☑ Secure or bring inside any furniture and other outdoor objects.

☑ Keep the refrigerator and freezer thermostats to their coldest settings and try to minimize opening and closing their doors.

☑ If you are told to do so, turn off all your utilities.

☑ Check that your gas lines and tanks are turned off.

☑ Evacuate if you are told to do so by officials, and follow their instructions.

☑ Keep curtains and blinds closed. These can act as added protection from flying debris.

☑ Keep doors to the outside closed and locked.

☑ Stay inside and in an interior room, preferably in the basement or on the ground floor.

Outdoors

☑ If time and conditions allow it, move your boat onto a mooring. If not, tie up securely, allowing for significant water level rise, higher than ordinary.

☑ Remember that the eye of the hurricane is calm and therefore deceptive; it may simply mean the storm is halfway over. Stay safe until you are sure the storm has passed.

☑ Look for flooding, and stay off flooded roads and washed-out bridges.

☑ Be alert for tornadoes; hurricanes can

sometimes produce these as a by-product of their severity.

☑ Watch out for flying debris, often more dangerous to life and property than the winds themselves.

A boat slams against a pier. The year 2004 was a wicked Atlantic hurricane season.

→ WHAT *NOT* TO DO

Indoors

☒ Do not go outside.

☒ Do not stand or crouch near windows and doors.

☒ Do not leave interior doors open; they can swing loose and become hazards.

☒ Do not be fooled by a lull in storm activity; the eye of a hurricane is calm, but strong winds pick up again.

☒ Do not stay in large, open rooms. It's better to take refuge in smaller rooms in the center of your home. A closet or hallway on the lowest level can provide safety.

☒ Do not remain exposed and standing. If the storm hits your home, lie on the floor under a table or another sturdy object.

☒ If you live in a high-rise, do not take the elevator to lower floors; use the stairs.

☒ Do not use your phone unless it's urgent. This will prevent logjams on telephone lines and free up "space" for emergency calls.

Outdoors

☒ Do not guess when the storm is over; wait for official reports or for the sky to clear for an extended period.

☒ Do not seek refuge in weak structures; take shelter in solid buildings.

☒ Do not ignore evacuation routes; mind officials' directions.

HOW TO: **RECOVER**

→ **WHAT TO DO**

Indoors

☑ Be on the lookout for wild animals, especially poisonous snakes that may have swept in.

☑ Take photos of any damage for insurance purposes.

☑ Contact a structural engineer or building inspector if you have doubts about your home's safety.

☑ Watch your pets, and do not allow them to stray.

☑ Use caution when walking in or around debris.

☑ Check your foundation and walls for any structural damage.

☑ Check all food for spoilage. If in doubt, throw it out.

Outdoors

☑ Wear proper and protective clothing when you are cleaning after a storm.

☑ Use caution in your yard and around your home.

☑ Check for power lines that may have loosened.

☑ Check for gas leaks: Smell for the odor; listen for any hissing.

☑ Be aware that flooding and debris flows can follow a hurricane, sometimes hours or even days after a storm event. Monitor news stations for flood reports.

An aerial view shows New York's battered coastline after Sandy in 2012.

Volunteers help homeowners reclaim neighborhoods after Katrina.

→ WHAT *NOT* TO DO

Indoors

☒ Do not drink or prepare food with tap water until you are sure it's not contaminated.

☒ Do not light any candles. This could ignite any gas present.

☒ Do not turn on flashlights for the first time indoors; the flame or flashlight battery could ignite leaking gas, if present. Step outside to turn your flashlight on, or do so before reentering your home if you evacuated.

☒ Never use a generator inside your home or any enclosed space.

Outdoors

☒ Do not drive unless absolutely necessary, and stay off the streets.

☒ Do not ever go near dangling power lines. If you spot them, immediately report their location to your local power company.

☒ Do not reenter your home if you smell gas.

Superstorm Sandy stranded
Seaside Heights' JetStar
roller coaster in the Atlantic.

EXTREMES

HURRICANES AT THEIR WORST

• Superstorm Sandy in 2012 devastated New York, New Jersey, and other parts of the Northeast, causing about $65 billion in damage and claiming 159 lives.

• Hurricane Katrina in 2005 was the costliest hurricane in U.S. history. It crashed onto shore in Louisiana and Texas, and further along the Gulf Coast, causing more than $125 billion in damage and claiming more than 1,800 lives.

• The worst cyclone storm in terms of deaths was in 1970 in the Bay of Bengal; as many as 500,000 people were killed when the storm hit East Pakistan and Bangladesh.

A land-spout tornado grinds across a farm road in western Kansas.

CHAPTER 4

TORNADOES

The season started quietly in the midsection of the United States, known for its ferocious spring tornadoes. The Great Plains stayed cold and dry, wintry. In fact, the entire 12-month span from May 2012 to April 2013 was "remarkable for the absence of tornado activity in the United States," according to a NOAA meteorologist. But things changed in the middle of May. "After a very slow start for the year," renowned storm chaser and researcher Tim Samaras wrote to his National Geographic colleagues on May 20, "it appears that 'Tornado Alley' is finally living up to its name."

Nineteen tornadoes roared through northeast Texas on May 15, with hail the size of baseballs. One town alone suffered six dead, hundreds injured, and whole neighborhoods blown to smithereens. Intense supercells formed up on May 19, kicking up multiple tornadoes. NOAA tracked 34 sightings; twisters scraped through seven Oklahoma towns and killed two near Shawnee. May 20 was worse for Oklahoma, though, as a brutal tornado stayed alive for 39 minutes, churning up a path 1.1 miles wide and 14 miles long along the southern edge of Oklahoma City, sending hundreds to the hospital and leaving more than 24 people dead.

This was the kind of weather Tim Samaras looked for. He and his team tracked 11 tornadoes during those three days, although, as he wrote in his email, his team "attempted an intercept on the storm that eventually produced the tornado near Shawnee," but they arrived

---

RED CROSS BEST PRACTICES VACATE YOUR MOBILE HOME

American Red Cross

Mobile homes are not safe during tornadoes. If possible, leave your mobile home and get to the nearest sturdy building or shelter. Heed public warnings and do not wait until the tornado is in sight. Do not consider a bathroom or hallway in a mobile home to be a safe interior space.

20 minutes too late. "Storm chasing can be very frustrating at times," he commented, and correctly predicted a quietus for the next few days.

But on May 31, in the words of the NOAA account, "a potent set of ingredients came together" and tornadoes blasted Oklahoma once again, including one deemed by NOAA "one of the most powerful tornadoes sampled by mobile radar and also the widest known tornado on record," cutting a swath more than 2½ miles wide. One, two, three different funnels churned out of supercells at once, forming up in record time with hurricane-force winds lower to the ground than usual.

The monster twister left eight people dead, including Tim Samaras, his son Paul, and his teammate, meteorologist Carl Young. In retrospect, all who knew him remembered Samaras's utmost concern for storm safety. His story stands as witness to the unknowable, more-than-human, overwhelming brutality of weather extremes.

More than a thousand tornadoes occur in the United States every year, more than in any other place on Earth. A good half of them occur during the late spring in the Plains—a region called Tornado Alley for their prevalence. They are violent, forceful, and sudden. The most destructive of them spawn from massive supercell thunderstorms, forming up on average in a mere 13 minutes. They move fast; they can grow or change direction abruptly. On average, tornadoes cause an average of 70 fatalities and 1,500 injuries in the United States each year. Those who live in tornado-prone

Did You Know?
↘ NATURE'S SIGNAL

While looking after your pets, you may want to look to them for your own safety. There have been numerous instances of pets getting agitated and exhibiting strange behavior before a tornado. Apparently, some dogs howl, cats head for more confined spaces, and birds will stop going to feeders.

An image of a supercell thunderstorm reveals its awesome power.

Describing Tornadoes

A tornado is a narrow, fiercely rotating column of air stretching down from a thunderstorm to the ground. It forms when warm, humid air rotates as it rises into the storm cloud.

Tornadoes grow in many dimensions: the breadth of the storm as it engulfs the air; the width of the track it carves out on land; the speed at which it travels across the land; the time and distance it remains formed up as a twister; and the speed of its spiraling winds. A tornado a mile or so wide can strafe the ground for more than 50 miles; the strongest tornadoes have rotating winds of more than 250 miles an hour. Tornadoes move at an average speed of 30 miles an hour, but some stand still and some speed up to 70 miles an hour. Most tornadoes move from southwest to northeast. But it's important to note that every one of these factors is difficult to predict until the storm happens.

Meteorologists and engineers estimate a tornado's strength by examining the damage after the twister hits. In the 1970s, University of Chicago meteorologist

regions must know the signs and the protocol; those who live elsewhere do best to stay informed.

Storm debris
is strewn
about a
Missouri
neighborhood.

and leading tornado scientist T. Theodore Fujita created a ranking system, expressing estimated tornado wind speed by assessing the physical damage caused. The National Weather Service upgraded it, and improvements since resulted in the Enhanced Fujita Scale, abbreviated "EF." Unlike the Saffir-Simpson hurricane scale, which is based on wind measurements and estimates before a storm hits, EF ratings are assigned after a storm has passed, based on examining the damage.

The EF ratings are:

→ **EF0 (65–85 mph):** Light damage. Peels surface off some roofs; some damage to gutters or siding; branches broken off trees; shallow-rooted trees pushed over.

→ **EF1 (86–110 mph):** Moderate damage. Roofs severely stripped; mobile homes overturned or badly damaged; loss of exterior doors; windows and other glass broken.

→ **EF2 (111–135 mph):** Considerable damage. Roofs torn off well-constructed houses; foundations of frame homes shifted; mobile homes completely destroyed; large trees snapped or uprooted; light-object missiles generated; cars lifted off ground.

→ **EF3 (136–165 mph):** Severe damage. Entire stories of well-constructed houses destroyed; severe damage to large buildings such as shopping malls; trains overturned; trees debarked; heavy cars lifted off the ground and thrown; structures with weak foundations blown away some distance.

→ **EF4 (166–200 mph):** Devastating damage. Well-constructed houses and whole frame houses completely leveled; cars thrown and small missiles generated.

→ **EF5 (winds above 200 mph):** Incredible damage. Strong frame

---

NOAA BEST PRACTICES IN TALL BUILDINGS

If a tornado approaches and you are in a tall building, go to an enclosed, windowless area in the center of the building on the lowest floor possible away from glass. Interior stairwells are usually good places to take shelter, and if not crowded, allow you to get to a lower level quickly. Stay out of elevators.

houses leveled off foundations and swept away; automobile-size missiles fly through the air in excess of 100 yards; high-rise buildings have significant structural deformation; incredible phenomena will occur.

As with many other extreme weather events, public announcements differentiate between a "watch," meaning to stay alert, and a "warning," meaning there is known danger.

Tornado Watch: A tornado watch signifies the possibility of multiple tornadoes, often in an area as large as 25,000 square miles. If a tornado watch is issued for your area, prepare for severe weather and stay vigilant, tracking radio, television, or Internet to know when warnings are issued.

Tornado Warning: A tornado warning means a tornado

Gear and Gadgets
↘ BUILD A SAFE ROOM

If you live in a tornado-prone zone, the best protection you can plan is a designated safe room. Someone in a safe room that is built according to FEMA guidelines will have "a very high probability of being protected from injury or death," according to the agency.

An inside view of a storm shelter

An existing room can become a safe room, either in the basement or in the interior of a lower floor of your house. You can also add an exterior safe room, either on the ground or underground. There are also prefab safe rooms you can purchase and install. These claim they can withstand an EF5 tornado—the most violent kind. Some of these offer air-filtration systems, solar power, fully functional plumbing and septic systems, as well as infrared surveillance systems and escape tunnels.

To consider your options and understand required building specifications, consult FEMA P-320, "Taking Shelter From the Storm," which can be downloaded from the FEMA website.

A tornado funnel cloud strikes downtown Miami, Florida, in 1997.

has been seen or indicated by radar in an area usually covering several counties or parts of counties. A warning indicates a serious threat, and you and your loved ones should respond immediately.

Where and When?

Where on Earth? In general, conditions in the middle latitudes, roughly 30° to 50° north or south, support the most tornadoes. Within this band, cold polar air meets warmer air from the south, brewing up thunderstorms when the two meet. Add to those conditions the variations in airflow at different levels of the troposphere in these midlatitudes, facilitating the wind sheer required to form a tornado.

Where in the United States? Although tornadoes can occur nearly everywhere, they predominantly strike in the center of the continental United States, east of the Rocky Mountains and in a band from Texas and the Deep South up to lower Michigan. Ironically, these tornado-prone regions also tend to be the nation's most fertile agricultural zones, thanks to the prevalence of showers and thunderstorms.

In the United States, two areas are most subject to frequent tornadoes: Florida and so-called Tornado Alley. Florida's many thunderstorms,

Continued on page 133

A powerful tornado decimated parts of Moore, Oklahoma, in 2013.

EXTREMES

TORNADOES PAST TO PRESENT

• History's most destructive tornado occurred in 1925. The "Great Tri-State Tornado" blew across Missouri, Illinois, and Indiana, causing 219 miles of destruction.

• In 1840, the Great Natchez Tornado formed along the Mississippi River and stripped the forests of trees on each side of the riverbanks. The tornado's winds plucked small boats out of the water.

• The 2013 Moore tornado of May 20 reached EF5 supertornado wind strength status; it left a trail 14 miles long, destroying about 1,300 homes and killing 25.

EXTREME WEATHER BASICS
Unpredictable Tornadoes

Tornadoes form in the updraft rising into a thunderstorm. Supercells that spin out the strongest tornadoes depend on large-scale wind and atmospheric pressure patterns from the ground up to 35,000 feet. These include jet stream winds as fast as 150 miles an hour, upper air disturbances approximately 18,000 feet above sea level moving across the United States, southerly winds roughly 5,000 feet above the ground hauling in humid air to feed thunderstorms, and cool, dry air moving across the ground from the west or northwest to push up humid surface air and help create twisting motion.

FORECASTING TORNADOES

Computer models are quite good at forecasting at least two or three days ahead of time when the right conditions for numerous, strong tornadoes will begin and which areas they should affect. The NWS Storm Prediction Center often issues alerts pointing to a risk of a tornado outbreak in a specific part of the country two or three days in advance. Local broadcast and online meteorologists and newspapers usually pass along these outlooks.

Unfortunately, forecasters cannot pinpoint where a tornado will hit until shortly before the twister forms; even then, paths can be uncertain. When you hear an alert that tornadoes are possible in a day or two, you should abandon plans for activities that will keep you far from shelter on the day tornado weather is predicted. Also, talk with family members and refresh your emergency plan.

An updraft rises into a thunderstorm, creating a tornado.

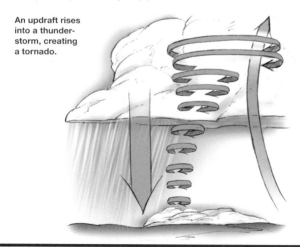

Neighbors embrace after surviving a monstrous tornado near Oklahoma City.

tropical storms, and hurricanes make the state tornado prone. Tornado Alley is the colloquial name for the loosely defined stretch of the United States that experiences the majority of the county's tornadoes, roughly from central Texas northward to northern Iowa, and from central Kansas and Nebraska east through Indiana.

When in the year? Although tornadoes can occur in every state in the United States, on any day of the year, and at any hour, there is a tornado season that generally tracks south to north. On the Gulf Coast, they occur earliest, from February to April. In the southern U.S.

Plains, they are most frequent during May and into early June. In the northern U.S. Plains and the upper Midwest, most occur in June or July.

When in the day? Because tornadoes often build out of thunderstorms, and thunderstorms happen later in the day, after they've gained force from solar energy and latent heat, it follows that tornadoes most often occur in the afternoon and evening, between 4 p.m. and 9 p.m.

What's Happening?

It takes a special set of circumstances to make a thunderstorm spawn a tornado. To understand the process, first picture a massive supercell thunderstorm cloud, with updraft winds already dynamic, fueled by significant temperature differences:

1. Warmer air rises and cooler air falls. The storm itself may be moving across the ground as well, or it may stand still.

2. Falling rain drags down air near the storm front, generating a spinning motion of air parallel to the ground. Spinning roll clouds—a bank or wedge—often form up.

3. Warm humid air rising into the storm tilts the vortex of air upward, creating a vertical column rising up into the center of the storm. That area of rotation can measure up to six miles wide and becomes the birthplace of a tornado.

4. Pulses of wind coming down with precipitation falling from the rear of the storm wrap around the column of spinning air and strengthen it into a tornado.

What's It Like?

Meteorologists often describe a tornado in the abstract, but what should people on the ground be on the lookout for? The answer might seem to be simple: a funnel-shaped force coming out of clouds in the distance. But if you see that shape, chances are you have stayed looking too long.

Aside from fierce thunderstorms and public warnings, there are telltale signs that a tornado may be approaching or forming nearby. According to the NOAA Storm Prediction Center in Norman, Oklahoma, daytime signals can be:

→ A dark bank of clouds with the appearance of rotation parallel to the ground.

→ Swirls of dust, dirt, and debris lifting up from ground level.

→ Dead calm right after heavy hail or rainfall.

→ Thunderous rumble that lasts for more than a few seconds.

Good Idea
↘ TUNE IN TO WEATHER INFO

Live weather reports are compiled online constantly by the Weather Information Network *(broadcast-weather.net).* Through it, you can set up local watch and warning alerts across multiple devices, such as your personal computer or mobile phone. The network provides live forecasts, radar images, news, and updates via streaming radio broadcasts, as well as audio streams and clips.

An EF5 tornado destroyed a home and the large trees that once surrounded it.

Nighttime signals include oddly colored lightning flashes at ground level or lightning illuminating clouds and showing their shape dipping down toward the ground. The most important thing is, if you suspect a tornado forming, act right away to protect your loved ones, take shelter, and tune in for weather alerts and information.

Water Spouts

A waterspout is a tornado over water, typically a large lake, bay, or the ocean. In the United States, the Florida Keys see the most waterspouts—several hundred a year. They also occur in the Atlantic east of Florida, in the Gulf of Mexico, and occasionally in the Great Lakes and on the West Coast.

Waterspouts come in two types: tornadic and fair weather. Tornadic waterspouts begin as tornadoes on land and then turn into waterspouts when they move over water. Fair weather waterspouts, the milder of the two, form only over water, beginning on the water's surface and building into the sky.

Waterspouts form in five stages, best imagined from above. First, a light-colored "disk" appears on the surface of water. Then a spiral pattern of light and dark-colored surface water bands begins to spiral from the dark area. A ring of sea spray, called a cascade, starts swirling around a center something like the eye of a hurricane.

The waterspout then takes shape, an apparently hollow funnel with a spray vortex that can rise several hundred feet or more above the water's surface and may create a visible wake or train of waves. The waterspout finally dissipates when warm air flows into its vortex and weakens it.

Typically, waterspouts last up to 20 minutes, often a shorter period of time, but they can be dangerous. They have overturned boats, damaged large ships, and killed people. Even weak waterspouts can churn up water and toss loose items around on a boat deck. If you see a waterspout from a boat, do all you can to move in the opposite direction. See if the waterspout is moving, and move at a 90° angle from that, letting it pass you by. If possible, seek safe harbor. On land, seek shelter.

After a Tornado

Dealing with life after a storm can sometimes be more difficult than preparing for the storm

Good Idea
↘ THE SAFEST POSITION

Once in sturdy shelter, assume a protective position during the impact of the storm. If possible, position yourself under a sturdy table. Face an interior wall. Crouch with your knees and elbows on the ground. Place your hands over the back of your head to protect your neck and head.

Schoolchildren practice a protective position to take during a tornado.

A waterspout appears in the Gulf of Mexico near Alabama.

Storm chasers use technology, including radar apps, to monitor severe weather.

itself. Stress is a common result from tornadoes, even long after they have gone. Anxiety and fear, along with the loss of a home, valuables, pets, or loved ones can bring about emotional and physical exhaustion. This should not be ignored, and needs to be treated.

As in any traumatic situation, post-traumatic stress disorder (PTSD) can result. Medical professionals can help, and there are centers designed to treat the issues. Many resources are available for children, who are especially susceptible to PTSD, including a national network: the National Child Traumatic Stress Network. According to this organization, parents should be on the lookout for children who, after a tornado, exhibit:

→ Feelings of insecurity, anxiety, fear, anger, sadness, despair, or worries about the future.

→ Fear that another tornado will happen.

→ Beliefs in untrue causes of tornadoes.

→ Disruptive behavior.

→ Unusual dependency and/ or phobias.

→ Physical ailments or sleep problems.

→ Problems at school.

If these signs progress and become chronic, professional treatment should be sought. The American Psychological Association also recommends joining local support groups with others who have suffered from natural disasters.

There's an App for That
Available for download from iTunes and/or Google Play, these apps may be helpful for tornadoes.
→ The **American Red Cross Tornado App** provides an array of tornado information, from quizzes and historical information about tornadoes in your area to an audible siren, triggered by a NOAA Tornado Warning nearby. Call ****REDCROSS (**73327677)** for a text message linking you to download sites or visit *www.redcross.org/mobile-apps/tornado-app/*.
→ **TornadoSpy+** uses crowdsourcing to provide tornado maps, warnings, and alerts; it also allows users to report and upload photos of any tornado activity they spot.
→ The **Tornado Chasers** app includes diagrams of the anatomy of a tornado and

---

Did You Know?
↘ AMAZING FLYING DEBRIS

With winds that can exceed 300 miles an hour, it should be no surprise that tornadoes can carry some very large and unexpected things—including cows. They have carried trains, cars, and trucks; toppled trees; ripped off roofs; and lifted asphalt from the ground. In one instance, a tornado created a flying mattress.

Residents sift through debris to find belongings.

According to the NWS's Storm Prediction Center, a tornado that blew through Massachusetts in 1953 launched mattress pieces from Worcester to Boston Harbor, more than 40 miles. Debris can also fly high into the air, so much so that airplane pilots thousands of feet high have witnessed material lofted by tornadoes.

a comprehensive visual guide to clouds; it also includes maps of national weather warnings for the United States, United Kingdom, and Canada—all the way down to the current information about your location.

→ **Tornado Alert** is a useful community-driven tornado early warning system. Any user who spots a tornado can send an alert to all other users of the app within 20 miles; alerts are delivered, on average, in less than five seconds. It also alerts users of a "Tornado Warning" or "Tornado Watch" in the area within one minute of the alert being issued.

Protect Your Pets

Tornadoes threaten pets, too. Some animals are sensitive to changes in severe weather and may try to hide, so it's important to keep your eye on them before things get out of hand.

The American Humane Association advises you think through pet safety procedures before, during, and after a tornado. Have an emergency kit prepared for your pet as well as your family, including a three-day supply of food, water, and medicines if necessary. Keep the following in mind:

→ If it's not safe for you outside, it's not safe for your pet; bring it inside at the first indication that a tornado may be possible. If possible, have a crate ready for each animal and put it under sturdy furniture.

→ Make your tornado-proof area pet-friendly, and have a stash of pet supplies there.

→ If your pet has a place it goes to hide when scared, practice

FEMA BEST PRACTICES BEWARE AFTERWARD

Leave your safe room or return home only when authorities indicate it is safe. If you suspect any damage to your house, immediately disconnect utilities: Shut off electric power and close gas and propane tank valves to avoid fire, electrocution, or explosions. Use a flashlight to inspect for damages: Candles can spark explosions if a gas or power line has been damaged. Don't use any device that burns gasoline, charcoal, propane, or natural gas: Carbon monoxide can build up and cause injury or death. If you smell a leak, turn the gas off and open all windows.

Cage or crate your animals to keep them safe during severe weather.

getting it out of there and into your tornado-proof area.

→ During a tornado, take your pets with you when you evacuate. Be sure they are wearing their identification tags.

→ After a tornado, give your pet time to reorient. Scents and landmarks may no longer be familiar.

→ Don't let your pet eat food or drink water that could have been contaminated during the storm.

→ After a tornado, keep dogs on leashes and cats in carriers. Be on the lookout for harmful objects left in debris.

→ Always keep pets away from downed power lines.

Tornadoes in the Future
Researchers continue to find evidence of a "robust increase" not only in thunderstorm occurrences and severity in the eastern United States, but also in the weather extremes that thunderstorms generate. Recent history supports their prediction: In the last few years, severe storms and tornadoes have produced more devastation, combined, than any other weather phenomena. In 2012, 11 major weather disasters (including wildfires) in the States created at least $1 billion in damages; of those, 7 were caused by severe thunderstorms and tornadoes. ■

Surviving a Tornado

An EF5 tornado forms, with a parent supercell structure and wall cloud.

RANDY DENZER has been fighting fires for 20 years. He's also a storm chaser and is active in the storm-spotter community, chasing down tornadoes and helping to educate people about safety. His first rule is "don't die." But the May 4, 2007, tornado in Greensburg, Kansas, which virtually leveled the city, almost had him breaking that very rule.

"That night, the Greensburg night, we had a hell of a storm firing up," Denzer recalls. "We kind of missed our big window of opportunity during the day. We were driving back to Dodge City that night and on our way back, we see these big, giant storms going up, you know, the Greensburg storms going up."

One of Denzer's other rules, however, is not to storm chase at night.

"We were in contact with some teams that were on the south side of [the storm]. Those teams were actually kind of telling us, 'Hey, there is a big tornado ahead, but it's already crossed the road.' So based on that information, we decided to do something against what we normally do, which is the whole night-chasing thing. But it really wasn't night chasing. When we drove down, we had been told that people had a clear view of the tornado."

According to Denzer, "Mother Nature sometimes throws you a loop that there's nothing you can do to prepare for." Which is exactly what happened to him in Greensburg. Interestingly, Denzer never got to see the tornado that almost hit him, but he later learned it was a close call.

The firefighter says he and his team knew they were in trouble when the winds picked up and got to 80-plus miles an hour. "We were actually having debris strike us. But we never lost control. We skipped the bullet," he says.

Panicking is something that Denzer says there is no room for when storm chasing. "You can't panic because if you panic, you're going to screw up." For example, when he and his team inadvertently found they were amid the storm, "We were calling each other. We were looking for trees and power lines, and made sure that we navigated out of the area the best we could, and we did," Denzer says.

There are four key mandates to staying safe during a tornado, according to Denzer. He calls these mandates "ACES":

"**A**" is for awareness, which means knowing the environs you are in and looking out for hazards. It also means keeping your wits about you during a storm.

"**C**" is for communication, which is key during a dangerous event. Denzer says being able to call people to garner more information about a storm and where the dangers lie can mean the difference between life and death. It also means letting others know that you are safe and where safe areas may be.

"**E**" is for escape routes. Denzer says every storm chaser should know how to get out of the way of a tornado—fast.

"**S**" is for safety zones. Just like with escape routes, having several safety zones identified is critical to survival. Even if these safety zones are in another county away from the tornado area, Denzer says they are important to identify for times when or if it becomes too dangerous to remain near the storm.

"If you're going into a dangerous situation, whether it's severe storm spotting or chasing, whatever you want to call it, no matter what, if you're sitting in your house or following it in a car, it's dangerous; it's a dangerous situation," Denzer says.

> "You can't panic because if you panic, you're going to screw up."

Understanding Tornadoes

Storm chasers monitor
an approaching tornado
in western Kansas.

Joshua Wurman, *president of the Center for Severe Weather Research in Boulder, Colorado*

→ **How do you gather data for your tornado research?**

We have a fleet of mobile weather radars, called Doppler on Wheels, and four heavy-duty pickup trucks, which have weather instruments on them. The pickups each carry five or so tornado pods that we deploy in "picket lines" in front of a storm to sample the winds, temperature, and relative humidity both around and inside the tornadoes. The goal is to answer two questions: How and why are

tornadoes formed? And, what is their structure?

→ **What can you see with your radar?**

The radar sends out pulses of microwaves, and they scatter off of turbulence in the air, off of bugs, raindrops, and, in the case of tornadoes, debris like gravel and foliage. The fact that we have two radars enables us to calculate the vorticity of winds, which is the strength of rotation, and the updrafts and downdrafts. Two radars are ten times better than one.

→ What have you discovered so far?

That winds near the ground during a tornado are much stronger than we thought. If you're on the 20th story of a building and open a window, it's usually windier up there than if you're on the 4th story, right? But in tornadoes, it's the other way around. In one tornado we measured, the winds 15 feet above the ground were stronger than what we saw at 30 feet, and so on. We've also discovered, for the first time, a triggering mechanism for a tornado. The cause was an extra surge of air in the downdraft at the rear of the thunderstorm that wrapped around it, increasing the rotation near the tornado. For the first time, we were able to make an observation with our radar about why a particular storm made a tornado when it did. This is a very exciting result that might help us make better predictions. There's still a ways to go here, but we think it's a major contribution.

→ What does more damage in tornadoes, the wind or debris?

Wind can push a building down. It can break your window, then lift your roof off. But it isn't the wind that breaks your window. It's the wind lifting a rock and throwing the rock through your window. So it's a combination. But how do they interplay? We don't have enough data . . . yet.

→ Do we know what the maximum wind speeds are inside a tornado?

Some computer simulations have suggested extremely high wind speeds might be possible—sonic speeds almost. But those have never been observed. My radars have measured the highest wind speeds ever documented: a little over 300 miles an hour. That was in Moore, Oklahoma, in 1999. We also had winds of about the same magnitude in El Reno, Oklahoma, in 2013, except that it happened in a small multiple vortex.

→ Is there any evidence that climate change has affected tornadoes?

The short answer is no. The long answer is that we don't even know what to expect. You'd think that as you get more warmth, you'd get more thunderstorms. More thunderstorms, more tornadoes. However, the jet stream is likely to be weaker in a globally warmer environment, which means fewer thunderstorms will rotate. So it's hard to say.

HOW TO: **PREPARE**

→ **WHAT TO DO**

Indoors

- ☑ Build an emergency kit and have a family communications plan to connect and/or reconnect with each other during and after a tornado.

- ☑ Educate yourself on the likelihood of tornadoes hitting your area.

- ☑ Identify ahead of time your best source for weather information. Prepare for no power and know how you will get info even without it.

- ☑ Listen for tornado warnings and weather reports. Remember a "watch" means threatening conditions, whereas a "warning" means tornadoes in the area.

- ☑ Investigate home insurance options. Even though most homeowners insurance covers tornado damage, it's important to make sure your property is valued and covered properly, especially if you live in a tornado-prone area.

- ☑ Build or designate a safe room.

- ☑ Consider having a helmet and goggles ready, to provide a degree of protection from flying debris.

- ☑ Bring a car seat inside for extra protection for an infant.

Outdoors

- ☑ Learn to know the weather warning signs of tornadoes: a dark, greenish sky; a wall cloud—dark, low, isolated thunder cloud; a loud, insistent roar; clouds of debris; large hailstones; and, of course, a funnel cloud forming up under a thunderstorm cloud.

- ☑ Make certain to clean up the yard of any loose debris, which could become dangerous with the onslaught of high winds.

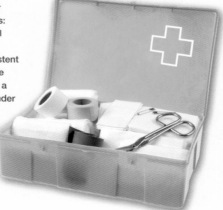

Many people who live in tornado-prone areas are building shelters.

→ WHAT *NOT* TO DO

Indoors

☒ If you have recently moved, do not assume your new community provides weather information and shelters in just the way your old one did. Inform yourself, especially if in a tornado-prone zone.

☒ Do not leave the house if a tornado watch has been issued.

☒ If possible, do not remain in a mobile home if a tornado watch has been issued. Seek sturdier shelter nearby immediately.

☒ Do not plan to be outdoors if a tornado watch has been issued.

Outdoors

☒ Do not leave any outdoor items such as grills, furniture, trash cans, or potted plants outdoors around your house. These items can get swept up and become flying weapons that cause personal and property hazards.

☒ Do not assume that no visible funnel cloud means no tornado is coming. Often the swirling winds are not visible until they pick up dirt and debris.

HOW TO: **SURVIVE**

→ **WHAT TO DO**

Indoors

☑ Respond immediately to a tornado warning

☑ Gather your prescription medications, wallet, and keys only if you have time.

☑ Go to your safe room. Lacking that, go to a basement or an interior room on the lowest floor. Consider a bathroom, a closet without windows, or a closet under the stairs.

☑ Try to put as many walls as possible between you and the outside.

☑ Leave a mobile home immediately and go to a more sound building or a designated shelter.

☑ Put an infant into a car seat for added protection indoors, but don't waste time running out to the car to get the seat if a warning has already been issued.

☑ If you are in a high-rise or tall building structure, get to a small interior room or find a hallway on the lowest floor possible.

☑ Wear sturdy shoes so you can walk for a long distance or run if you are forced from your location.

Outdoors

☑ If you are driving and your vehicle gets hit by flying debris, pull to the side of the road and park.

☑ If you are caught in your car and cannot drive anywhere safe in time, remain in your vehicle, not in the driver's seat, with your seatbelt on.

☑ Lower your head below the windows and cover it with your hands and any blanket or coat you might have.

☑ Find a ditch or sloping area below roadway level. Lie down and cover your head with your hands.

☑ No matter where you are outdoors, look out for flying debris. Flying debris is responsible for most tornado fatalities and injuries.

During a tornado, take shelter in the basement if you can.

→ WHAT *NOT* TO DO

Indoors

☒ Do not open any windows no matter what type of building or structure you are in. It is a myth that open windows equalize the pressure and can prevent your house from exploding.

☒ Do not remain near windows, doors, or near the outside perimeter of the structure you are in.

☒ Do not seek shelter in the upper levels of the home or building you are in; get as low to the ground as possible.

☒ Do not wait until you see a tornado before you take cautionary measures.

Outdoors

☒ Do not seek shelter underneath an overpass or bridge. You are much safer finding a low, flat location.

☒ Do not risk trying to outrun a tornado. Staying put or finding safe shelter close by is less risky than trying to outpace a tornado.

☒ Do not attempt to follow or chase tornadoes on a whim.

HOW TO: **RECOVER**

→ **WHAT TO DO**

Indoors

☑ Check yourself and others for injuries.

☑ Wear sturdy shoes or boots, and wear long sleeves and gloves when traipsing through or touching debris.

☑ Use battery-powered lanterns instead of candles if you lost power.

☑ Hang up any telephones that may have fallen off their hooks.

☑ Listen to public safety officials and cooperate with their instructions.

☑ Be aware that there may be structural damage to your home.

If so, contact your local city or county building inspectors.

☑ Shut off your electricity by using the main circuit breaker if there is frayed wiring or you see sparks, or any possible signs of burning.

☑ Leave your house immediately if you smell gas or suspect a gas leak. As soon as possible, call your local gas company, police or fire department, or the state fire marshal's office.

☑ Make sure you clean up medicines, drugs, flammable liquids, or other potentially hazardous materials that may have spilled during the tornado.

Outdoors

☑ Report any electrical hazards to the police and the utility company.

☑ Use caution when entering a damaged structure.

☑ Watch where you step, inside and out—50 percent of tornado-related injuries are suffered during rescue attempts, cleanup, and other post-tornado activities. Nearly one-third of those injuries come from stepping on nails.

☑ Dress for debris: Wear hard-soled shoes, pants and long-sleeved shirt, or a work jumpsuit of a thick material such as denim.

☑ If you did not do so already, shut off valves and switches for all utilities: electricity, gas, propane. Look, smell, and listen for any evidence of system failure, such as frayed wires, leaking gas, or broken pipes.

Dealing with the aftermath of a tornado can be bewildering.

→ WHAT *NOT* TO DO

Indoors

☒ Do not try to move anyone who is seriously injured—unless they are in danger of getting even more hurt. Get medical assistance.

☒ Do not stop monitoring storm reports.

☒ Do not use anything that burns fuel or charcoal indoors. Carbon monoxide (CO) is emitted by these fuels, and can be deadly.

☒ Do not leave candles burning when they are unattended. And make sure they are in safe holders away from curtains, paper, wood, or anything else that can catch fire.

Outdoors

☒ Do not go anywhere near or touch downed power lines. Even objects near downed power lines can be dangerous, and current can travel through water or cement.

☒ Do not go into tornado-affected areas unless assistance has been requested. You may interfere with relief efforts.

☒ If you were instructed to evacuate, do not return home until you are told it is safe.

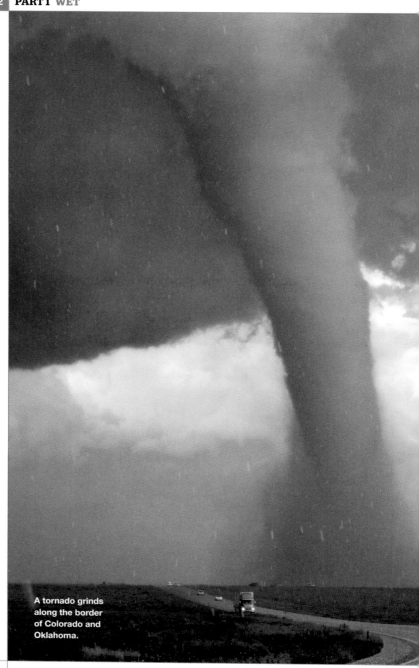

A tornado grinds
along the border
of Colorado and
Oklahoma.

EXTREMES
TORNADO STRIKES

• In April 1989, a deadly tornado struck Bangladesh, killing 1,300 people and injuring 12,000. Poor construction was partly responsible for the deaths.

• The 1925 "Great Tri-State Tornado" (in Missouri, Illinois, and Indiana) is the deadliest to ever hit the United States, killing some 700 people.

• On May 22, 2011, an EF5 tornado hit Joplin, Missouri, killing about 157 people. It was the single deadliest tornado since modern record keeping began in 1950.

PART 2

CHAPTER 5
DROUGHT

CHAPTER 6
WILDFIRES

"THE CLOUDS APPEARED, AND IN A WHILE THEY

Dry is a condition typically defined by what is lacking: water. And as the world grows increasingly scarce of accessible fresh water, dry weather is becoming dangerously pervasive. Without water we cannot live for more than a few days.

Almost to the drop, the same amount of water has existed on the planet for millions of years. Earth doesn't experience a water shortage—regions do. In some places, the weather seems to be getting wetter; elsewhere, conditions seem dry and getting drier.

Drought occurs naturally, and the rhythm of wet and dry will even out for most places. But a drought can last through many growing seasons, and for those in its midst, it feels unending.

Human industry intersects with Earth's water cycle. We count on fresh water from our lakes, rivers, and streams, from aquifers and from reservoirs, for household and industrial use. We manage water with

these expectations in mind. As more people, more factories, and more livestock make demands on Earth's water, more regions face water shortages of extreme proportions.

This is drought of a different sort: The demand for water surpasses the supply. The intersection of that sort of drought with a naturally dry period pushes conditions to extremes.

In 2012, more than 70 percent of the land area of the United States, including Alaska and Hawaii, experienced "abnormally dry or drought conditions." The summer of 2012 was the driest on record for the Plains, as dry as any Dust Bowl summer. Average corn yield dropped by a quarter.

AND WENT AWAY, DID NOT TRY ANY MORE."

— JOHN STEINBECK, *The Grapes of Wrath*

To the west, 2013 was the driest on record for California, and 2014 began with wildfires in the forested landscape of Humboldt and also in chaparral hillside neighborhoods near Los Angeles. Water level in reservoirs, particularly in the central part of the state, fell far below 50 percent capacity.

Water shortages, higher food prices, threatening wildfires: Dry conditions can endanger daily life in any number of ways. These extremes, like so many others caused by weather, are beyond the control of the individual. The best way a person or a family can respond is to understand the possibilities, stay prepared, plan ahead, and weather through the dry times safely together.

Yosemite National Park thirsts for water.

Drought conditions—as shown in Spain—are found throughout the world.

CHAPTER 5

DROUGHT

The dust was so thick that children had to wear goggles on their walks to school. Inside houses, wet sheets were draped across doors and windows, and rags were crammed into crevices to keep dust at bay. But every effort was futile. A fine, dry soil permeated everything.

The Dust Bowl was the most destructive drought the United States had ever seen. By 1934, drought had essentially turned the Great Plains, already a windy and semiarid region, into a desert. Dry weather, combined with overplowing and excessive grazing, brought on dust storms so severe they were dubbed "black blizzards." Towering walls of dust rolled across the prairies like fog.

All told, some 50 million acres of land and millions of people were affected during the nearly decadelong dry spell.

Since then, advances in agriculture and soil management have largely relegated such conditions to history books. Yet human efforts can only go so far. Long stretches of dry weather still pose urgent problems. Those living in drought conditions suffer today, and economic repercussions can endure for months and even years to come.

Recent Droughts

The past few years have reminded many of the Dust Bowl. In July 2012, the lower 48 states were suffering the most expansive drought since December 1956. Across the

---

Did You Know?
↘ NATURE'S SIGNAL

A thin snowpack in winter is a sign that a summer drought is likely because freshwater supplies often run low. Winter snow and ice melt to help refill rivers, lakes, and other sources of fresh water we tap for our everyday use.

nation, 2,245 counties representing 71 percent of the United States were designated as disaster areas due to drought that year. Nearly two-thirds of all American farms were located in drought-struck areas, impacting cattle, corn, soybeans, and other crops. As the next year began, in early January 2013, the U.S. Department of Agriculture declared that 597 counties remained disaster areas due to drought and heat.

Cattle farmers accustomed to watering cows with natural ponds and streams had to buy and haul in water from faraway sources. Corn farmers harvested as little as 10 percent of their fields' projected yields. Beef prices rose, and depleted grain crops meant reduced production and higher prices of other meat animals such as poultry. Because of the U.S. position in the global food market, these effects rippled around the world.

You didn't have to be a farmer to feel the drought's impact, however. The city of Phoenix, Arizona, was engulfed by a miles-wide, 5,000-foot-tall dust storm on July 21. Mississippi River barges stood still, stranded and grounded near Memphis, Tennessee. Texas Forest Service officials estimated the state lost some 300 million trees in rural areas.

Good Idea
↘ IT TAKES A VILLAGE

The National Drought Mitigation Center encourages every community to become drought-ready by tracking its drought history, monitoring current conditions, and formulating a drought response plan. A free downloadable booklet, *Drought-Ready Communities: A Guide to Community Drought Preparedness,* includes worksheets, exercises, tools, drought-monitoring resources, planning sections, response recommendations, case studies, and further resources. Find it at *drought.unl .edu/portals/0/docs/ DRC_Guide.pdf.*

A community water meeting

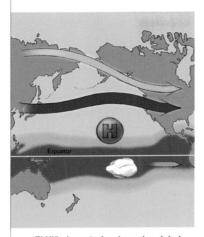

El Niño is part of an irregular global climate pattern called the Southern Oscillation. It means warmer Pacific Ocean temperatures.

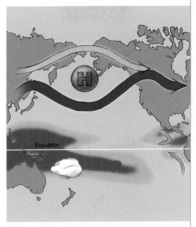

La Niña, the counterpart to El Niño, is also part of the Southern Oscillation. It means cooler Pacific Ocean temperatures.

So is this the new normal? Can we expect widespread droughts every year? Some studies suggest yes. Best to recognize the threats and learn survival techniques to prepare for and live through periods of severe drought.

El Niño and La Niña

Although there are many variables that cause droughts, the tempestuous siblings of the weather world, El Niño and La Niña, are major contributors. The two comprise opposite phases of what is known as the El Niño-Southern Oscillation (ENSO) cycle. The ENSO cycle is the scientific term for the fluctuations in temperature between the ocean and atmosphere in the eastern and central Pacific.

El Niño is the warming of ocean surface temperatures of the central and eastern Pacific, which disrupts patterns across the globe, from increased rains in northern Peru and Bolivia to drought in Southeast Asia, Australia, and India. In North America, El Niño can bring wetter-than-average conditions over portions of the U.S. Gulf Coast and Florida, with drier-than-average conditions in the Ohio Valley and the Pacific Northwest. El Niños often bring more fierce winter storms than average to the U.S. West Coast, but also tend to reduce the number of Atlantic Ocean

Reservoirs are recording lower water levels.

tropical storms and hurricanes that threaten the Atlantic and Gulf of Mexico coasts.

El Nino's counterpart, La Niña, is the cooling of ocean surface temperatures in the same waters. Global climate impacts courtesy of La Niña tend to be opposite those of El Niño. In Indonesia and parts of Australia, La Niña can bring flooding rains; in Argentina and the U.S. Plains, La Niña can bring on drought.

Many scientists propose that climate change might be inciting the impact of ENSO as warmer oceans add more kick to storms and weather patterns. The theory has been supported by, among others, an international team of scientists who analyzed tropical tree-ring records, allowing them to generate an archive of ENSO activity of unprecedented accuracy. They discovered that ENSO was more

Gear & Gadgets
⬊ MEASURE YOUR WATER USE

One of the first steps in water conservation is knowing how much water you regularly use. Research shows that people conserve more when they learn how much they use, saving as much as 15 percent of their total consumption—and in turn their water bills drop.

You will find a number of websites that help you make this calculation. For example, use the U.S. Geological Survey (USGS) Water Science School's questionnaire at ga.water.usgs.gov/edu/sq3.html. Insert your own typical daily habits—bath or shower, dishwasher, flushes, drinking water, etc.—and it calculates your daily water consumption for you.

But that's just a daily estimate. To really measure your water use, consider installing an indoor water monitor that tracks usage by faucet or appliance. Small LCDs even attach to your refrigerator door to remind you of how much water you are using. The devices are convenient and tap into the new generation of smart meters, which utilities are embracing to manage water flows and be alerted when leaks happen.

Water meters calculate use and can create savings.

active in the late 20th century than at any time in the previous seven centuries, implying, they say, "that this climate phenomenon is responding to ongoing global warming."

The time between ENSO events is irregular, but they tend to recur every three to five years, according to NOAA. Once developed, usually between June and August, both El Niño and La Niña activity tends to last for around a year, although at times the effects can endure for 18 months or more. Being up to date with current ENSO activity can help you prepare for associated weather events in your region; check *elnino.noaa.gov* for current ENSO status.

The Return of the Dust Storms

Dry times mean more dust. A recent study supported by the United States Geological Survey notes that drier conditions expected as a result of climate change will likely reduce perennial vegetation cover and result in increased dust storms. Massive dust storms in Arizona over the past few years have blinded motorists, downed power lines, and grounded airline flights. In 2012, NOAA noted that in the last ten years, more than 100 dust storms had been reported in the state of Arizona.

A Dust Bowl–type event will probably not happen again, but contemporary dust storms still damage property damage, cause fatal car accidents, divert air traffic, and have an immense economic impact on farmers. Dust storms also raise concern about valley fever, a fungal

---

RED CROSS BEST PRACTICES RECYCLE WATER

American Red Cross

Keep in mind that water can be reused in many ways. Watering houseplants or the garden is a great use of previously used water. When taking a shower, place a bucket in the shower with you to catch some of the extra water and never pour water down the sink; try to think of another use for it. This is called gray water.

The Colorado River, seen here in Utah, is running dry.

disease contracted when people inhale spores kicked up into the air by clouds of dust. Approximately 150,000 cases of valley fever are reported every year, and probably more that have gone undiagnosed. Mild cases often resolve themselves, so occurrences of the fever could be more widespread than statistics indicate.

Managing Earth's Water

We live on a planet abundant with water—but not infinitely so. Most of it is salt water in the ocean; much of Earth's fresh water is frozen in polar ice caps; and of all the planet's fresh-water resources, less than one percent is suitable for human use. Furthermore, Earth's water supply remains constant, yet as Earth's human population grows, so does the demand for fresh water.

The U.S. Geological Survey estimates that considering drinking, cooking, bathing, flushing, housekeeping, gardening, and the like, each American uses between 80 to 100 gallons of water daily. Remarkably, that's only a fraction of the total water that many people require; the average American lifestyle is fueled by nearly 2,000 gallons a day, some of that sucked from other places around the world.

A farmer and local official discuss a drought's impact on the soybean crop in 2012.

It takes water to do everything from producing and transporting food to making clothes to running the power plants that generate electricity. Producing a cotton shirt, on average, requires 700 gallons of water; a pair of jeans requires around 2,600 gallons, most of that water going to grow the cotton.

If water needs increase, droughts hurt more, and water management is all the more important. Some of the states with the highest projected population growth also have the highest domestic per capita water usage. Nevada, for example, is one of the states that rates at the highest level for daily water usage, and the U.S. Census Bureau projects a population increase of 114 percent there by 2030.

Managing water is a personal, family, and community responsibility. Being prudent with water is always important, and using water even more efficiently is a goal all can share. Find ways to bond together with others nearby and change habits; don't wait until drought makes it an obligation.

The Long Reach of Drought
We live in a world where water, and plenty of it, is taken for

granted, but severe droughts around the world, including California's severe drought of 2014, have made us ever more aware of how drought's impact reaches far beyond the immediate in time and space.

In the developing world, drought strikes at the core, spreading famine and disease. We in the modern world may feel immune to such life-and-death impacts, but in fact a serious drought can ripple through our lives, lasting longer and affecting many more than just those who live in the immediately affected area.

Economic impacts start with lost crops and increased agricultural costs, all pushing grocery prices higher. The

Continued on page 170

Good Idea
↘ MAKING A RAIN BARREL

Rain barrels help save for a non-rainy day. They generally have three components: a top hole, an upper drain, and a lower drain. Here's how to make your own: Buy or salvage a 55-gallon plastic drum. Cut a hole in the top for collecting rainwater. Insert a skimmer basket—the same type you'd use for a garden

A rain barrel collects runoff through a gutter.

pond or swimming pool—to filter out debris. Cover the basket with a fiberglass window screen so mosquitoes and other disease-carrying insects cannot infect the barrel. Add a top drain with a plastic faucet fixture and leave it open to prevent barrel overflow. Make the bottom drain with a plastic faucet attached to a garden hose. Keep this faucet closed until you want to use the water on the lawn or garden. Position the rain barrel strategically, uphill from the place you need the water. Place it under eaves or gutters to catch the biggest flow.

Sheep graze, despite the dry, dusty terrain.

EXTREMES
DROUGHT FACTS

• The Dust Bowl lasted from 1931 to 1939 in the United States. It was caused by a prolonged period of dry weather combined with overfarming in the Great Plains.

• During the 1950s, a drought lasted for five years throughout the Great Plains and the Southwest. Temperatures reached 100°F for much of the summer in Dallas, Texas.

• A three-year drought in about a third of the United States from 1987 to 1989 was the costliest natural disaster to affect the United States—until storm-related damages surpassed its total of $39 billion.

California drought reduced agricultural production by a total of one million acres, according to one estimate.

Drought causes losses elsewhere in the economy as well: the timber industry, affecting paper and building material prices; parks and natural areas, affecting travel and recreational opportunities; and power and other utilities, raising the price of fuel and electricity.

Environmental impacts can be long-term. Drought can bring on soil erosion, affect how wildfires burn, and contribute to loss of wildlife habitat. Drought complicates bird migration patterns and puts increased stress on many animals, especially endangered species whose habitats

Good Idea
⬎ PLANT FOR THE DRY TIMES

One great way to do your part to conserve water locally is xeriscaping, a movement started by the Denver, Colorado, water department in 1978 and now generally accepted as a good idea, no matter how drought-prone your neighborhood.

The word comes from the Greek *xeros* — dry — and it means choosing native drought-resistant plants for landscaping rather than plants (including lawn grass) that need extensive watering to survive and look good. Xeriscaping techniques can change yards and gardens, making hand-watering less necessary and keeping them beautiful through the driest months.

Consider planting native drought-tolerant plants.

A concerned farmer checks the soil and hopes for rain.

A depth marker on the wall of a swamp shows that water levels are dropping.

and food sources are already at risk.

And drought affects human health and safety tremendously. Many analysts believe that higher temperatures, which can cause drought conditions, have played a part in the increase around the world of such devastating diseases as dengue fever, West Nile virus, and cholera. Closer to home, dry conditions can favor propagation of nuisance species such as ticks, body lice, and fire ants.

Drought changes air quality, interrupting the natural water cycle. Communities see allergies and asthma on the rise.

Drought also changes quality as well as quantity of available water when wells and reservoirs dry up. Coastal areas see salt water creeping into freshwater sources.

Staying Well During Drought

The impact feels overwhelming—so many consequences, such a domino effect. Although you cannot change the course of extreme weather for the sake of your family, there are a number of ways to lighten the load.

→ **Monitor household water.** Reduced rainfall can put extreme demands on water sanitation facilities. If the color or taste of your water changes, contact local authorities and arrange to have it tested before using it to bathe, drink, or eat.

→ **Wash and peel fruits and vegetables.** Farmers here and abroad may rely on recycled water to irrigate during drought, which raises the likelihood of harmful bacteria on the skins of the fruits and vegetables they grow.

→ **Be careful when eating fish or seafood.** Drought conditions change the quality and quantity of water in rivers, lakes, and bays. Fish, shellfish, and other animals that mature in a setting with less than enough fresh circulating water can carry toxins and disease.

→ **Keep air circulating.** Drought conditions may require a

Did You Know?
↘ SHIPPING WATER

Seemingly far-fetched schemes have been floated to deal with severe water shortages. Some schemes have been tried: Concerns that fresh water–deprived countries in Asia might try to buy water in bulk from the Great Lakes and have it shipped to them led to action by the eight states bordering the lakes and the U.S. Congress to put the brakes on the idea of bulk export. However, the town of Sitka, Alaska, has signed agreements to export bulk water to thirsty customers in countries such as India and other countries in the Middle East.

Shipping fresh water might become big business.

EXTREME WEATHER BASICS
Defining Drought

There is no clear definition of drought among meteorologists, because droughts result from constellations of causes, and their start and end points are never clear. Droughts can last for months or years and can be very local or nearly continental. They usually occur with heat waves, but they can also be the long-term effect of diminished snowfall months before and miles away.

We now understand that large-scale patterns of ocean temperatures relate to precipitation trends over faraway regions, helping meteorologists issue alerts to the possibility of drought or for excessive rain or snow in coming months. The best known of these patterns is the El Niño-Southern Oscillation (ENSO) cycle, which includes El Niño and its sibling, La Niña, which have roughly opposite effects, and a neutral phase in between.

Scientists also have strong evidence that a swing in surface temperatures of the Atlantic Ocean—called the Atlantic Multidecadal Oscillation—is linked to dry and wet periods in North America and Africa. The Atlantic seems to swing between warm and cool phases lasting 20 to 40 years, with its average temperature during a warm phase approximately 1°F above that of a cool phase.

Even pressure patterns far from the ocean appear linked to this cycle. North American droughts (including the Dust Bowl of the 1930s) seem to occur during the warm phases, while African droughts occur during the cold phases.

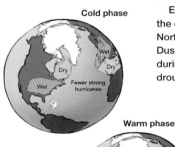

FORECASTING DROUGHT

Knowledge of these global patterns and real-time data on what's going on helps NWS forecasters produce the U.S. Seasonal Drought Outlook, which outlines areas where a drought is likely to continue, grow worse, ease up, or end, and where new droughts could begin over the next three months.

Scientists are researching the Atlantic Multidecadal Oscillation for its links to dry and wet periods.

Droughts can bring more pet illnesses such as parasites and heartworm disease.

community to conserve energy, thus forcing households to use less air-conditioning than they are used to. If that occurs, open windows and allow natural airflow to ventilate your house as much as possible.

→ **Filter the air you breathe.** If family members are prone to allergies or asthma, take extra precautions, including providing face masks, during drought, as spores, pollen, dust, and other irritants suspended in the air increase when soil and air are very dry. Keep nasal passages hydrated with saline solution, available in any pharmacy.

→ **Stay clean.** Family members should wash as much as or even more often than usual during a drought, despite water restrictions. Use waterless hand sanitizer at every sink. Sponge bathe with a bowl of warm water, soap, and a washcloth, just as you would take a bath or shower.

There's an App for That
Available for download from iTunes and/or Google Play, these apps may be helpful during periods of drought.

→ A free **Dust Storm** app, developed by the University of Arizona, provides dust storm alerts and safety tips for any region of the country.

→ Local water utilities may offer water awareness apps. For example, the **San Diego**

Drivers are caught in an Arizona dust storm.

County Water Authority app provides water news, issues, and other features.

→ **Wet Or Dry** by EZ Apps provides drought and precipitation outlook maps for regions across the United States. Designed for iPad, it is available from iTunes.

→ **H20 Tracker** helps you estimate your household water usage with an eye to conservation.

→ If you water your lawn, the **Sprinkler Times** app or computer program calculates an optimal schedule to reduce overwatering and save water.

Protect Your Pets

Some extreme weather events cause obvious threats for pets; drought is much sneakier. If you have outdoor pets, consider the following dangers:

→ **Fleas and ticks:** More wildlife comes in your yard, looking for water, and this can lead to more fleas and ticks in your yard, which can lead to more fleas and ticks on your pets. Talk to your vet about preventative measures.

→ **Parasites:** Drought can make otherwise healthy bodies of fresh water stagnant, creating an optimal breeding ground for parasites. Keep pets away from murky standing water.

→ **Heartworms:** Be especially on the lookout for mosquitoes, which transmit heartworm disease to both dogs and cats. You can discuss prevention with your vet, and also make sure to eliminate sources of standing water.

→ **Predators:** Drought affects vegetation that wildlife depends on, which can throw the food web off and may result in predators approaching your property seeking prey. Take preventive measures to keep your pets safe: Walk dogs on leashes, keep an eye on pets when outside, bring pets inside at night, don't feed pets outside, and keep trash areas especially tidy to prevent attracting unwanted wildlife.

→ **Anthrax:** *Bacillus anthracis,* the anthrax bacterium, survives for decades in soil and can become activated during times of drought or flooding. Animals can inhale or eat spores, or the spores can enter the body through wounds or insect bites. Dogs and cats seem to have an innate resistance; sheep and cattle are more likely victims. On rare occasions, infected animals have been known to transmit anthrax to humans through skin wounds, but usually infected animals die within hours and do not share the disease. ■

RED CROSS BEST PRACTICES FORM GOOD HABITS

American Red Cross

Find ways to reduce water use, no matter if you live in a drought-ridden area or not. For example, install a low-flow showerhead. Never leave water running while performing tasks such as washing dishes or brushing your teeth.

FIRST PERSON: Dr. Jason Smith, M.D., emergency medicine specialist; former Green Beret and Special Forces Combat Diver

Surviving Extreme Dehydration

Soldiers train to be prepared for extreme weather conditions.

SPECIAL FORCES combat soldiers are no doubt tough. But they are human just like the rest of us, and susceptible to the same physical maladies as we are. Take the 26-year-old Green Beret who suffered from dehydration so acute he nearly lost his life. Without disclosing the soldier's name, Dr. Jason Smith, who combat-trains Special Forces operatives, explains how dehydration sets in and why it's so important in dry times to manage your fluid intake.

As background, Dr. Smith explains that this soldier had been in combat deployment for nine months in a mountainous, cold-weather region in Afghanistan. There he was unable to

do much running, swimming, or other physical workouts beyond the exertion demanded of him in day-to-day combat. And his body had acclimated to cold to temperate weather conditions.

Back in the States, the soldier was stationed in a hot climate and went through training during the summer. "The training course is physically arduous," Smith says. "Days begin before 4 a.m., and often last through 9 p.m. or later."

Several hours of calisthenics begin the typical training day, along with a nine-mile run, and six additional hours of physical and mental rigor. Although trainees are advised to drink two or three gallons of water a day, this soldier didn't. He let his water intake lapse and drank only about half of the recommended amount.

During hot, dry times, many may feel the temptation to drink less fluid and ration, as he did. But medical specialists say you shouldn't conserve. In fact, you should drink water when you feel thirsty and avoid rationing; your body will naturally store as much as it needs. The Green Beret learned that the hard way.

The signs were there for medical personnel to see: His heart rate was markedly elevated. His breathing was rapid and shallow. He was able to answer questions, but he was very slow to do so. He was easily confused. His temperature was elevated, but he had no symptoms or evidence of infection. He was sweating profusely.

He had gone into rhabdomyolysis—a condition caused by an unusually high level of muscle breakdown products circulating in the blood. He suffered acute renal failure and multiple severe electrolyte imbalances.

Doctors immediately took action and put the soldier on a vigorous

intravenous rehydration solution program, which saved him from dying of dehydration. The experience shows that no matter how rough and tough the person, you need water to survive.

Dr. Smith also highlights the need for electrolytes: "When we dehydrate to the point of renal failure, our kidney cells start 'not being able to do their jobs' of optimally filtering. Therefore, our electrolytes [sodium, potassium, phosphates, magnesium, etc.] are not being selectively filtered and/or excreted properly. This leads to abnormal levels of these electrolytes in the bloodstream and the cells. When this happens, cells and biochemical processes begin to malfunction. Examples include heart cells not squeezing hard enough . . . liver cells not detoxifying the blood enough . . . and brain cells not thinking quickly enough."

So drink plenty of water. And in case the situation will arise in which potable water is in short supply, have a store of electrolyte-enhanced liquids such as Gatorade or Powerade in order to stay hydrated and healthy.

> No matter how rough and tough the person, you need water to survive.

EXPERT WITNESS: Richard Seagar
Coping With Extreme Drought

Extensive droughts are reaching places such as Lake Mead, Arizona.

Richard Seager, *research professor at Lamont-Doherty Earth Observatory of Columbia University*

→ **In August 2012, 78 percent of the United States was in drought conditions. That was pretty much unprecedented in modern times, wasn't it?**
Yes, it was. There have been one or two years during the Dust Bowl and during the 1950s drought that looked like that. But in summer of 2012, the drought even reached up to where I am in New York.

→ **Would you describe drought as simply a lack of rain?**
No, temperature is also important. If you increase the temperature of the atmosphere, that increases the water-holding capacity of the atmosphere and hence extracts more moisture from the surface through evapotranspiration. What you're concerned about usually is the amount of moisture in the soil that is available for crops and plants to use.

→ **In general, do scientists believe that climate change will cause wet areas of the world**

to get wetter and dry areas to get drier?

That is generally agreed upon. Pretty much every climate model agrees with that as a basic rule of thumb.

→ Are we already seeing the impact of climate change on droughts?

Beyond the background rise in temperature, it's really hard to find the human-induced signature in precipitation. But by averaging over large regions, we do find evidence that the hydrological cycle globally is changing over the past decades in the way the climate models predict it should do, due to rising greenhouse gases. The way that nature is evolving is certainly hinting that, yes, there is an emerging human component that's making drought in the American Southwest, for example, more likely.

→ In one of your papers you wrote that "the American West could be in for a future in which the climate is more arid than at any time since the advent of European settlement."

Yes, what the models predict is that the Southwest—southern California, Arizona, New Mexico, Texas, and northern Mexico—will become drier as a consequence of rising greenhouse gases. And that's just steadily going to get worse over the course of the current century and, indeed, shifting into a much drier climate than any we have seen since the period of European settlement.

→ You also wrote that by mid-century, levels of dryness in the Southwest could be as bad as they were during the Dust Bowl—and that could be the new norm.

Yes, what in the past was a level of aridity that was part of a drought that went on for several years, like the Dust Bowl did, would become the new climatological norm.

→ Will that be a disastrous consequence, do you think, or something that populations can adjust to?

I think, in terms of the available water resources, it actually can be adjusted to. There's quite a lot of wiggle room in Western water resources to cope with a reduction, though it would require some reallocation of water. In particular, agriculture would have to make do with less water so that more water could be used for municipal purposes. And that's not an easy adjustment, though it's certainly something that could be done. It probably falls short of a catastrophic disaster, but we shouldn't belittle the size of the adjustments that may need to be changed.

HOW TO: **PREPARE**

→ **WHAT TO DO**

Indoors

- ☑ Check your house for leaks, and repair any dripping faucets. A drip a second wastes more than 3,000 gallons of water a year. One way to check is to turn off all water sources and check your water meter to see if it moves.

- ☑ Replace faucets with low-flow models. These restrict the amount of water that comes out of your plumbing.

- ☑ Install an instant hot-water heater for your sink. The longer it takes for water to heat and pour, the more water it takes.

- ☑ Insulate your water pipes. This keeps your water hotter and also prevents pipes from breaking.

- ☑ Choose water-efficient appliances.

- ☑ Consider buying low-volume, or low-flow, toilets that use less than half the water of older models.

- ☑ Consider replacing your shower head with an ultra-low-flow version.

Outdoors

- ☑ Xeriscape to create a landscape. Use more mulch and stones and less grassy lawn that requires a lot of watering.

- ☑ Plant drought tolerant vegetation. Some plants, such as cacti and low-water grasses, require less water than others, and can cut as much as two-thirds of the water you might use for thirstier types. Also, some water utility companies offer incentives and rebates for you to plant water-wise plants.

- ☑ Check your soil type and adjust it in your garden. Sandy soil drains more quickly than soil with more clay in it. Therefore, sandier soil requires more water. Add

more organic matter (such as compost, rotted manure, or commercial soil conditioners), which absorb and hold water better.

- ☑ Compost. Just five pounds of compost mixed with 100 pounds of soil can hold an additional 25 gallons of water.

A gardener removes food from a composting pile. Composting saves water.

→ WHAT *NOT* TO DO

Indoors

✗ Do not waste water by pouring it down the drain. There may be another use for it, such as watering indoor plants or your garden.

✗ Don't use your kitchen sink disposal as a garbage bin. Disposals require a lot of water to operate. Toss garbage in the bin or better yet, start a compost pile.

✗ Do not use a brick, stones, or other crusty objects in place of a low-flow device for your toilet. These can cause damage to your plumbing.

Outdoors

✗ Do not overwater your garden. About half of the water used outdoors goes to waste from evaporation or runoff. Watering once or twice a week is sufficient.

✗ Do not let your garden hose run. Use a shutoff nozzle. An unrestricted garden hose can use water at a rate of as much as 12 gallons a minute.

✗ If you have a pool, do not leave it uncovered. As much as 95 percent of pool water that is lost to evaporation could be saved if a pool cover is used.

HOW TO: SURVIVE

→ WHAT TO DO

Indoors

☑ Put a bucket in your shower to catch splash water that you can use for plants or the garden.

☑ Use automatic dishwashers, but only if they are fully loaded. "Light wash" settings consume less water.

☑ Hand-wash dishes by filling two containers—one for cleaning with soapy water and another for rinsing with clear water.

☑ Wash vegetables in a large bowl or dish instead of with running tap water.

☑ Keep drinking water in the refrigerator rather than having the tap run for cool water.

☑ Use a washing machine only for full loads, and wash for a shorter amount of time.

Outdoors

☑ Check your soil moisture. If it's still moist, you don't need to water your lawn or garden. Also, if your grass springs back when you step on it, it doesn't need watering.

☑ Always water the landscape in the morning or evening, when temperatures are cooler and water doesn't evaporate as quickly.

☑ Make sure your sprinklers are aimed properly for your lawn—not the sidewalk or street.

☑ Irrigate in multiple sessions for shorter lengths of time rather than one dousing to help your lawn absorb moisture and avoid runoff.

☑ Allow your lawn to be sacrificed in times of extreme drought to preserve trees and large shrubs.

☑ Use an automated, commercial car wash that recycles water if you must wash your car. Commercial car washes consume as much as 100 gallons less water a wash than hand washing.

Consider washing your dishes by hand to save water.

→ WHAT *NOT* TO DO

Indoors

☒ Do not flush the toilet more than you must, and don't use it as a receptacle for paper products, bugs, cigarettes, and other types of waste.

☒ Do not take baths. They can use three times as much water as the average shower.

☒ Do not rinse dishes before putting them in the dishwasher.

☒ Do not waste tap water that flows as you wait for it to warm. Heat water on the stove or in a microwave.

☒ Do not let the water run as you brush your teeth, wash your face, or shave.

☒ Do not use warm tap water to thaw meat or other frozen foods.

Outdoors

☒ Do not overwater your lawn. It's estimated that 50 percent of landscape irrigation is wasted due to overwatering, runoff, and evaporation.

☒ Do not water your lawn during or immediately after it rains. A soaking rain can eliminate the need for watering for as long as two weeks.

☒ Do not leave sprinklers or hoses on and unattended.

☒ Do not use water from a garden hose to clean the driveway or sidewalk; use a broom or blower instead.

HOW TO: **RECOVER**

→ **WHAT TO DO**

Indoors

☑ Remember the hardest part of being without water. Take steps to avoid those problems again. Shore up supplies for future droughts by planning ahead and conserving.

☑ Consider a full examination of your plumbing to see if installing water-saving appliances or fixtures makes sense.

☑ Do the math: Water-efficient plumbing such as dual-flush toilets and low-flow faucets may be pricey up front, but they can decrease your freshwater use and lower water bills over the long run.

☑ Establish the habit of rationing water.

☑ Set family time limits for showers.

☑ If you must water your lawn, install a timer that cuts off water after a reasonable period.

☑ Consider other ways to self-meter your water use, including installing electronic meters.

Outdoors

☑ If you continue to water your lawn or garden, be aware of the sprinkler's trajectory to avoid sending water onto sidewalks or driveways.

☑ Plant more shade-loving species. They will require less hand-watering.

☑ Plant more drought-tolerant vegetation.

☑ Consider installing a household gray water system that recoups water going down the drain and diverts it into storage tanks for irrigation use. Some systems even have filters to rid the water of detergents and other infectious chemicals.

☑ Keeping your gutters, pipes, and pool filters clean and clear prevents backups and spillage, which is wasted water. Preventive maintenance can help shore up the water supply.

☑ Learn better watering techniques. Watering too much too quickly results in runoff and wastes water. Watering slowly allows water to seep into soil where it is needed.

☑ Invest in soaking hoses rather than sprinklers for watering the garden. Slow drips directly into the soil minimize evaporation and make the best use of water resources.

Good Idea
↘ DUST STORM DOS AND DON'TS

I n a dust storm, the best thing to do is to stay indoors or seek inside shelter. If you are outside, here are some tips.

What to Do

• Use a mask to cover your nose and mouth. If you don't have a mask, use a moistened bandanna or other piece of fabric.
• Dab petroleum jelly inside your nostrils. It can help prevent drying of your mucous membranes.
• Remove your glasses or contacts if you wear them.
• Wrap as much of your skin in clothing as possible to protect it against blowing dirt and debris.
• If you travel, mark your direction with stones or other objects as landmarks can change.
• If you are driving, pull completely off the roadway.
• If you cannot pull off the road safely, proceed slowly, using the center lines as your guide, and sound your horn.
• When you have pulled off the road, turn off all vehicle lights, including emergency flashers; approaching vehicles may not realize you are parked and may use your lights as a guide.

What Not to Do

• Do not attempt to drive through a dust storm or sandstorm
• Do not stop in the travel or emergency lanes. That leaves you vulnerable to collision.
• Do not count on regular eyeglasses to protect your eyes.

A dust storm blows in, making driving perilous.

Drought-dried lakes
are becoming more
common in the
United States.

EXTREMES
WHERE DRY IS DRY

• The 2012 drought in the Midwest and Southwest was more extensive than any since the 1950s. Approximately 80 percent of agricultural land was affected.

• The "Millennium Drought" in Australia lasted ten years, from 2000 to 2010, with some areas taking longer to recover. Rainfalls declined over the course of a decade in parts of the country.

• The Atacama Desert stretching from the border of Peru into Chile is known as the driest place on Earth. There are stretches where rain has never been recorded.

Wildfires, such as this one in Virginia, can burn day and night for weeks.

CHAPTER 6

WILDFIRES

On August 17, 2013, a hunter's illegal campfire set California's Stanislaus National Forest ablaze. What would become known as the Rim Fire raged across the Sierra Nevada forests and skirted Yosemite National Park, ultimately scorching more than 250,000 acres of some of the wildest areas in the state. The fire destroyed 11 residences, 3 businesses, and dozens of outbuildings, and did untold damage to the habitat that serves as home to California's precious wildlife.

From chipmunks and cattle to bobcats and bears, animals were killed, injured, and displaced. For those animals whose populations are already threatened—the great gray owl, the Sierra Nevada red fox, and the Pacific fisher—the Rim Fire may have proved especially tragic. As John Buckley, executive director of the nonprofit Central Sierra Environmental Resource Center, noted, "only birds that could fly the farthest and animals that could run the fastest survived."

Destructive wildfires like the Rim Fire have been getting worse in recent decades; they're lasting longer and burning larger areas. Although limited fires benefit wildlands in a number of ways, once out of control they can be fast-moving, destructive, and terrifying. They can also be wildly unpredictable. Winds or convection currents lift pieces of burning material called firebrands aloft, shooting them miles away, where they ignite

---

Did You Know?

↘ WHERE THERE'S FIRE, THERE'S SMOKE

The most dangerous part of a fire can be the smoke, rather than the flames. In a burning building, stay low and crawl out: Smoke and poisonous gases rise. If you cannot leave, close off the room and all its vents. Don't try to escape through a door with smoke coming through it. Find a different route instead, even if it's a window.

new spot fires, and spread fear and damage far and wide.

Which is to say, a wildfire can end up at your front door in minutes, with little time for you to react. That's why advanced planning is so key, as well as knowing how to see a fire coming and what to do when you cannot get out of its way.

What Is a Wildfire?
Although many people call any large-scale burn event a "forest fire," it's important to distinguish different types, especially considering how natural forces and human intentions interact

in the setting and control of a fire. Begin your knowledge of the threat of fire in your region by understanding terminology. These distinctions also remind us of how many ways a wildfire can get started:

Wildland fire: A wildland fire is any non-structure fire that occurs in the wild. This is the broadest term and encompasses three more specific types of fires: wildfire, prescribed fire, and wildland fire use.

Wildfire: A wildfire is any unplanned and undesirable fire

Good Idea
↘ WHAT TO DO IF YOUR CLOTHES CATCH FIRE

Remember three words: STOP, DROP, and ROLL.

• STOP means just that. Do not attempt to extinguish the fire by running; that will only serve to fan the flames. Stop where you are.
• DROP means lower yourself and stay as low to the ground as you can. Protect your face with your hands.
• ROLL means turn your body over and over until the flames are smothered and extinguished.

The same mantra holds true if someone else catches fire. If he or she is unable or unwilling, knock the person to the ground and smother the flames with a large piece of material (such as a coat or a rug) until they are completely extinguished.

Children gaze upon a large fire. The flames can mesmerize.

that occurs in the wild. A wildfire can be one that started accidentally, either naturally or by human causes, and it can also be a deliberate fire that went out of control.

Prescribed fire: A prescribed fire has been deliberately ignited under the supervision of a managing agency and meets specific ecological objectives. For someone to set a prescribed fire, a plan must be submitted and approved, conforming to local and national guidelines.

Wildland fire use: Accidental wildfires can be managed and turned to advantage for resource management. This term refers to a wildfire that has been turned into a prescribed fire.

What Causes Wildfires?

Lightning strikes certainly do cause some fires. In the northern Rockies, for example, scientists estimate that lightning probably causes around 90 percent of them. But in the United States as a whole, 90 percent of wildfires start not by natural causes but because of human activities.

Carelessly discarded cigarettes, auto ignition sparks, burning debris, unattended campfires, and (regrettably) arson can all lead to fires that then spread out of control. As forested land gets further developed for housing and recreation, the risk of human-caused accidental fires increases. Sometimes the human footprint alone

A firefighter battles the stubborn flames of a big blaze.

can be to blame; the 2011 Las Conchas Fire in New Mexico, which spread across more than 150,000 acres near Los Alamos, started because an aspen tree fell onto a power line.

A human presence may be largely responsible for starting wildfires, but the fate of a fire—its duration, extent, and intensity—is largely determined by natural forces such as climate, topography, and natural growth in its path. High temperatures, droughts, wind, and other weather patterns, both immediate and long-term, all shape the path by which a wildfire develops, behaves, and concludes.

Why Fires in the West?

Wildfires can spark anywhere, but there are certain parts of the continental United States more prone to them than others. The areas most at risk are in the West and Southwest, especially California, Nevada, Arizona, Utah, Colorado, New Mexico, and western Texas, plus the northern edge of Montana and certain parts of Oregon. All these areas are rated as "extreme danger zones" by the U.S. Forest Service.

Did You Know?
↘ NATURE'S SIGNAL

If you see or smell smoke during the day or see a red-orange glow at night, a fire is nearby. If you hear crackling or see sparks, the wildfire could be less than a mile away.

Orange glow and haze are nature's signs of fire.

A complex combination of factors contributes to the vulnerability or resistance of a wooded area to a spreading fire. The species and age of trees, the density of their growth pattern, the elevation, soil composition, and climate—including current temperature and recent rainfall patterns—all affect fire's potential. And all these factors add up to making the American West more fire-prone than the East.

Many forests rely on winter snow for moisture. As mountain snow melts, it saturates the soil, supplies the streams, and adds to natural water reserves. Without this essential step in the water cycle, forests dry out and become more flammable. Winter droughts mean that snowpack-dependent ecosystems become parched much earlier than normal, and this condition can make for an extended, fiercer fire season.

In the arid West, when trees die, they stay on the landscape for many decades, even a century or more. Because the climate is so dry, standing dead trees and fallen debris don't rot as quickly as they do in the East. Unburned forests build up a huge volume of combustible material over the decades, fueling wildfires more virulently.

Good Idea
↘ HOW TO PUT OUT A FIRE

With all types of fire—electrical, liquid, or organic—get safe first and immediately call a fire professional. But if you must handle a fire in front of you, follow these guidelines:

• An electrical fire, common in house fires, should be extinguished by turning off any source of power. Then, by means of fire extinguisher or smothering, flames can be extinguished. Never use water on a fire unless you know for certain what is burning.

• A liquid fire (grease, oil, flammable liquid) can be extinguished with a fire extinguisher or by means of smothering. (Never throw water on a liquid fire; it worsens flames.)

• An organic fire (wood, paper, etc.) can be extinguished by fire extinguisher, water, or smothering.

The massive Waldo Canyon fire burns in the mountains above Colorado Springs.

Air quality and temperatures factor in as well. Heat waves east of the Rockies usually come with high humidity, and the warm, wet air tends to hamper fires. The drier summer heat of the West desiccates the forests during higher-temperature times of year, which may make them even more susceptible to flame.

The Good News About Fire

Not every large-scale fire does bad things. Fires were burning through the natural world long before anything human caused them. Many plants and animals—and the landscape itself—need occasional fires as part of their cycle of life, death, and replenishment.

Some evergreen trees produce durable, resin-filled cones that depend on fire to melt the seal and release their seeds. Giant sequoias, for example, germinate best after a fire has swept through them. The heat from a fire helps the cones release seeds into bare soil fertilized by ash, creating the perfect environment for them. Fire also aids giant sequoias by killing white fir trees before they grow too tall; when left to their own devices, the firs act as ladders for fire to climb to the sequoia's crowns, resulting in more punishing harm.

Fires consume dead, decaying vegetation accumulating on the forest floor, thereby clearing the way for new growth.

Fireweed flowers grow at the base of a charred tree.

Fire returns nutrients to the soil quickly and can open up dense areas and help maintain meadow habitats. Several animal species use these open areas for food and shelter.

All these reasons make fires helpful to forests, but we're human and we tend to fear fire instinctively. Not until recently has science driven our firefighting protocol. Beginning in the early 20th century, fire management meant fire suppression: Rather than letting small fires burn their course, firefighters stamped out wildfires as quickly as possible.

By the 1970s, the tide had turned, with research supporting the plan to let some fires burn for the sake of the ecosystem. But what's good for the forest is not necessarily good for a subdivision. Into the 1990s, exurban sprawl expanded ever farther into wildlands, adding the risk of property damage to the equation, and a need to analyze whether to let natural forest fires take their course. These matters grow ever more complicated: The Cerro Grande Fire in New Mexico in May 2000 burned 47,000 acres and damaged 235 homes—and it was a fire intentionally set by Park Service personnel to manage the forest.

Who's at Risk?

According to researchers, nearly a third of the nation's residences—houses, apartments, and so on—stand in what they call the wildland-urban interface. That means more people are living near forests where fires can (and, in some cases, even should) burn. Further, the number and intensity of large-scale wildfires has increased over the past 30 years. Neighborhoods near forests need to become "prepared to safely accept wildfire as a part of their surrounding landscape," notes the U.S. Department of Agriculture in its report "Wildfire, Wildlands, and People," downloadable at *www.fs.fed.us/openspace/fote/reports/GTR-299.pdf.*

Here are a few key steps that you, your family, and your community can take to turn a fire-prone neighborhood into a fire-adapted one:

→ Design structures to be ignition-resistant. Box in underhangs, eaves, soffits, and so on. Use glass, preferably double-paned or tempered, for windows and skylights.

→ Use building materials that are nonflammable or fire-resistant. If you retrofit anything for fire resistance, make it your roof, using top-rated fire-resistant materials such as composition shingles, metal, clay, or concrete.

→ Landscape your yard for ignition resistance. Clear, mow, and water consistently in the 30-foot perimeter around your house. Selectively maintain tree growth in the 100-foot perimeter around your house.

→ Remove flammable materials on the outside of your house, including fencing, vegetation, firewood storage, and so on.

Continued on page 202

USDA BEST PRACTICES CODE OF THE WEST

USDA Some rural communities in the U.S. West are adopting their own "Code of the West," a grassroots manifesto of public awareness and community effort to create fire-adapted neighborhoods together. If you have recently moved into a fire-prone rural area, ask your neighbors or civic leaders about efforts already underway to work together.

The Red Eagle
wildfire of 2006
burns tall in
Montana.

EXTREMES
BLAZING FIRES

• One of the worst wildfires in the United States was Colorado's Black Forest fire in 2013. The most devastating in the state's history, it burned 486 homes, forcing thousands to evacuate.

• In 2008, the South One wildfire that blazed in Virginia's Great Dismal Swamp smoldered for four months because it burned so deeply into peat soils.

• One of the biggest fires in the United States occurred in Wisconsin in 1871. The Great Peshtigo Fire burned 1.5 million acres and killed between 1,200 and 2,400 people.

Use fire-resistant materials for balconies, decks, and garages.
→ Work to help establish local codes and minimum standards for ignition-resistant homes if they don't already exist.
→ Agree on safe zones within the community and safe evacuation routes to leave the community if necessary.
→ Maintain the forest within and near your community to reduce immediate fire danger.

Learn the Drill

Although fire drills in schools are routine, less than 20 percent of households in the United States have or have practiced a home fire-escape plan, according to experts. The U.S. Fire Administration, part of FEMA, recommends the following four steps to create a domestic fire-drill plan, especially for families who live in wild-fire-prone areas:
→ Make sure there are two ways out of every room, and be sure everyone in the family knows them.
→ Agree on a meeting place near home if you have to leave quickly, where firefighters can see you and know you are out.
→ Know and share the emergency number for your local fire department.
→ Practice your family escape drill together.
→ Keep floors, hallways, and stairs clear of debris and clutter, and share the fire-drill plan with babysitters and frequent visitors.

Gear and Gadgets
↘ DUAL-SENSOR ALARMS

When it comes to smoke and fire alarms, it's all about the sensors. That's why it's important to get dual-sensor alarms, or install two types of alarms. Dual-sensor alarms combine heat detection and smoke detection into one device. Ionization technology is what is best at detecting heat: fast, flaming fire. Photoelectric smoke alarms excel at quickly detecting smoke from a smoldering fire. It's also a good idea to use interconnected models, so if an alarm goes off in the basement, it will warn you via your alarm upstairs near your bedroom. If you're a bad cook and/or burn toast a lot, look for models with a "hush" button.

Firefighting slurry deposited by a plane squelches a wildfire in Black Forest, Colorado.

A minister prays with an evacuee at a shelter in southern California.

Community Preparedness

Communities in high-risk areas should be proactive and diligent about wildfire preparation. Because many fire evacuations generally come with at least a three-hour notice, if you are prepared, you may have time to assist neighbors, the elderly, or other community members who are in need of help.

Also, you may want to set up a cooperative agreement with community members in different parts of your town to share resources and accommodations if one party is evacuated and the other is not. If evacuation is imminent, local emergency responders such as police and fire departments will direct you to a nearby shelter. You can also find the nearest shelter with your smartphone. Text SHELTER plus your zip code to 43362 (4FEMA).

What to Expect

More than 9.3 million acres burned in the United States in 2012; the fires were massive in size, with 51 fires exceeding 40,000 acres, and 14 of those exceeding 100,000 acres.

In June 2013, U.S. Forest Service Chief Tom Tidwell explained to the U.S. Senate Committee on Energy and Natural Resources that Florida, Georgia, Utah, California, Texas, Arizona, New Mexico, and Colorado all suffered the largest and/or most destructive fires in their history in the last six years.

Compared to 40 years ago, wildfires burn on average twice as many acres each year today.

The rise in large fires in the West comes along with higher temperatures and ever earlier snowmelts, which has resulted in longer fire seasons; since the 1970s, the length of the fire season has increased by more than two months. Tidwell blames part of it on severe drought, which leads to extreme fire weather. Numerous other experts agree. Don Wuebbles, who shared the 2007 Nobel Peace Prize for his part in the Intergovernmental Panel on Climate Change, warns that warmer temperatures and changes in precipitation could very well double the acreage consumed by fires each year on average in the next 30 years.

Good Idea

↘ HOW TO CREATE A SAFETY ZONE

According to FEMA, here is the best way to create a 30- to 100-foot zone of fire-resistant space around your home:

- Rake leaves, dead limbs, and twigs, and dispose of them at your local landfill.
- Clear all flammable vegetation, and make sure to remove all leaves and rubbish from under structures.
- Trim your treetops so there is at least a 15-foot space between tree crowns (30 feet for conifers), and remove tree limbs within 15 feet of the ground.
- Remove all dead branches that extend near or over the roof. Call your local power company and have them clear any branches from power lines.
- Make sure to remove any vines from the walls of your home.
- Clear a ten-foot area around any propane tanks you may have, and place a screen over your barbecue grill using one-quarter-inch mesh.
- Store such things as gasoline, rags, and other flammable items in approved safety cans, and then place the cans a safe distance away from your home or garage.
- Stack your firewood pile at least 100 feet away from your home and uphill, if possible.

Keep logs far enough from your home, creating a safety zone.

EXTREME WEATHER BASICS
Wildfires and Weather

Wildfires and weather are inexorably linked. Normal seasonal dryness, such as in much of the U.S. West, or drought in other regions sets the stage for wildfires by drying out grasses, brush, and trees to supply fuel. Although people are responsible for most wildfires, some begin with "dry lightning"—thunderstorms with lightning that hits the ground but with rain that evaporates on the way down. These are most common in the West.

As a fire's smoky hot air rises, it creates gusty, changing winds around the fire as air rushes in to replace the rising air. Wildfires are most dangerous when atmospheric conditions favor "plume-dominated fires." These include light winds aloft that won't disturb a column of hot air rising above the fire and relatively cold air aloft that keeps the rising hot air more buoyant. The rising air creates a pyrocumulus cloud that can develop into a thunderstorm, but rarely one with heavy rain.

The gusty, changeable winds causing air blowing across the ground to rise into the plume can endanger firefighters by sending flames rushing toward them. Even worse, at times plumes have collapsed, sending strong blasts of fiery winds upon firefighters too quickly for them to escape. Fast-moving cold fronts can also cause quick wind shifts that endanger firefighters.

FORECASTING WILDFIRES

The NWS sends incident meteorologists to the scene of large wildfires to alert firefighters when sudden wind shifts are possible, and also to produce forecasts firefighters use to plan strategies.

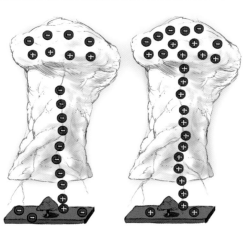

A violent interchange of positive and negative electrical charges between clouds and ground causes lightning, a natural cause of wildfires.

Take precautions to protect your pets during a wildfire.

Protect Your Pets

Pets need to be prepared for wildfires too. The American Humane Association offers the following tips on its website.

BEFORE THE FIRE

→ Evacuate your pets as early as you can.

→ Have on hand a list of boarding facilities, pet-friendly hotels, and emergency shelter locations.

→ Make sure your animals are wearing collars with current information.

→ Consider microchipping your animals for backup identification.

→ Stock extra pet supplies in your vehicle.

→ Practice loading cats and dogs in pet carriers before you have to.

→ Practice loading large animals into a trailer and driving them before you have to.

AFTER THE FIRE

→ Do not allow pets to wander around fire-struck buildings.

→ Keep dogs on a leash and cats in a carrier until you know house and yard are safe.

→ Watch for objects that could cause injury or harm to your pets.

→ Give pets time to reorient themselves. Familiar scents and landmarks may be altered and cause your pet confusion or to become lost.

→ Keep pets away from downed power lines and debris.

A fire in Saratoga Springs, Utah, leads to an evacuation of the area.

→ A free **Wildfire Info** app for iPhones and iPads maps and lists all active wildfires in the United States, including perimeter maps for all fires. Premium versions, one for firefighters and one for homeowners, include a fire weather overlay map, weather/fire danger calculators, and other incidentals. Wildfire Pro is available for Android, too. Visit an app store or *www.firewhat.com/app/*.

→ Using satellite data, the free app **Burnt Planet** pinpoints hot spots, ranging from wildfires to small controlled fires, from around the world.

→ For Colorado residents, **Colorado Wildfire Watch** from the state's Division of Fire Prevention and Control updates info on wildfires and relief efforts.

→ **Wildland Toolkit** by Peakview Software, $5.99, is a professional firefighter tool used to predict wildfire behavior. Highly technical but of interest to those studying fire behavior.

There's an App for That

Available for download from iTunes and/or Google Play, these apps may be helpful as you prepare to face dangers from wildfires:

→ The **Red Cross Wildfire App** offers state-by-state wildfire updates and preparation tips, plus a function to let loved ones know that you are safe. Call **REDCROSS (**73327677) from your smartphone; for a download link, visit *www.redcross .org/mobile-apps/wildfire-app,* or search an app store.

RED CROSS BEST PRACTICES GOING HOME AGAIN

After a fire, inspect your home carefully before entering. Broken power and gas lines or foundation cracks can signify that your home may still be unsafe. Hissing sounds and a gaseous smell are indicators of a dangerous gas leak. Check with your fire department to make sure your house is structurally sound before entering, especially if you notice any of these signs of danger.

American Red Cross

FIRST PERSON: Darrell Fortner, firefighter and business owner, Colorado Springs, Colorado

Wildfire Hits Close to Home

A father and son watch as the family home burns in Colorado.

DARRELL FORTNER and his wife, Jennifer, lost their home during the epic 2013 Colorado wildfires outside Colorado Springs. Ironically, Darrell runs a tree-trimming operation, Dundee Tree Service, that helps mitigate and prevent forest fires. But when a blaze reaches massive proportions, as this one did, burning some 16,000 acres, there is little anyone can do but evacuate.

Thankfully, Darrell and his wife were not inside their home when the fire reached their land; they were out doing errands. A neighbor called and informed them how close the fire was to their house. So they did what most people would do, but should not: They headed home, fast.

"The fire was three times higher than the tree line, and the wind was going about 40 to 50 miles per hour. It was just unbelievable," Darrell says. "I looked down the road, Black Forest Road, and it was so dark in smoke, no one could go through that unless they had gas masks, and even with that they would be blinded because you couldn't even see through it . . . The sheriff wouldn't let me in, and I'm glad they didn't, because if I got in, I probably would have stayed."

The Fortner house was much more than a simple structure to Darrell and his wife. It was a symbol of his hard work, his family. It was in the truest sense of the word, a "home."

"We lost a lot of cats and all four of our German shepherds," Darrell added. "The firefighters buried them all right there. That was so gracious of them and loving. They put stones around their grave . . . My wife and I married 20 years ago, and that was our first home together, in that house."

And it wasn't as if Darrell hadn't taken the right precautions. He had built a fire protection zone around his house and says he had trimmed the surrounding trees properly. He even kept vehicles and equipment a fair distance away. "I have an area of land that is 100 feet wide and 700 feet long. I mitigated, I cut down every tree literally on my property for 200 feet on each side," Darrell says.

But the fire didn't pay attention to Darrell's safety steps. "The fire went east at first and then about 6:45 [p.m.] it turned back and went back south and came in the back end of my property, where the neighbors' trees were really close to ours . . . My house was actually out in the open with lots of aspen trees around it, lots of deciduous trees, and small evergreens."

Despite all the loss, Darrell says he was fortunate: Two of his neighbors died from smoke inhalation during the fire.

"I've been in this situation all over the United States—helping people with fires and saving their homes; hurricanes and helping people take away debris and things; and I'm seeing what they're going through. I've never been through it myself until now, and now I really understand exactly what they are going through."

> "No one could go through that unless they had gas masks, and even with that they would be blinded."

Firefighters water hot spots amid the blaze.

EXPERT WITNESS: Steve Running

Bigger and Hotter Wildfires

A night burn operation occurs on a forested hillside.

Steve Running, *Regents Professor of Ecology at the University of Montana*

→ Have wildfires been getting worse in the western United States?
Yes, we're seeing bigger fires today. And once they get going, they're burning for a longer period of time. They're also burning across a wider area of the landscape.

→ The average fire used to last about a week, right? And now megafires can last more than a month.
What happens is firefighters usually try to put out any fire that breaks out near human settlements; some wilderness fires are allowed to burn. Most they can successfully control within the first few days. But when all the conditions go wrong, especially with the wind, a fire can get too big too fast. At that point, there's really nothing humans can do to stop it. That's something the public doesn't understand. We don't expect NOAA to stop hurricanes before they reach the beaches in Florida. So why do we expect the Forest Service to stop these enormous wildfires at the edge of town? The Yellowstone Park fires in 1988 burned until the snow fell.

→ How is climate change related to this trend?
In a couple of ways. First off, the

mountains of the West used to carry snow well into the summer. When Lewis and Clark tried to cross Lolo Pass in Montana on June 21, 1806, on their way back east, they encountered 20-foot-high snowdrifts. Nowadays, the snow up there's gone by May 1st. The snowpack melts early enough that higher-elevation forests have time to dry out. Then all it takes is for a lightning strike to hit, and it can get going quickly. We're seeing forests that haven't burned for centuries becoming vulnerable. And summer rainfall in the western mountains is limited, and quickly evaporates away in a few days.

→ Is that early melting due to higher temperatures in the West?

Oh, yeah. That's been well established in the science literature. Snowpacks on average have been melting about two weeks earlier than they used to, say, 50 years ago. Also more winter precipitation is coming as rain.

→ There have also been more record hot temperatures in the summer, right?

Yes, the higher summer temperatures we've seen dry out the forests quicker, so more of them are vulnerable to ignition. Once you have the system dry enough to be ignitable, it's just a Russian roulette of when an ignition might occur.

We also have a dramatically longer fire season. In California it's now almost a year-round vulnerability. You can have wildfires in what is supposedly the dead of winter down there. Up here in Billings, Montana, we've had wildfires in January. That used to be impossible. It was just plain too cold.

→ So is this how it's going to be? Are we going to have monster fires every summer?

Not everywhere and not every summer. Montana's had a couple of easy fire years lately, while Colorado has had a couple of terrible ones. Some years will be wetter and cooler than others or simply have the good luck of few lightning storms. But in an overall sense, this is the new normal. We're continuing to warm up. The snowpack is continuing to melt earlier, and nothing in future climate trends is likely to alter this trajectory.

HOW TO: **PREPARE**

→ **WHAT TO DO**

Indoors

- ✓ Treat your house, or build with noncombustible materials, especially roofs, siding, decking, or trim. FEMA recommends fire-retardant chemicals be evaluated by a nationally recognized laboratory, such as Underwriters Laboratories.

- ✓ Have your chimney inspected every six months, and clean it once a year. Make sure your dampers are working, and have a spark arrester installed that meets the requirements of National Fire Protection Association Standard 211, as FEMA recommends. You can order through nfpa.org. Contact your local fire department for exact specifications.

- ✓ Use mesh screens as fire retardants under porches, decks, and floor areas.

- ✓ Have a dual-sensor smoke alarm for every level of your home, and place them near bedrooms.

- ✓ Test your smoke alarms every month, and change the batteries every year.

- ✓ Teach each family member how to use a fire extinguisher, and show them where it's kept. FEMA recommends an ABC type of extinguisher.

- ✓ Install fire-protective shutters and drapes, if you can.

- ✓ Consider buying a generator in case of electricity loss if power lines are affected by a blaze.

Outdoors

- ✓ Landscape with fire-resistant shrubbery and trees. Pine, evergreen, and fir trees are more flammable than hardwood trees.

- ✓ Clean your roof and gutters on a regular basis.

- ✓ Obey ordinances when burning yard waste, and keep fire tools and extinguishers close at hand.

- ✓ Check that your garden hose is long enough to reach any area of your home.

- ✓ Make sure you have a water source close by such as a small pond, cistern, well, swimming pool, or hydrant.

- ✓ Use extreme caution with flammable liquids and fuels, as well as with portable appliances such as lanterns, stoves, or heaters.

- ✓ Install freezeproof exterior water outlets on at least two sides of your home, and place outlets at least 50 feet from your house.

Keep your chimney clean and inspected.

→ WHAT *NOT* TO DO

Indoors

☒ Do not use decks, patios, and balconies as storage locations for combustible materials such as newspapers and magazines, rags, or clothing.

☒ Do not leave vented spaces, such as soffits, eaves, and crawl spaces, open. Box in with fire-resistant materials, including even a $1/8$-inch metal screen, to block hot embers from flying and spreading fire.

☒ Do not be caught without an emergency kit and an evacuation plan, especially if you live in a fire-prone area.

Outdoors

☒ Do not leave debris that can easily burn outside the house, including piles of wood, lawn furniture, barbecue grills, tarp coverings, and flammable liquids (such as oil or gas cans).

☒ Do not toss cigarettes, matches, or any other burning material from your car or discard them on the ground. Use an ashtray.

☒ Do not leave a fire outside unattended. When leaving a campsite, or if you plan on sleeping through the night, make sure your campfire is completely out. Douse it with water, and mix the ashes and embers.

☒ Do not do any backyard burning of waste in windy conditions, and don't forget to check local restrictions.

HOW TO: SURVIVE

→ WHAT TO DO

Indoors

- ☑ Close all windows, vents, and doors to thwart a draft.

- ☑ Turn off all natural gas, propane, or oil supplies to your home.

- ☑ Fill your tubs and sinks with water, and outside fill your garbage cans and buckets. If you have a pool or hot tub, fill it. This slows and discourages fire paths.

- ☑ Keep fire tools such as rakes, axes, handsaws or chainsaws, buckets, and shovels at hand and ready to use.

- ☑ Close any outside vents, including those for your attic and basement. Make sure pet doors are closed, too.

- ☑ Take down any flammable drapes or curtains, and close all your shutters, blinds, and window coverings. Close all doors inside the house to prevent draft. Open the damper on your fireplace, but close the fireplace screen.

- ☑ Stash valuables (including important documents) inside your car so you can depart quickly. Valuable items that won't be damaged by water should be put in a pool or pond.

- ☑ Clear room areas and move flammable furniture to the center of your home, as far away from windows and doors as possible.

- ☑ Turn on every light in every room of your house as well as the outside lights. This makes things more visible in heavy smoke conditions.

Outdoors

- ☑ If time allows, clear combustibles, including firewood, barbecue grills, and fuel containers from your yard.

- ☑ Make sure your garden hoses are connected to water faucets, and place sprinklers in especially vulnerable places such as your roof and by fuel tanks. Turn them on if the fire encroaches.

- ☑ Look for a low-lying area that is clear of debris and vegetation and head for it.

- ☑ In emergency situations only, you should stay in your car. It is less dangerous than trying to outrun a fire on foot. According to FEMA, metal gas tanks rarely explode.

- ☑ Make sure to turn off the water if you must evacuate.

- ☑ If the fire consumes the area around you, lie on the ground, douse your clothing with water, and cover yourself with a blanket or soil. Breathe through a moistened cloth.

Take your pets with you when evacuating.

→ WHAT *NOT* TO DO

Indoors

☒ Do not try to wait out a fire; evacuate immediately.

☒ Do not neglect what you are wearing: Wear shoes you can run in, long pants, a long-sleeved shirt, and have gloves and a handkerchief to protect your face.

☒ Do not assume someone else has called 911 or the fire department; call and describe any fire sightings.

☒ Do not count on electricity working. Unplug all unnecessary appliances, including garage door openers which you can open by hand. Keep your garage doors closed.

☒ Do not remain standing. Get as close to the ground as possible, and crawl to avoid gases and heat (which rise).

☒ Do not ever go back inside a burning building.

Outdoors

☒ Do not attempt to outrun a fire. Instead, look for a body of water such as a pond or river to jump in.

☒ Do not remain on the uphill side. Rather, seek shelter on any nearby downslope.

☒ Do not drive through heavy smoke. If you must, park away from trees and brush.

☒ Do not drive too fast through a wildfire area. Watch out for pedestrians and other vehicles. Roll up your windows and close all air vents in your vehicle.

HOW TO: **RECOVER**

→ **WHAT TO DO**

Indoors

☑ If you have gotten burned, or are with burn victims, immediately cover all burn area and cool the injury. Call 911.

☑ Check your home for any signs of fire, damage, or lingering dangers such as embers. Especially check your attic and roof areas.

☑ Maintain a fire watch for a few hours after the fire has passed, checking for smoke or other signs of fire.

☑ Ask a neighbor to maintain lookout over your property if your home has become unsafe to remain in.

☑ Keep an eye out for ash pits, and keep clear of them. Mark them if necessary.

☑ Take care of your pets and animals. Hidden hot spots can injure them if they walk on embers.

☑ Use masks and proper tools and equipment to clean up ash. Follow health guidelines.

☑ Hose down or douse debris with water to stop dust particles from blowing.

☑ Wear leather gloves and heavy-soled shoes to protect hands and feet.

☑ Properly dispose of any flammable liquids, cleaning products, and fuel containers. Keep them well away from anyplace where they could be at risk of heat or sparks.

Outdoors

☑ Put on sturdy shoes, and cover yourself with as much clothing as possible to protect any exposed body areas. This will also protect from sparks, embers, and burning ash.

☑ Evacuate, and choose a path away from the fire. Keep a constant lookout for changes in any speed or direction of the fire. Do this at regular intervals.

☑ Call a friend or family member to alert them of your location and the direction you are taking.

A man inspects all that remains of his home after a fire.

→ WHAT *NOT* TO DO

Indoors

☒ Do not reenter your house until officials give you the okay to do so.

☒ Do not guess at inspection signs; if a building inspector has placed a sign on your home, stay out until you receive instructions.

☒ Do not eat food that has been exposed to fire.

☒ Do not use water that may have been contaminated.

☒ Do not try to open your safe or strongbox right away. These can stay hot for hours, and contents can burst into flames.

☒ Do not go near power lines or poles that have fallen or are damaged.

Outdoors

☒ Do not let scorched earth remain. Help soil recover by replanting or mulching rather than trying to start from seeds. The right vegetation depends on the locale where you live.

☒ Do not think fire won't hit the same area twice; it can recur.

☒ Do not ignore the possibilities of floods. Scorched earth allows water to flow more easily on the surface and often creates floods. Take flood control measures when you rebuild.

Wildfire plumes
waft high into the
atmosphere in
New Mexico.

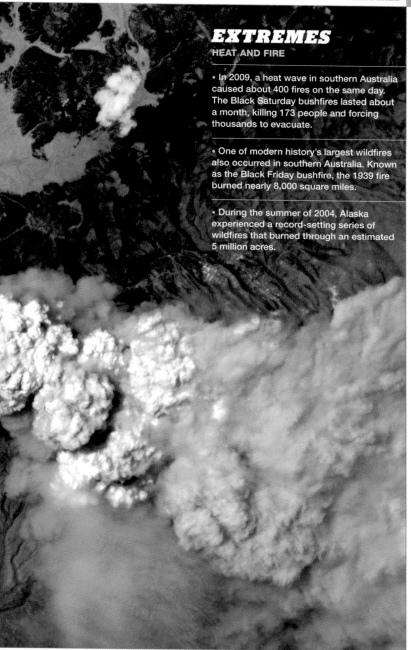

EXTREMES
HEAT AND FIRE

• In 2009, a heat wave in southern Australia caused about 400 fires on the same day. The Black Saturday bushfires lasted about a month, killing 173 people and forcing thousands to evacuate.

• One of modern history's largest wildfires also occurred in southern Australia. Known as the Black Friday bushfire, the 1939 fire burned nearly 8,000 square miles.

• During the summer of 2004, Alaska experienced a record-setting series of wildfires that burned through an estimated 5 million acres.

PART 3

"THE FUTURE AND IT IS HOT."

It's changing our planet. The oceans are warming, and so is the land—with consequences yet to be fully reckoned. The atmosphere is changing too, as higher temperatures change global weather patterns. In some places, we are seeing intense storms and frequent floods; in others, severe droughts and destructive wildfires. In this section, you'll learn what you can do to prepare for and survive in a world with more heat.

Humanity has never faced a situation quite like this before. Since the rise of civilization, there's never been a global rise in temperature as rapid as what we're seeing today. Since the 1970s, the global mean temperature has risen by more than 0.7°F. Looking ahead, temperatures may vary over short periods due to different influences, as they have in the past. But over the long term, scientists say, global mean surface temperatures are expected to keep rising, in some models by as much as 8.6°F by the end of this century, compared to the 1985–2005 period.

Because of this relatively sudden rise, certain regions are likely to become even hotter than they are now, even as others become cooler, wetter, or drier. This is because higher temperatures affect the water cycle, which in turn affects precipitation. As temperatures rise, evaporation rates will increase. That means more moisture will be circulating throughout the atmosphere, creating the potential for more intense rainfalls or snowstorms.

In the Arctic and higher latitudes, higher temperatures will continue to alter the landscape by melting ice and raising sea

IS NOW.

— JAMES HANSEN, director of NASA Goddard Institute for Space Studies

levels. Warm regions, too, will feel the heat, experiencing extended heat waves, prolonged droughts, and, in some places, increased risk of wildfires.

The source of all this heat is clear. The world has warmed and continues to warm because of the impact of greenhouse gases like carbon dioxide in the atmosphere, which acts like a blanket to retain energy from the sun. How long this warming will last and by how much it will increase will depend in part on our greenhouse gas emissions. How the world's nations handle limits and meet targets is still being determined.

In this section, we highlight the practical problems that higher temperatures bring and offer suggestions for how to cope with them.

A haboob, or massive dust storm, looks to overtake Phoenix in 2011.

Temperatures
are rising
around the
globe.

CHAPTER 7

RISING TEMPERATURES

After the "no-show" winter of 2011–12, when snow coverage in the continental United States ranked third lowest on record, the month of March coasted in with the warmest spring yet; across the nation nearly 15,000 high temperature records were broken. A few months later, July finished as the hottest month ever recorded in the United States. In many places, temperatures of 100°F and higher lingered for days.

In the end, 2012 was officially recognized as the hottest year on record for the contiguous 48 states and the second worst for extreme weather events. The year's average temperature of 55.3°F exceeded the previous record by a full degree and was more than 3.2°F warmer than the average for the 20th century. Every state in the nation experienced above-average temperatures in 2012, with 19 states setting records, according to NOAA. A persistent drought covered 61 percent of the country at its peak, withering crops across the farm belt and causing power plants to reduce the amount of power they produced (or to use water warmer than regulations called for to cool their systems). Low river levels disrupted Mississippi River barge traffic.

The rest of the world was unusually warm as well. The average global temperature for 2012 was 58.2°F, making it one of the 10 warmest years on record, all of which have

---

FEMA BEST PRACTICES HEAT INDEX

Be aware of both the temperature and the heat index. The heat index is the temperature the body feels when the effects of heat and relative humidity are combined. Exposure to direct sunlight can increase the heat index by as much as 15°F.

Children play in a water fountain. People look for ways to beat the heat.

occurred during the past 14 years. The trend was clear, according to the Intergovernmental Panel on Climate Change (IPCC), a body established in 1988 by the United Nations and World Meteorological Organization "to provide the world with a clear scientific view on the current state of knowledge in climate change and its potential environmental and socioeconomic impacts." "Each of the last three decades has been successively warmer than any preceding decade since 1850," the IPCC noted in September 2013. "In the Northern Hemisphere, 1983–2012 was likely the warmest 30-year period of the last 1,400 years," the IPCC report added. All told, the IPCC concluded, the global average temperature has risen by about 1.5°F from 1880 to 2012.

Reaching a "Tipping Point"?
Once the Earth's average global temperature reaches a certain level, many scientists believe disruptive changes may be triggered that cannot be reversed. At the 2009 Climate Change Convention in Copenhagen, representatives from around the world set a goal of holding global mean warming below an increase of 3.6°F (2°C) above preindustrial levels—which means we may be

dangerously close to that "tipping point."

The more the world warms, the greater the likelihood of widespread calamities, wrote Jim Yong Kim, World Bank Group president, in a recent report. If the average global temperature increases by 7.2°F (4°C) in the decades ahead, we could see the inundation of coastal cities, increasing risks for food production, unprecedented heat waves, water scarcity, damage to coral reefs, and other losses of biodiversity. Such a world would be "so different from the current one that it comes with high uncertainty and new risks that

Gear and Gadgets
↘ GAUGING THE HEAT

There are various types of thermometers on the market. Many mercury thermometers are a thing of the past, and mercury is treated as hazardous waste, according the United States Environmental Protection Agency. Moreover, the National Institute of Standards and Technology announced in 2011 that it would no longer calibrate mercury thermometers, which means these thermometers' accuracy cannot be counted on.

Different types of materials that are sensitive to heat and cold—expanding when heated and contracting when cooled, just like mercury or alcohol, for example—are now used to gauge temperatures. Both analog and digital versions are available. Many digital versions have wireless sensors and can accurately determine the weather specific to your home location. And yes, "there is an app for that." Online apps link to the Internet and feed weather data to your handheld device. Once you set your location, all sorts of temperature alerts can be established.

Hygrometers should also be considered. These measure the amount of humidity in the air. This is an important gauge, especially when temperatures begin to rise, because humidity reduces the body's ability to cool itself by sweating.

By knowing the temperature and humidity levels, you can better assess how hot it might be and feel outside and take appropriate safety measures.

Handheld weather station

threaten our ability to anticipate and plan for future adaptation needs," he warned.

Global Impacts

The trend toward higher temperatures could have serious consequences, scientists have predicted:

Ocean Warming: The oceans will continue to warm during the 21st century, the IPCC reported. During the past few

---

Did You Know?
↘ NATURE'S SIGNAL

A creepy result of increased temperatures is the potential for an exponential boom in insect breeding. Flies, for example, depend on warmer weather to develop. Higher temperatures over longer periods mean multiple generations can emerge in the same season. Flies develop from larva more quickly when the temperatures get warm. Moreover, warmer temperatures increase growth rates. So as global temperatures rise, more flies are born over shorter periods of time. And we could see huge swarms. In May 2013, people fled cities and towns and shut tight their windows and doors across the Balkans to keep swarms of flies at bay. The flies blanketed surfaces like snow from a blizzard, according to news reports. Unusually warm temperatures after damp weather caused the outbreak. Other bugs could produce similar outbreaks as global temperatures rise—along with massive cases of the willies.

Higher temperatures will bring bigger swarms of insects.

Myriad factors contribute to rising temperatures, including carbon emissions.

The ground level can sink as the level of seawater rises.

decades, most of the temperature increases have taken place in the upper levels of the sea (from the surface to a depth of 2,300 feet). In the decades ahead, heat is likely to penetrate from the surface to the deep ocean, which could affect ocean circulation.

Snow and Ice: Glacial melting will also continue, the IPCC predicts. During the past two decades, the Greenland and Antarctic ice sheets have continued to lose mass. Glaciers have also shrunk worldwide, and Arctic sea ice and Northern Hemisphere spring snow cover have decreased in extent. As the 21st century proceeds, Arctic sea ice cover is likely to shrink further and get even thinner, the IPCC predicts. The spring snow cover is also likely to decrease in the Northern Hemisphere as global temperatures rise.

Sea Level: From 1901 to 2010, global mean sea level has risen by 0.6 feet (0.19 m), the IPCC reported. About three-fourths of the sea level rise since the early 1970s has come from melting glaciers and ocean thermal expansion. More sea level rise is expected during the 21st century.

What's Causing the Warming?
The Earth gets its heat from the sun. Sunlight and ultraviolet rays (relative shortwave energy) heat the Earth's surface, while

infrared radiation (longer wave energy) is reradiated to the atmosphere. On its way back to space, some of this outgoing radiation is absorbed by greenhouse gases such as carbon dioxide, effectively trapping it in the lower atmosphere. When in balance, the right amount of radiation remains to keep the planet at workable temperatures. This process is known as the greenhouse effect. Without greenhouse gases, Earth would be a much different place, with an average global temperature around 0°F instead of the current 59°F.

Continued on page 237

FEMA BEST PRACTICES URBANITES AND HEAT WAVES

Be aware that people living in urban areas may be at greater risk from the effects of a prolonged heat wave than are people living in rural areas. Because asphalt and dark roofs are more common in cities, and because dark surfaces store heat longer, urban dwellers should be keenly aware of heat ailments and learn the warning signs of hyperthermia. Get trained in first aid to learn how to treat heat-related emergencies.

Be aware of the urban heat island.

A forest is ablaze in
Custer State Park,
South Dakota.

EXTREMES
HOT AND GETTING HOTTER

• In 2003, a massive heat wave struck Europe, where an estimated 70,000 people died due to high temperatures. Entire rivers dried up, grapes turned to raisins on the vine, and crops shriveled.

• In March 2012, temperatures in the United States were so high that more than 7,000 daily records were tied or broken.

• The highest surface air temperature recorded on Earth—134°F—was in Death Valley, California, in July 1913.

Polar bears find less Arctic sea ice from which to hunt.

But when concentrations of greenhouse gases are too high, they retain too much energy, and the planet begins to warm up. Today atmospheric concentrations of carbon dioxide, methane, and nitrous oxide—three of the most important greenhouse gases—have increased to levels not seen during the past 800,000 years.

In theory, changes in sunlight could also cause increased warming. But since the 1970s, satellite measurements of solar energy reaching Earth have shown no increases except those associated with the ups and downs of the 22-year solar cycle. That means the sun cannot be blamed for the current warming trend, the IPCC concludes.

A Surge of Greenhouse Gases

Earth has experienced periods of dramatic warming before. About 56 million years ago, parts of North America saw a jump in annual temperatures by as much as 9°F, and the consequences were dramatic: droughts, floods, insect plagues, and extinctions. The cause of this spike was a sudden injection of carbon into the atmosphere, possibly from massive volcanic eruptions or melting methane deposits. Wherever it came from, it took the planet 150,000 years to recover. Now,

---

Gear and Gadgets
↘ VAMPIRE POWER USERS

They've suddenly popped up all over your house: electronic gadgets that quietly suck away power while you're not looking. The more power we consume, the more greenhouse gases power plants emit to keep up. That cell phone charger? If its plugged in (and warm), its still consuming electricity. Your aging desktop computer or big-screen TV? Same story. Any electronic device with a clock or remote control could still be using power, even if it is turned off. The easiest way to slay these vampires? Cluster devices on a power strip and shut them down together.

EXTREME WEATHER BASICS
Warming Up

Why is our planet getting hotter? To consider this question, let's take another look at the greenhouse effect—a relationship between Earth and sun that supports life as we know it, but, if thrown out of kilter, could cause tremendous changes in temperature, climate, and weather.

Solar energy is absolutely essential to life as we know it. Likewise, it powers the weather that we experience. Gases blanket the Earth—the atmosphere—and solar energy travels through the atmosphere, warming it very little before it reaches the Earth's surface, providing heat and light.

Some energy radiates from Earth's surface. Certain gases in the atmosphere absorb some of it and the atmosphere becomes warmer. The warmed greenhouse gases radiate energy in all directions, including back toward Earth's surface. These gases are called greenhouse gases because, like a greenhouse, they keep some of the warmth within the atmosphere. It is a natural process that life on our planet depends on.

But there are concerns. Climate scientists have concluded that the greenhouse effect has been accelerated by gases humans have been adding to the atmosphere by burning fossil fuels since the beginning of the industrial revolution in the 18th century.

Carbon dioxide (CO_2) is a major greenhouse gas. It has a natural cycle on Earth that includes time in the air, in water, as part of living things, in rocks, and buried deep in the Earth in coal, oil, and natural gas. As humans burn fossil fuels, more CO_2 is being pumped into the atmosphere. An atmosphere containing more CO_2 traps more energy within the atmosphere, thus warming the Earth.

FORECASTING RISING TEMPERATURES
Debates continue, often on political rather than scientific grounds, as to how well scientists can observe or forecast a long-term warming trend on Earth. Predictions of future climates depend on computer models using complex mathematical formulas that represent interactions within and among the atmosphere, oceans, land, and ice-covered places on Earth. Forecasts give a general climate picture, not specific weather details.

The greenhouse effect appears to be increasing.

Seawater floods Venice's Piazza San Marco.

in a disturbingly similar way, we're doing it again.

Since the industrial revolution began in the mid-1700s, human activities have contributed many billions of tons of extra carbon dioxide into the atmosphere. The main source of this carbon dioxide has been the burning of fossil fuels. Methane, nitrous oxide, and several other gases have also played significant roles.

These emissions continue today. And scientists say that the result will be even higher temperatures around the globe. In its latest report, the IPCC laid out four scenarios for temperature increases during the period between 2081 and 2100 compared to the period between 1986 and 2005. In the best-case scenario, in which greenhouse gas emissions are actually reduced, the report predicts a range of possible temperature increases from 0.5°F to 3.1°F. In the worst-case scenario, in which greenhouse gases have increased, the report predicts a range of increases from 4.7°F to 8.6°F. It also notes that, under all scenarios except the most moderate one, warming will continue beyond 2100.

Carbon Dioxide: Although carbon dioxide is naturally present

Carbon emissions have increased since the industrial revolution.

in the atmosphere as part of Earth's carbon cycle—where it circulates among the atmosphere, oceans, soil, plants, and animals—human activity is adding much more. Atmospheric concentrations of carbon dioxide have increased by almost 40 percent since preindustrial times, from approximately 280 parts per million by volume (ppmv) in the 18th century to 391 ppmv in 2011. The largest single source of carbon dioxide emissions in the United States is the combustion of fossil fuels such as coal to generate electricity, followed closely by the combustion of fossil fuels such as gasoline and diesel fuel for transportation.

Methane: Methane is the second most prevalent greenhouse gas emitted in the United States from human activities. In 2011, it accounted for about 9 percent of all greenhouse gas emissions from sources such as leakage from natural gas systems and the raising of livestock. The gas is also emitted by natural sources such as wetlands. Methane is more abundant in Earth's atmosphere now than at any time during the past 650,000 years.

Nitrous Oxide: Although nitrous oxide contributed to only about 5 percent of U.S. greenhouse gas emissions in 2011, its molecules stay in the atmosphere for an average of 120 years before dissipating. The impact of one pound of nitrous oxide on heating up the atmosphere is more than 300 times that of one pound of carbon dioxide. Nitrous oxide is also produced by both natural and human activity. Adding nitrogen to the soil through the use of synthetic fertilizers accounted for about 69 percent of total U.S. nitrous oxide emissions in 2011. It is also the product of the breakdown of nitrogen in livestock manure and urine. Ice core samples show that nitrous oxide concentrations were stable for 11,500 years; but since the industrial revolution, they have risen about 18 percent, with a swift increase toward the end of the 20th century.

Signs of Climate Change

A few degrees can make a big difference in the global ecosystem. Although it might not seem that a slight uptick in temperature could be significant, the impacts can be broad and dramatic. The EPA lists the following as signs of climate change; as you'll see, they're far more serious than merely a sultry summer afternoon. Many of these, and/or their effects, are discussed further throughout this book:

Changing rain and snow patterns: As temperatures rise, more moisture evaporates from land and water into the atmosphere. More moisture in the air generally means more rain and snow can be expected from a storm—as well as more heavy downpours.

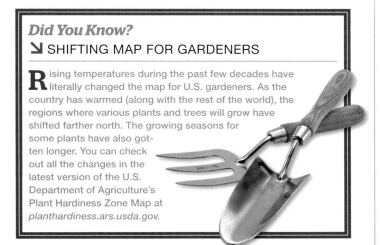

Did You Know?
↘ SHIFTING MAP FOR GARDENERS

Rising temperatures during the past few decades have literally changed the map for U.S. gardeners. As the country has warmed (along with the rest of the world), the regions where various plants and trees will grow have shifted farther north. The growing seasons for some plants have also gotten longer. You can check out all the changes in the latest version of the U.S. Department of Agriculture's Plant Hardiness Zone Map at *planthardiness.ars.usda.gov.*

Cattle in a feedlot emit methane, which is linked to global warming.

More droughts: Increased evaporation leaves less water in the soil. As a result, some parts of the world that are normally dry have experienced even longer or more severe droughts.

Warmer oceans: The atmosphere affects oceans, and oceans influence the atmosphere. As the temperature of the air rises, oceans absorb some of this heat and also become warmer. An increase in temperature may alter ocean currents and, in places like the tropics, promote stronger storms.

Rising sea levels: Water takes up more space as it gets warmer. Each drop of water expands only a little, but when you multiply this expansion over the depth of the ocean, it adds up and causes sea level to rise. Sea level is also rising because melting glaciers and ice sheets are adding more water to the ocean.

Shrinking sea ice: In the winter, the area covered by ice in the Arctic Ocean grows, and in the summer it shrinks. During the past few decades, the region has been warming faster than others, causing a loss of sea ice. In September 2012, the Arctic Ocean had the lowest sea ice extent on record, 49 percent below the average for that month during the period from 1979 to 2000.

Melting glaciers: Glaciers are large sheets of snow and ice that are found on land all year long. You can find them in the western United States, Alaska, the mountains of Europe and Asia, and many other parts of the world. Rising temperatures have caused glaciers to melt faster than they can accumulate new snow.

Increased ocean acidity: As the amount of carbon dioxide in the atmosphere has increased, a lot of it has been absorbed by the oceans—about 40 percent. Carbon dioxide reacts with seawater to form carbonic acid, which makes the ocean more acidic. This acidity can be harmful to corals, plankton, and other sea creatures.

Less snowpack: Snowpack is the total amount of snow and ice on the ground. In high mountainous areas and other cold spots, snowpack builds up during the winter and melts in the spring and summer. With rising temperatures, some places will get less snow and more rain; thus, the snowpack won't be as deep. And when the air is warmer, snow melts faster. From 1950 to 2000, the April snowpack in some parts of the western United States declined by 75 percent.

Thawing permafrost: Permafrost refers to a layer of soil or

Synthetic fertilizers add to nitrous oxide levels.

A villager in Bangladesh walks along a cyclone-battered area.

rock that is frozen year-round. Permafrost is found in much of Alaska, parts of Canada, and other countries in the far north. You might think a place with permafrost would be barren, but plants can still grow in the soil at the surface, which is not frozen during warmer parts of the year. However, there may be a thick layer of permafrost underneath. As air temperature rises, so does the temperature of the ground, which can cause permafrost to thaw or melt.

Best Ways to Keep Cool

There are wiser ways to keep cool during hot weather than simply turning up the air-conditioning. Every little effort helps. These new habits will ease your discomfort during a heat wave—and, considering that we are in for rising temperatures in the coming decades, they may be useful practices to follow no matter what during the hotter parts of the year.

Organize your living space: Hot air rises, and even with good ventilation, rooms upstairs will be hotter than rooms downstairs. So in the heat, relocate most of your activities—maybe even sleeping—to the lower floors of your house. Basements dug underground will stay a constant cooler temperature. Keep curtains and blinds drawn during daylight to minimize solar gain. Appliances, including computers, televisions, and incandescent lightbulbs, generate heat while turned on, so be vigilant about turning off everything not actively in use.

Organize your daily schedule: As much as possible, do as those who live in the tropics do: Consider the middle of the day siesta time, or at least the time to stay put without planning much physical activity. Wake up earlier and complete household and garden chores before the sun beats overhead. Reschedule work time later in the day. When days are longer, you can get a lot done and still have a mid-day respite.

Plan your meals: Reconsider your menu and perhaps even your meal schedule during the hottest of times. Eat raw foods that don't require cooking to reduce your stove and oven use. Substitute nuts and dairy products for meat, not only so you generate less heat in the kitchen but also because those

Good Idea
↘ MAKING A CROSS BREEZE

Configure windows for cross ventilation and stack ventilation. Cross ventilation allows the natural path of the wind to cool an indoor space. You need to figure out the direction of the wind. Once you determine this, open a window or door so the wind can flow in. If you have a

Create cross breezes to keep airflow cool.

fan, place it facing inward to blow fresh air into the space you are trying to cool. Next, open a window or door that is diametrically opposite (or close enough) to allow the air inside to flow out. Again, if you have a fan, place it here facing out. Monitor the direction of the wind in case the windows and doors have to be switched.

Stack ventilation is the same concept, except the open window or door allowing air in is on the bottom floor and the open window or door allowing air out is on a higher floor and on the opposite side. This draws warmer air out of a building and vents lower levels.

foods generate less metabolic activity—less body heat—as you digest them. Graze rather than eat a full meal for the same reason. Drink plenty of fluids, especially water, with and between meals.

Know the Symptoms

Higher temperatures mainly just make us less comfortable, but sometimes the discomfort may signal a health problem that requires medical attention and treatment.

Heat cramps—painful and involuntary constriction of limb muscles—are not harmful in and of themselves but often signal the onset of more serious problems, primarily heat exhaustion and heatstroke.

Did You Know?

⬎ UPS & DOWNS OF TEMPERATURES PAST

Scientists began measuring temperatures more than 400 years ago, when Galileo invented the first thermometer around 1592. But the Earth's average temperature wasn't routinely recorded until the 1880s. Paleoclimate models allow temperatures to be estimated much farther back in time than this, though. By using computer models, scientists can look millions of years into the past and estimate climate, including temperatures. They do this by recreating climates with information gathered from tree rings and air bubbles trapped in ice cores, for instance. With these data points, they can reconstruct the ups and downs in global average temperatures.

A liquid thermometer measures the air temperature.

Less snowpack means less fresh water during the snowmelt.

A woman texts in the rain. Different apps keep you weather wise.

Heat exhaustion's symptoms include vomiting, nausea, headache, and dizziness, as well as general exhaustion. If a person experiencing heat exhaustion does not respond quickly by resting and rehydrating, symptoms can progress to heatstroke, a serious condition.

Heatstroke is a potentially fatal condition that occurs when the body's own methods of cooling internally are not adequate for the job. Infants and the elderly are most susceptible. Symptoms include those for heat exhaustion as well as those that are more extreme: rapid pulse, lack of sweating, hallucinations and confusion, and even seizures. At its worst, heatstroke can induce coma.

Heat exhaustion and heatstroke are serious and life-threatening conditions that must be addressed immediately. At the first sign of any of these symptoms, make sure to rest and rehydrate.

For any of the more severe symptoms, seek immediate medical attention from your family doctor or in a local emergency room. Do not hesitate to call 911 if you are concerned.

There's an App for That

Among the most urgent impacts of rising temperatures are more frequent emergencies caused by extreme weather events outlined in this book. Available for download from iTunes and/or Google Play, the following apps are general weather and emergency apps that may be helpful across the board:

→ The **NOAA Now** app offers the latest news and emergency updates from NOAA. It also includes the nationwide ultraviolet index; ocean storms, including the latest information for the Atlantic, Eastern Pacific and Central Pacific cyclone basins; mainland storms, including the latest severe weather alerts; satellite views of the United States, the Northeastern and Western Pacific, and the Western Atlantic.

→ **RadarScope** is for the weather enthusiasts in need of a radar app. Along with a number of other tools, it displays NEXRAD Level III radar data. You can select one of the 156 different radar sites and plot your own location; it also displays NWS warnings.

→ The **AccuWeather** app is a good, straightforward tool with easy-to-read displays and other options, as well as information on specific health concerns and other personalized data.

→ **MyWarn** delivers severe weather alerts from the National Weather Service to its users within seconds of them being issued. The app "follows" the user with location-based services to constantly monitor the specific threats for any location in the United States, and notifies users if severe weather is forecast for their location, if they are in a severe weather watch, or if they are inside a warning area issued by the NWS.

→ The **Red Cross Shelter Finder** displays open Red Cross shelters and their current population on an easy-to-use map interface.

→ The official **American Red Cross First Aid app** provides instant access to the information you need to know to handle the most common first aid emergencies.

→ The **FEMA app** contains disaster safety tips, an interactive emergency kit list, emergency meeting location information, and a map with open shelters and open FEMA Disaster Recovery Centers. ■

CDC BEST PRACTICES KEEP HYDRATED

Drinking enough fluids is essential to preventing a heat-related illness. Do not drink only when you are thirsty, but continue to hydrate yourself, whether or not you are engaged in physical activities. Do not drink alcohol, extremely cold drinks, or very sugary drinks.

FIRST PERSON: Fred Eningowuk, an Inupiat resident
of Shishmaref, Alaska

A Way of Life in Danger

Due to thinning ice, subsistence seal hunting isn't what it used to be.

FRED ENINGOWUK is on the front lines for increased temperatures. He lives on the island of Shishmaref in Alaska, where his family has lived for generations. The Inupiat trace their lineage on the land back some 4,000 years. About 500 villagers now live in Shishmaref. But they are being uprooted due to changes in the climate.

Shishmaref sits on the Bering Strait on the edge of the Arctic Circle. Warmer temperatures have caused the ice there to melt and the land to erode. The community maintains a subsistence culture, where villagers live off what they hunt. Less ice means they cannot hunt as well. The ice allows them to travel on the frozen sea; otherwise they are stuck on their tiny island. In addition, their homes are getting swept away by the encroaching sea.

The Army Corps of Engineers says the entire community of Shishmaref must move; it's too vulnerable to storms and extreme weather.

"We've been having about a month earlier spring and about a month later autumn," Fred says. "I don't know what is going on with this spring, and I don't know why we are having these storms. We usually have our last storms in April, but right now (May) we have a storm. It makes life more difficult. It makes travel more difficult. For example, it's going to be covering some ice in some dangerous areas with this new snow. So everyone is really waiting for the north wind so we can start our spring hunting."

Fred explains that although the snowstorms that come are more severe, there is less snow on the ground. "Good snow," as he calls it, doesn't come until February of late, and this wreaks havoc on their sleds and all sorts of day-to-day items that get damaged due to exposure.

Yet, Fred, who gives his age as "50-plus," doesn't want to leave. "I grew up here so I'd rather stay here, you know. The older generations, we'd rather stay here. But we have to think about the next generation, too."

Moving to the mainland is an option. However, Fred isn't convinced that it is going to be any better over time. "We can be better off staying rather than relocating to the mainland because of the permafrost [melt] on the mainland; that could be a disaster waiting to happen," he worries.

And who can blame him? If the permafrost melt has caused coastal erosion and homes to fall into the sea off Shishmaref, why couldn't permafrost melt encroach upon life in mainland Alaska, or anywhere else for that matter? The only solution would be to abandon their coastal culture and heritage.

Fred says, "I'm afraid if we move from where we are, we'll lose our subsistence base . . . if we go over to the mainland we may not be able to hunt. We are used to a subsistence lifestyle that has revolved around the island. That's our way of life."

Stay or go, increased temperatures have changed Fred's way of life for good.

> **"We are used to a subsistence lifestyle that has revolved around the island. That's our way of life."**

Erosion is forcing evacuation.

EXPERT WITNESS: **Dr. Heidi Cullen**

Coping With Big Changes in a Warmer World

Pedestrians huddle under an umbrella in New York City. Heavy downpours have increased.

Dr. Heidi Cullen, *chief climatologist for Climate Central, a nonprofit science journalism organization based in Princeton, New Jersey*

→ How unusual is the rise in temperature that we've seen globally during the past 50 years?

It isn't the rise that's unprecedented. It's the rate of the rise. We've seen an increase of about one and half degrees Fahrenheit over the past century, which is really quite something. When we look back to the last ice age, we see this kind of warming happening on a thousand-year timescale. Today, we're seeing it happening in just decades.

→ One and half degrees doesn't sound like much, but it represents an enormous amount of energy, doesn't it?

Yes, massive. You've got to remember that more than 90 percent of the warming that's happened over the past 50 years has gone into the ocean. Only a very small amount has gone into the atmosphere. So what we're seeing in the weather is just the tip of the iceberg.

→ **Do you think the extreme weather we've been seeing is a reflection of climate change?**

If you look at heavy downpours—where a lot of rain comes in a very short time—we've seen a 74 percent increase in the northeast United States since the late 1950s. Just from the physics alone, we'd expect that if you increase the Earth's temperature, there will be more moisture in the atmosphere. So now when it rains, there's more energy in the system, more moisture in the system, to come out in the form of rain.

→ **Plus all those heat records that have been broken recently.**

Exactly. The summer of 2012–13 was the hottest on record in Australia, where they had these devastating wildfires and widespread flooding. It was a terrible year when it came to extreme weather. They called it the Angry Summer. A paper recently showed that global warming increased the chances of that kind of hot summer happening by more than five times. By the middle to the end of the century, that kind of summer could become the new normal.

→ **That's a scary idea.**

No, it's really not good. A world with 7 to 11 degrees warming is a radically different planet.

→ **How concerned should we be about extreme weather?**

When I look at how much of the heat is going into the oceans and how long the timescales are for the overturning of the oceans, the term that comes to mind is irreversible. Even if we go cold turkey with CO_2 emissions, it will take more than a thousand years for the temperature increase to begin to dissipate. What we are doing now will impact our kids and grandkids.

→ **What can we do on an individual or family level to prepare for our changing weather?**

First, you need to know what kind of risks you're exposed to. If you live along the coast, for example, you need to think about storm surge and sea level rise. What can you do to reduce your overall level of vulnerability? Does your home need to be elevated? Do you have important appliances in the basement? How else can you become more self-reliant? Each community will face a different set of risks. At the local level, I'm seeing signs that folks are really coming together—saying, you know what, we're going to do something about this. That makes me hopeful.

HOW TO: **PREPARE**

→ **WHAT TO DO**

Indoors

☑ Install fans.

☑ Hang shades and/or drapes to keep sun out.

☑ Shade windows facing west. These receive the most sunlight during the hottest part of the day.

☑ Caulk around windows and put weather strips around doors to keep cool in.

☑ Close the fire damper so cool air cannot escape.

☑ Use programmable thermostats so while you sleep or are away, temperatures can return to normal without manual consideration.

☑ Create an envelope of insulation with building materials that reduce drafts.

☑ Know your medical state. Poor blood circulation and certain medications can make you more vulnerable to hot weather.

☑ Make sure air conditioners are working properly by ensuring coils and filters are clean and refrigerant levels are appropriate.

☑ Check for sources of heat that you might not think about, such as incandescent lightbulbs and computers. Turn off all the electrical and electronic appliances you can.

Outdoors

☑ Consider installing highly reflective roofing, or light-colored roofing on your house. These, rather than darker materials, don't absorb as much heat.

☑ Build extended eaves, plant leafy trees, install awnings, or construct an arbor to help block the sun.

☑ Install solar panels, if you can. By using the sun's energy, you'll use less of your own and help keep your house and the planet cool.

Close the shades to
help keep cool.

→ WHAT *NOT* TO DO

Indoors

☒ Do not plan activities in higher floors or sun-filled rooms. Heat rises.

☒ Do not take down storm windows. These help insulate windows from higher temperatures.

☒ Do not ignore the attic. Attic fans can help cool the house fast.

☒ Do not forget to stay in touch with neighbors, especially elderly ones who are more vulnerable to rising temperatures.

Outdoors

☒ Do not take unnecessary trips in your car. Automobiles contribute greenhouse gases and other pollutants to the air.

☒ Do not waste water on yards or car washing during heat emergencies.

☒ Do not leave south- and west-facing windows unshaded during summer. Consider installing awnings or shutters.

☒ Do not forget to mulch the garden to hold moisture in soil as much as possible.

HOW TO: **SURVIVE**

→ **WHAT TO DO**

Indoors

- ☑ Figure out the hottest part of the days and where the sun shines most for shade.

- ☑ Freeze bottles of water. If the power goes out, they thaw and can provide a cool source of water.

- ☑ Freeze washcloths. These can be placed on the back of the neck to cool the body in times of higher temperature.

- ☑ Limit activity to thwart your body temperature from rising and the possibility of more serious health conditions.

- ☑ Seek out shade.

- ☑ Use air-conditioning or fans.

- ☑ Clear clothes dryer vents. Clogged vents push more hot air back into your home. They also pose a fire hazard if not cared for properly.

- ☑ Eat healthy. Regular, well-balanced meals keep the body strong and provide it with nutrients that heat can sap. Go with spicy meals. This can help the body sweat, which cools the skin.

Outdoors

- ☑ Have a ready source of water. Hydration is key to coolness.

- ☑ Seek out shady areas.

- ☑ Look out for signs of sunstroke, heatstroke, and cramps. Nausea, vomiting, headache, dizziness, weakness, and confusion are all signs your body is overheating.

- ☑ Wear light-colored, loose-fitting clothing and a sun hat whenever you go outside.

- ☑ If your pets stay outside, always provide them with fresh, cool water and be sure they have a safe, shady spot to rest and sleep.

Staying hydrated is one key to beating the heat.

→ WHAT *NOT* TO DO

Indoors

☒ Do not circulate fans in a clockwise direction; counterclockwise movement forces air downward and cools things more quickly.

☒ Do not keep the lights on and run high energy–consuming appliances (such as dishwashers) during the hottest part of the day. These not only increase the heat inside your home, but also strain the electric grid and present a greater likelihood of power outage.

☒ Do not keep all the windows closed if you don't have air conditioning.

☒ Do not consume diuretics such as alcohol and coffee. These reduce blood flow to the skin, and in turn sweat.

Outdoors

☒ Do not dress in dark clothes. This attracts and stores more heat.

☒ Do not conduct activities for long periods during the day; take breaks.

☒ Do not go from cold temperature (say an air-conditioned car) immediately into a hike at midday. Acclimate to rising temperatures first.

Lightning storms,
like this one in
Nebraska, can
threaten home safety.

EXTREMES
MORE LIGHTNING ON THE HORIZON

• The most deaths from a lightning storm occurred in 1971, when a Peruvian airline flight crashed from a lightning strike into the Amazon rain forest, killing 91 people.

• The village of Kifuka in the Democratic Republic of the Congo is hit by lightning the most in the world, averaging 158 lightning bolts a year.

• In the United States, the most lightning, with an average of 59 lightning bolts a year, occurs in Florida—mostly in the summertime.

Children play in a water fountain to keep cool.

CHAPTER 8

HEAT WAVES

It took Western Europe by surprise. For weeks during the summer of 2003, a brutal heat wave gripped populations from the United Kingdom and France to Italy and Spain. An estimated 70,000 people lost their lives in the sweltering crisis, with temperatures soaring up to 30 percent higher than normal. Many of the deaths, especially in France, were among elderly residents whose homes had no air-conditioning to help them cope with daytime highs of 104°F and nights almost as bad.

FEMA BEST PRACTICES UP YOUR FLUID INTAKE

Extreme heat dehydrates your body and causes you to lose essential salts and minerals. To prevent water loss, increase fluid intake (in particular intake of water) and avoid caffeine and alcohol, which dehydrate your body. Throughout the day, eat small meals rather than large ones, which boost metabolic heat and water loss.

It's important to replenish electrolytes during hot weather.

Baseball fans try to stay cool during a game. Don't try to brave the sun; find shade.

Heat waves may be the sliest of weather phenomena. With none of the drama that accompanies floods, lightning, tornadoes, or hurricanes, they sneak up on a region and lay waste to the most vulnerable among us. In the United States, they're responsible for more deaths than all of those other weather hazards combined. But few people fully understand just how pernicious they can be. Because of that, awareness is key.

The Mechanics of a Heat Wave
In simple terms, a heat wave takes place when high atmospheric pressure forms over an area and settles in, baking everyone unfortunate enough to be stuck in it. In an area of high pressure, air from above is sinking toward the ground, warming and compressing as it sinks. The high pressure acts as a barrier blocking other weather systems from moving in, which is why some heat waves last as long as several weeks. The high pressure also discourages winds and prevents clouds from forming over the area, both factors that allow temperatures to soar. The National Weather Service

defines a heat wave as at least three consecutive days with high temperatures of at least 90°F. They are the stubborn bullies of the weather world.

What to Expect

Things appear to be heating up. Between June 28 and July 7, 2012, the city of St. Louis suffered through ten straight

Gear and Gadgets
↘ BREATHABLE FABRICS

L ess isn't always more when it comes to dressing for the heat. In fact, covering up as much as possible can avoid sunburn. Fabric choice is key here. Many types of material don't "breathe," meaning they don't allow air to circulate through the fabric to evaporate sweat. Cotton and linen are perhaps the most commonly thought of fabrics that allow for this.

Technological advances in how fabrics are made have greatly improved "breathability," however. Now different kinds of material not only speed up breathability, but also accelerate evaporation. This cools the body. Fabrics such as the patented and trademarked CoolMax and Dri-Fit designed for athletes are going mainstream. They wick moisture away and at the same time distribute cool air onto the skin. Other fabrics come with ultraviolet blockers, protecting from the sun's bands of radiation that affect us most.

Sure, seersucker looks great, linen feels nice, and cotton is an easy choice for lightweight clothing. But to beat the heat in the 21st century may mean picking up some apparel made with 21st-century technology.

Certain fabrics "breathe" better and thus work better in the heat.

days of temperatures exceeding 100°F. Eight of those ten days set new records; seven of the ten reached or exceeded 105°F. In March of the same year, NOAA's National Climatic Data Center reported that more than 7,000 daily record high temperatures were broken or tied across the United States during the month. Residents of Chicago were subjected to nine consecutive days of record high temperatures in March, eight of which exceeded 80°F; six of those nine days were on the winter side of the vernal equinox.

More hot weather may be on the way. The National Center for Atmospheric Research (NCAR) predicts that heat waves will become even more intense, more frequent, and longer lasting in the second half of the 21st century. In its Fifth Assessment Report, the Intergovernmental Panel on Climate Change agrees that it is very likely that heat waves will happen more often and last longer.

A 2013 study from the Potsdam Institute for Climate Impact Research predicts that climate change will incite a "robust, several-fold increase in the frequency" of heat waves by 2040. According to their models, we're about to enter "a new climatic regime in which the coldest summer months by the end of the century will be substantially hotter than the hottest experienced currently." But perhaps the

Did You Know?
↘ NATURE'S SIGNAL

You don't necessarily need a thermometer to figure out the temperature—a cricket will do. By counting the number of times a cricket chirps, you can calculate how many degrees it is outside. Here's how to do it: Count the number of times a cricket chirps every 14 seconds, add 40 to that number, and the total is the temperature in Fahrenheit. Cricket chirps have been scientifically proven to be related to air temperature, so it's no myth. The faster the chirps, the hotter the temperature.

People cool off near the Eiffel Tower.

Extreme heat particularly affects the elderly and the very young.

National Resources Defense Council, a nonprofit international environmental advocacy group, puts it all into perspective most dramatically with its report estimating that 150,000 Americans could die by the end of the century because of the excessive heat events caused by climate change, an estimate that includes only the country's top 40 cities.

Heat Islands

Cities are hot spots. As open land is converted into an urban environment, areas that were once permeable and moist become impermeable and dry. As a result, cities turn into "heat islands," sectors that are warmer than their surrounding, greener areas. In a city of a million or more people, the annual mean air temperature may be 1.8° to 5.4°F warmer than neighboring rural areas, the Environmental Protection Agency (EPA) explains. In the evening, the difference between city and country may be as high as 22°F because of the slow release of heat that the urban infrastructure captures during the day. This helps explain why heat waves take such a toll in cities. Air pollution doesn't help. The stagnant atmospheric conditions typical of a heat wave tend to trap pollutants in urban areas, adding severe pollution to the already deleterious effects of the heat. For these reasons, urban inhabitants should have increased vigilance in paying attention to the signs of heat illness, especially among the most vulnerable. Heat waves kill mostly poor people who live in houses or apartments without air-conditioning.

Killer Heat:
Know How It Harms

The human body dissipates heat in three ways: through circulation, by sweating, and to a lesser extent, through respiration. When the temperature rises, however, and especially when the weather is humid, the body's ability to maintain its proper temperature can be compromised.

If the body is unable to cool down through circulatory means or by sweating—or when the body cannot compensate for fluids and salt lost through perspiration—its core temperature begins to rise. At this point, problems may occur, ranging from heat cramps to heatstroke, the most severe of heat illnesses.

The body is considered to have heatstroke when its temperature reaches 104°F or higher. The tissues most vulnerable to heat are nerve cells, and because the brain is comprised of almost entirely nerve cells, it is especially sensitive to the body's rising temperature. In addition, cooling efforts include increased blood flow to the skin, which makes the heart work harder; that combined with dehydration from sweating results in cardiovascular strain. Along with the resulting damage to the brain and heart, very high body temperatures may also harm other vital organs and muscles.

When an individual is suffering from heatstroke, his or her body temperature can reach debilitating temperatures within 10 to 15 minutes. The longer treatment is delayed, the worse the damage can be. In the absence of any emergency treatment, the results can be fatal.

Heat affects everybody differently. People at greatest risk for heat-related illness include

Continued on page 271

CDC BEST PRACTICES COOLING OFF

Be aware that in temperatures in the high 90 degrees Fahrenheit, fans do not prevent heat-related illnesses. Take a cool bath or shower, or cool off in an air-conditioned room or shelter to remain safe. Even a few hours in air-conditioning can help cool you off.

Electric power
can surge during
extreme heat waves.

EXTREMES
RECORD-BREAKING HEAT

• The longest heat wave in history occurred in Marble Bar, Australia, when temperatures held above 100°F for 160 days.

• The year 2012 was the hottest on record for the United States. Temperatures were above normal for every month from June 2011 to September 2012. This had not occurred since record keeping began in 1895.

• The place with the highest average annual temperature for the longest period—93°F—is Dallol, Ethiopia.

A young man
keeps his body
core cool.

those at either end of the age spectrum—infants and children up to 4 years of age, because their central nervous systems are developing, and people 65 and older, because the central nervous system begins to deteriorate. Other factors that impact how the body regulates temperature include obesity, fever, heart disease, mental illness, poor circulation, prescription drug and alcohol use, and sunburn.

Heed the Relative Humidity
The skin is responsible for around 90 percent of the body's heat-dissipating needs through sweating. But sweating in and of itself does not cool the body; it needs to happen in conjunction with evaporation. Heat is released from the body as cooling evaporation on the skin occurs, allowing superficial vessels to return cooler blood back to the body's core to counteract rising temperatures.

When the relative humidity is high, evaporation is hampered; the moisture has no place to go when the air is already saturated with water molecules. When the temperature rises above

---

Good Idea
↘ DO-IT-YOURSELF REHYDRATION

Long bouts of perspiration and drinking excessive amounts of pure water can create an electrolyte imbalance in your body. This is marked by dizziness and cramps among other ailments. Always consult a physician, but in an emergency situation you can make your own oral rehydration solution:
• Mix ½ teaspoon of salt with 6 level teaspoons sugar to one quart room-temperature water. A half teaspoon baking soda can also be added if available.

A sugar-salt combo can help you rehydrate.

• Blend and drink (or serve) in small amounts (by the spoonful) every few minutes. Do this until urine becomes clear in color.

EXTREME WEATHER BASICS
How Heat Waves Happen

Heat waves begin high above ground. There, at altitudes of 10,000 feet or higher, jet stream winds roar along at speeds of a hundred miles an hour or greater. These winds, generally moving west to east, follow a wavy path that sometimes curves north and sometimes south.

When the jet stream curves north, it forms ridges in which air is slowly sinking toward the ground. As the air sinks, it warms at a rate of 5.5°F for every 1,000 feet.

By contrast, when the jet stream curves south, it forms a trough in which air is slowly rising. That helps clouds and precipitation to form.

From time to time, "blocking patterns" form in the waves, which stops their west-to-east movement. Such blocks cause heat waves to form under ridges in the summer. Not only does the air sinking from above heat up, but it also blocks rising air that could form clouds and rain, which allows the undimmed sun to continue heating the ground. A heat wave lasts until the blocking pattern ends, allowing a trough to arrive with cooler air and clouds.

FORECASTING HEAT WAVES
Because upper air patterns are easier to predict than many other weather phenomena, forecasters are usually able to issue heat wave alerts a few days in advance. Predicting when a blocking pattern—and thus a heat wave—will end is harder.

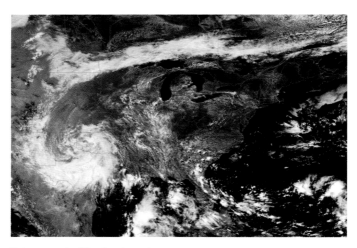

Hot, muggy air stifles the atmosphere.

Increased humidity can make the air feel hotter than indicated on the thermometer.

90 degrees in humid weather, the body's main cooling mechanism—sweating—can be dangerously jeopardized.

The term "relative humidity" gets tossed around a lot, and you may know that a relative humidity in the 45 percent range generally feels quite agreeable; that's the sweet spot at which most people tend to be most comfortable. Relative

---

Gear and Gadgets
↘ BED FANS

As nighttime heat increases in frequency, staying cool while you sleep is ever important. Bed fans can do the trick. These are height adjustable and designed to be aimed at your bed coverings. They are narrow and flat surfaced and sit neatly bedside to circulate air between your sheets, unlike traditional fans, which circulate air above the covers. Moreover, rather than cooling the whole room or house, bed fans specifically cool your body. This can save on electricity costs. Many come with wireless remote controls and have adjustable speed settings.

A worker takes a break to drink water. It's important to stay hydrated in the heat.

humidity is a measure of the amount of water vapor in the air compared with the amount of water vapor that the air would be fully saturated with at that particular temperature. Thus, the higher the relative humidity, the more water is in the air, resulting in decreased evaporative cooling and the potential for overheating.

Understand the Heat Index
Developed in 1978 by broadcast meteorologist George Winterling (who called it "humiture"), the heat index is a measurement of how hot it feels when relative humidity is added to the temperature. It's the counterpart to the wind chill factor. Because the dynamic between temperature and humidity can lead to dire health consequences for people, the NWS later adopted the heat index to give a numerical value to the relationship.

When studying the Heat Index, you can see what a dramatic effect relative humidity has on perceived temperature. For example, if the air temperature is 96°F and the relative humidity is 65 percent, it actually feels like a scorching 121°F. Keep in mind that the heat index values were designed around shady, light wind conditions; full sun exposure can increase the value up to 15°F—which is to say, in full sun

Did You Know?
↘ POWER OUTAGES

Heat waves can also cause power outages. This is because more power is used during heat waves than at any other time of the year. Too many people run their air conditioners at full blast at the same time, which puts more stress on the power system. Power stations, or substations, have built-in circuit breakers that kick in when demand becomes too much for the system to handle or when there are other transmission problems (such as downed power lines).

As we add more and more electrical devices to our homes (computers chargers for our phones, tablets, etc.), power demand has increased, putting more strain on power stations—even without extreme weather surges such as heat waves. But add increased demand due to weather, and systems could black out more frequently. Major weather-related power outages have increased from between 5 and 20 a year in the mid-1990s to between 50 and 100 a year.

WHAT TO DO
→ Listen on a battery-operated radio for updates about service restoration.
→ Use flashlights if possible. Candles and other flammable lighting sources (such as gas lanterns) are fire hazards.
→ Mind the elderly, and those with special needs, especially those in upper floors of buildings. Elevators probably won't operate during an outage.
→ Use caution when handling dry ice. Use gloves and an insulated container.
→ Try to keep only a single item plugged in so you know when the power is restored. This prevents damage to appliances and other devices when the power comes back on.
→ Use emergency generators wisely. They can be dangerous if not used properly. When in doubt, contact a licensed electrician.

WHAT NOT TO DO
→ Do not open and close refrigerator or freezer doors frequently. Food stays frozen for up to two days with doors closed.
→ Never touch or ever go near downed power lines.
→ Do not use cooking grills indoors as they emit carbon monoxide, which can be deadly.

Did You Know?
↘ HEAT AND RAILROAD TRACKS

Hot weather can bend and/or buckle railroad tracks. When the temperature hits 95°F, transportation authorities regularly send out inspectors to look for trouble spots. In the summer of 2010 heat wave, commuter trains in metropolitan areas suffered severe delays as tracks bent due to the extreme heat. In the heat wave of 2012, trains derailed. And, according to the U.S. Environmental Protection Agency, "more frequent and severe heat waves may require track repairs or speed restrictions to avoid derailments."

Extreme heat can bend or buckle train tracks.

the 96°F temperature and relative humidity of 65 percent in the previous example could ring in at a staggering 136°F.

The NWS issues heat alerts based mainly on heat index values. When the heat index is predicted to be greater than 105° to 110°F (depending on local climate) for at least two days in a row, the NWS begins issuing alerts.

Beware of Temperature and Temperament

It's not just the vital organs that suffer during heat waves; high temperatures can lead to hot tempers too. Numerous studies suggest a link between temperature and aggression. A 2004 study from researchers at the University of London and Lancaster University examining U.S. data found a link between strong seasonal patterns and several types of violent crime. The researchers concluded that stress hormones produced by the body in response to heat might lead to aggression. They also looked at workplace data and found a potential link between heat and incidents of labor strikes and people quitting jobs. Another study from Australia found that hospital admissions for mental and behavioral disorders increased by 7.3 percent during heat waves.

Ramifications

Heat waves are also tough on infrastructure. Among the most common problems are power outages when the electricity grid is tapped beyond its capacity by the use of air conditioners. Blackouts can last for days, leading to major disruptions. They can also exacerbate health dangers when people lose the power to keep their homes cool.

Roads buckle, pavement shatters, planes can get stuck in soft spots in the tarmac,

The power grid gets stressed during hot summers.

People stand in front of a grid showing power distribution in Los Angeles.

and train rails get kinks as they warm, leading to potential derailments. The D.C. commuter rail service, Virginia Railway Express, notes that an 1,800-foot length of rail will expand almost one foot with an 80-degree change in temperature, necessitating "heat orders" given to railroad engineers to reduce their speed.

High temperatures can also heat and dry soil so that it pulls away from buried water pipes. Hardened and shifting soil combined with increased pressure from water usage create strain to pipeline walls and make older pipes more vulnerable to bursting. Heat waves in the summer of 2011 burst hundreds of crucial pipes in California, Kansas, Oklahoma, Texas, Indiana, Kentucky, and New York, temporarily leaving consumers across the country without water.

Community Considerations

Some cities have addressed the severe effects of heat waves with response systems that may include news warnings, lists of single elderly residents, disaster centers that allow people to spend time in an air-conditioned place, water trucks, and door-to-door checkups of people who may be at risk. You can check with your municipality to inquire what precautions they have in place; if you belong to a community group, you can advocate for developing similar plans. On a personal level, you can make an effort to check in on family, friends, and neighbors who do not have air-conditioning, who spend much of their time alone, or who are more likely to be affected by the heat (the young, the elderly, pregnant women, and those with health problems, specifically). If you can, offer to take them for an after-noon outing during the warmest part of the day to the library, movie theater, mall, or other air-conditioned public place.

Local, state, and federal agencies as well as nonprofit organizations such as the Red Cross often provide "cooling centers" and shelters during extreme heat waves and power outages. An easy way to find out if there is a shelter in your area is to text SHELTER plus your zip code to 43362 (4FEMA).

There's an App for That
Available for download from iTunes and/or Google Play, these apps may be helpful in a heat wave:

NOAA
BEST PRACTICES STAY PUT DURING A DUST STORM

When driving in a dust or sandstorm, reduce your speed, turn on your headlights, and leave the road as soon as possible. Once off the road, turn off your lights. Other motorists may follow the lights as a guide and hit parked cars.

Visibility is reduced during a sandstorm.

RED CROSS BEST PRACTICES TIPS FOR COPING WITH HEAT

Keep these rules of thumb on hand to treat the three serious heat-related conditions: heat cramps, heat exhaustion, and heatstroke.

American Red Cross

1. Heat cramps. What to do: Move the person to a cool place and have him or her rest in a comfortable position. Lightly stretch the affected muscle and gently massage the area. Give an electrolyte-containing fluid, such as a commercial sports drink, fruit juice, or milk. You can also give the individual some water. Do not give salt tablets.

2. Heat exhaustion. What to do: Get the person to a cooler environment that has circulating air. Remove or loosen as much clothing as possible and apply cool, wet cloths to the skin. Consider fanning or spraying the person with water. If the person is conscious, offer small amounts of a cool fluid such as a commercial sports drink or fruit juice to restore fluids and electrolytes. Milk or water can also be given—about four ounces of fluid every 15 minutes. If the person's condition does not improve, or if he or she has a change in consciousness or vomits, call 911 or the local emergency number.

3. Heatstroke. What to do: Call 911 or the local emergency number immediately. Heatstroke can be deadly if not properly treated. Rapidly cool the body by immersing the person up to the neck in cold water, if possible. You can also douse or spray the person with cold water. Sponge him or her with ice water–doused towels over the body, frequently changing the towels. If you're not able to monitor the person's temperature, apply rapid-cooling methods for 20 minutes or until the person's condition improves.

A community group donates fans to families to help them stay cool.

→ The **FEMA** app provides disaster information and a map of FEMA Disaster Recovery Centers.

→ The **Red Cross Shelter View** app displays open Red Cross shelters and their current capacity on an easy-to-use map interface.

→ The **OSHA Heat Safety Tool** developed by the U.S. Department of Labor calculates the heat index and determines risk for workers; it also includes heat precautions (just in case you've lost this book).

→ The **Weather Underground** app, or any reliable weather service, can provide severe weather alerts and heat and air-quality warnings that can be helpful during a heat wave.

Protect Your Pets

You think you're uncomfortable in a heat wave? Imagine that you're wearing a fur coat and your only cooling mechanisms are panting and sweating through your feet. Pets are particularly vulnerable to the heat. The American Society for the Prevention of Cruelty to Animals (ASPCA) offers the following pet tips for when temperatures soar:

→ Make sure fresh, clean water is available, and make shady places available so pets

A cooling station in New Jersey helps keep elderly residents hydrated.

A golden retriever cools off in a water trough after working on the farm.

can cool off. Dehydration is a big concern.

→ Limit exercise to early mornings or later in the evenings when the temperatures are likely cooler. Also, check the sidewalks or the streets with the palm of your hand before you walk. If it's too hot for your hand, it's too hot for your pet's tender paws.

→ Keep pets indoors and bring outdoor pets inside, if possible, and allow them access to air-conditioning. For animals that cannot be brought indoors, find a shady, sheltered place for them to rest, and provide fresh water in stable containers (so they don't tip over).

→ Never leave your pet alone in a parked vehicle. A parked car can become like a furnace within minutes—even with the windows open—leading to fatal heatstroke.

→ Watch for symptoms of overheating, which include excessive panting or difficulty breathing, drooling, mild weakness, stupor, seizures, bloody diarrhea, and vomiting. The ASPCA advises contacting a veterinarian immediately if you suspect your pet is suffering from heatstroke.

Did You Know?
↘ EXTREME HEAT WAVES IN HISTORY

The most severe heat wave in history occurred in western Australia in 1923–24 when temperatures remained above 100°F for 160 days. More recently, both north and south Australia have had their fair share of heat. In 2009, Alice Springs in the north experienced 10 days in a row above 104°F. And in January 2014, southeast Australia was hit with temperatures of more than 104°F. In the south, Adelaide saw as many as 15 days above 95°F. In 2013, record heat was recorded for the country as a whole; in Queensland, the town of Birdsville suffered through more than a month of days above 104°F.

Europe has regularly experienced high temperatures since the turn of the century: in 2003, 2006, 2007, 2010, 2011, and 2012, drastic heat waves swept the region. During the 2003 disaster, temperatures soared as high as 117°F. In Paris, the thermometer stayed above 104°F for more than seven days.

In the United States, nearly 2,000 people died in 1980 when a heat wave hit the central and eastern parts of the country. In many places, temperatures remained above 90°F for most of the summer. Texas experienced the highest temperatures, above 115°F. In 1995, more than 700 people died when a heat wave hit Chicago, making this, according to the National Weather Service, the deadliest weather event in Chicago history.

Most recently, heat spells have set new records in the United States. In 2006, Woodland Hills, California, just outside the city of Los Angeles, recorded its highest temperature ever—119°F. In 2008, record temperatures were recorded on the East Coast. And in 2010, many of those records were again broken, with the Northeast seeing its highest temperatures in more than a century—only to see these records eclipsed in 2012, when more than 7,000 daily record temperatures were surpassed.

Extreme heat occurs in the Australian outback, home to Uluru.

FIRST PERSON: **David Donovan, a line worker with the Los Angeles Department of Water and Power**

Restoring Power After Crisis

Hurricane Hugo devastated homes along the Atlantic in September 1989.

WHEN THE power goes out, David Donovan is one of the guys who fixes it. You see workers like him high up on poles, underground, on the side of highways—in scorching heat and many times in deplorable weather conditions.

The amount of power linemen such as Donovan handle can be deadly. He says he regularly handles circuits with up to 138,000 volts. And a lot of that handling is done underground, where temperatures may reach 110°F, or 115°F.

Working in such heat is part of the job, part of what he has been trained for. Overhead work, such as atop poles or towers, can get scorching, too. "Okay, so that's part of my career," he says.

The most extreme heat he ever worked in wasn't part of his everyday job, however. "When Hurricane Hugo hit Puerto Rico, they sent 18 of us over to restore the island," Donovan says. "The devastation was phenomenal. The experience was over-the-top."

Because Puerto Rico needed more skilled workers to fix its power problem, professionals from mainland United States flew over to help. Donovan was among them.

"It was actually unbelievable," Donovan recalls. "The island was devastated by the hurricane. The poles were snapped and laid over, the power lines were down all over the island, so our job was to go in and restore power; rebuild the power lines from ground up. We did everything from reset poles to completely new sets of circuits and wires. We were working an average of 14-hour days. We were there for approximately three weeks."

"What you didn't expect was the humidity," he says. "It was so extreme none of us were used to it. But we weren't there on vacation; we were there to work. So, we're up at five o'clock in the morning, sitting down, trying to eat a breakfast, keeping our head away from our plate, because, as we sat there, the sweat would roll off of our foreheads into our food. Our bodies hadn't adjusted to the heat."

They drank plenty of fluids, he remembers, and they had to make sure that these fluids came from bottles, because the power lines were down. "That means the filtration plates were down, and drinking any of the water on the island could give us great contamination. One of the guys we worked with, one of our helpers, became severely ill, and we nursed him through this, and he had a rough few days that was touch-and-go, but we brought him back."

> "What you didn't expect was the humidity. It was so extreme none of us were used to it."

In addition to the heat, the work wasn't easy: Because there were few facilities, few workers, and few communication options, power workers had to rely on the sight of sparks at night to see where problems lay. "We'd start energizing those lines, and we'd climb up on the roof close and look for the explosions," Donovan says. All this made working in the heat more strenuous and difficult. "We just weren't used to the humidity, and we climbed poles, and we worked through it . . . It's part of the job."

Workers try to prevent a power blackout.

EXPERT WITNESS: Matthew J. Levy

Treating Heat-Related Emergencies

A senior in Tokyo suffers from heatstroke during a heat wave. Don't delay calling for help.

Matthew J. Levy, DO, M.Sc., an assistant professor of emergency medicine at Johns Hopkins University School of Medicine in Baltimore, Maryland

→ What kinds of emergencies do doctors see during a heat wave?
On the very minor end of the spectrum, you might have heat cramps or maybe a mild headache—the body's early warning indicators to itself that we're overdoing it too much. As the illness progresses in severity, vomiting sometimes happens, confusion sometimes ensues. Once the body starts having mental status changes—lethargy, confusion, seizures, coma, these kinds of things—the body's ability to compensate for its exposure to heat has failed, and the body's ability to compensate also gets messed up. That can make for a very dangerous situation.

→ People can die?
Very much so. As the heat illness progresses, you can have severe complications, where you have multiple systems on top of each other failing—you

might have someone with renal failure and they're unconscious because their core temperature is above 105° or 107°, or in some cases higher.

→ How can you tell if you need to call for help?

What I would tell my family is that the moment that someone is not "acting right" is the moment when we have a big problem. If someone is confused, perhaps more sleepy than they should be—if there are mental status changes—that's really the threshold when we realize that we're losing the game, so to speak. That's the time when professional medical help needs to be requested.

→ What if help is delayed? What should you do in the meantime?

If you have a toddler or an elderly relative in trouble because of the heat, let's say, you should remove any tight clothing they may be wearing. Get them out of the sun and into the shade. Get them to a breeze or fan. Get them off a hot floor or away from a surface reflecting heat and onto a cool surface. Get them wet. The evaporating water will take away some of the heat. Make sure they keep drinking water and fluids with electrolytes. Never wipe someone down with alcohol. We don't want them to shiver, which could

raise their body temperature. Don't give them Tylenol or Ibuprofen. It's not like a fever.

One problem with both the elderly and small children is that they may not realize they have a problem. Children go and go in the heat, and then they crash very quickly.

→ You also work in a hospital emergency room, right? Does it get pretty crazy during an extreme heat wave?

Yes, I work in an urban academic hospital. Things are seldom not busy. But during a heat wave we do see a shift. Besides direct impacts of heat exposure like heatstroke, we also see indirect complications, in which people with poorly controlled diabetes, obesity, heart disease, hypertension, respiratory problems, and other conditions can't adapt to the stress. When it's so hot and muggy and smoggy, it can push vulnerable populations like these—especially among the elderly, those with chronic illnesses and children— over the edge.

HOW TO: **PREPARE**

→ **WHAT TO DO**

Indoors

☑ Make sure window air conditioners fit snugly, and insulate them if not.

☑ Examine and properly insulate air-conditioning ducts.

☑ Use temporary window reflectors that can be installed between windows and drapes or shades. These can be aluminum foil–covered cardboard, or another material that reflects heat.

☑ Check the weather stripping on doors and windows to ensure cool air stays inside.

☑ Determine which windows receive morning or afternoon sunshine, and cover them. (According to FEMA, outdoor awnings or louvers can reduce heat that enters a home by as much as 80 percent.)

☑ Keep storm windows up all year to shade and provide insulation.

☑ Tune in to weather forecasts and stay informed of upcoming temperature changes.

☑ Know your neighbor, especially those who are elderly, young, sick, or overweight. They are most susceptible to heat.

☑ Learn about and how to treat heat-related illness; take a first aid course.

☑ Keep a supply of drinking water and nonperishable foods.

☑ Keep coolers in the house.

☑ Turn your refrigerator and freezer to a colder setting; they'll stay cooler longer if the power goes out.

☑ Have spare containers of water for cooking and washing.

☑ Have a corded phone if you have a landline; it will work better than a cordless phone, which goes out when the power goes out.

☑ Use surge protectors to safeguard electronics.

☑ Back up your computer data.

☑ Fully charge cell phones, tablets, and laptops.

☑ Keep a supply of fresh batteries.

☑ Have flashlights and portable radios handy.

☑ Fill your vehicle's gas tank.

☑ Have an alternative source of power for anyone on life-sustaining equipment.

A woman adjusts the drapes. Afternoon sun is the strongest.

Outdoors

☑ Postpone outdoor games and activities if a heat wave is threatened.

☑ Listen to NOAA Weather for weather reports from the National Weather Service that can affect you.

☑ Have backup plans to find a cool place indoors (such as libraries, schools, movie theaters, shopping malls, and other community facilities).

☑ Have loose fitting and light colored items in your wardrobe that you can wear during hot spells.

→ WHAT *NOT* TO DO

Indoors

☒ Do not let your food spoil. Keep food in the freezer and/or an icebox so it will stay colder for longer during a potential blackout during a heat wave.

Outdoors

☒ Do not waste water on washing your car during a heat emergency.

☒ Do not take where you live for granted: People who live in urban areas are at greater risk of a prolonged heat wave than are people living in rural areas. Dark surfaces such as asphalt and rooftops attract and hold heat longer in urban environments.

HOW TO: **SURVIVE**

→ **WHAT TO DO**

Indoors

- ✓ Drink more fluids (unless your medical professional directs otherwise). Even if you believe you are staying cool and being inactive, heat can take its toll quickly so be sure to watch for the warning signs.

- ✓ Check regularly (at least twice a day) on those the sun affects most such as infants, young children, the elderly, and those with heart disease or high blood pressure.

- ✓ Stay indoors and on the ground floor. Remember, heat rises.

- ✓ Lighter, well-balanced meals help the body regulate and keep temperatures down. Avoiding foods high in protein will keep your metabolic rate down and keep your body heat lower.

- ✓ Turn the lights down or off. This will not only keep things cooler, but it will also pose less of a drain on power stations (which become vulnerable to outages when demand rises).

- ✓ Take a cool shower or bath.

Outdoors

- ✓ Cover all exposed skin with high SPF (sun protection factor) sunscreen.

- ✓ Wear a wide brimmed hat to protect your head and face from the sun.

- ✓ Drink fluids.

- ✓ Limit strenuous activity.

- ✓ Seek out shady places and take breaks often.

- ✓ Dress in loose-fitting, light-colored clothing.

- ✓ Use a buddy system if working in excessively hot conditions.

A hat works as a sun protector on a baby.

→ WHAT *NOT* TO DO

Indoors

☒ Do not exercise or do strenuous work during the afternoon, the hottest part of the day.

☒ Do not drink alcohol, caffeine, or consume large amounts of sugar; these dehydrate the body.

☒ Do not drink extremely cold liquids; they cause stomach cramps.

☒ Do not eat foods high in protein; they increase metabolic heat.

☒ Do not take salt tablets unless instructed by a physician.

☒ Do not rely on fans to cool down if the temperatures get too hot. When the temperatures get into the high 90s, fans won't prevent heat-related illness.

Outdoors

☒ Do not leave infants, children, or pets in a parked car. Ever.

☒ Do not go outdoors, if possible. Stay indoors or in an air-conditioned place.

☒ Do not go quickly from one extreme temperature environment immediately into another. This can bring on dizziness and nausea.

Beachgoers enjoy
the sand and water of
Ocean City, Maryland.

EXTREMES

NOTABLE HEAT FACTS

• Key West, Florida, keeps the highest annual average temperature in the United States: 77.8°F.

• On February 22, 1918, in Granville, North Dakota, the temperature rose 83°F (from minus 33° to 50°) in just 12 hours.

• The hottest temperature ever recorded in Europe was in Athens, Greece, in 1977, when it reached 118.4°F.

PART 4

CO

CHAPTER 9
COLD WAVES

CHAPTER 10
BLIZZARDS

"THE AIR BITES IT IS VERY

COLD

It's January 2014, and winter is in full swing. Minneapolis temperatures never rose above 0°F for 62 hours straight. Chicago set a record with a low of minus 16°F (and a wind chill of minus 34°F). In fact, 50 weather stations across the U.S. Midwest set record lows. On January 6, the average temperature in the continental United States was 17.9°F.

On a planet whose temperature is rising, how can it happen that we have record snowfalls and epic temperature drops? How can our winters get colder when science describes climate change going in the opposite direction? Going forward, temperatures are expected to spike, in some models rising as much as 10°F this century. The relatively sudden rise, rather than gradual warming over time, means certain regions will become much hotter or cooler, or wetter or drier. This is because higher temperatures affect the water cycle, which in turn affects precipitation.

Even though Arctic air and waters are generally growing warmer than in the past, they are still far from "warm." During the long polar night, air in and near the Arctic still grows bitterly cold. Much of the time the polar vortex—a band of high-altitude winds flowing around the globe—keeps cold air in or near the Arctic. From time to time it bulges, pushing cold air far to the south.

Some scientists have proposed that Arctic warming is making the polar jet stream more wavy, which could allow it to push cold air into the south more often than in the past. At the same time, a more wavy pattern

SHREWDLY; COLD."

— WILLIAM SHAKESPEARE, *HAMLET*

also brings more warmer air into the Arctic than has happened in the past. The result would be an increased warming of the Arctic.

Even in a warming world, cold outbreaks will continue to push many a modern convenience to the breaking point. Ice drags power lines down. Pipes freeze; cold winds whistle, revealing cracks around windows. Snow and ice make driving treacherous.

For those who live in a region where freezing temperatures are the norm, adjustments during cold spells are routine. But for those in regions unaccustomed to such blasts, preparing for the cold ahead may be a new requirement. No matter where you live, it's best to take notice.

Record-low temperatures were set in Europe in 2012.

Drifting snow and
freezing temperatures
bring chaos to roads
and walkways.

CHAPTER 9

COLD WAVES

In early 2014, tens of millions of people in the eastern United States found out what a polar vortex feels like. Sliding south over Canada, a big chunk of this ominous-sounding phenomenon sent temperatures plunging from the Great Lakes to Florida—in some places by as much as 30 degrees below average.

What's a polar vortex? It's a pattern of high-altitude winds normally found in the Arctic. In that region, the coldest air stays within a loop, flowing around a center of low barometric pressure. Pressure differences outside and inside the vortex create winds that circle the Arctic, keeping the Arctic cold in place, right where it belongs.

But sometimes the vortex can wander far from its normal position up north—bringing record-breaking cold waves with it.

One of the worst on record happened in early February 1899, when a series of extremely cold areas of high atmospheric pressure moved from over the Arctic and Canada into the United States. On February 10, the strongest blast brought 0°F temperatures to the Gulf of Mexico coast. In Logan, Montana, the thermometer dropped to a staggering minus 61°F; people in Pittsburgh, Pennsylvania, saw a single-day record of minus 20°F.

By February 11, residents of Washington, D.C., were subjected to temperatures that

---

RED CROSS
BEST PRACTICES BUNDLE UP

American Red Cross

When going outside in cold weather, always dress in layers. Light layers of loose clothing preserve the most body heat. Keep your extremities covered: waterproof boots and layers of socks for your feet, mittens and gloves layered over your hands. Always cover your head and neck with a hat and scarf or scarves.

dipped to minus 15°F, the coldest temperature ever recorded in the capital. In Florida, snow flurried in Fort Myers, and Tallahassee saw minus 2°F; on Valentine's Day, it was 29°F in Miami. On Lake Michigan, tugs were frozen out of port for days. Ice jams on the Ohio, James, Tennessee, and Cumberland Rivers created devastating floods. On February 17, for only the second time in recorded history, the Mississippi River brought ice to the Gulf of Mexico.

It has been called the "greatest Arctic outbreak in history" and "the mother of all cold waves." Hundreds if not thousands are thought to have perished in the cold; with little data, we may never know. At minimum, hundreds of thousands of poultry, sheep, pigs, and cattle died—many frozen where they stood.

Fast-forward to the 21st century. Although we still experience extreme cold waves, our advanced weather forecasting capabilities leave us much better warned. Even so, between 1999 and 2011, there were 16,911 deaths—an average of 1,301 per year—in the United States associated with "exposure to excessive natural cold." And as the year 2013 ended, one locality after another reported the effects of a chilling cold wave: Bismarck, North Dakota, minus 31°F; nearly six feet of snow in parts of upstate New York. Snow blanketed a good third of the continent, west to east from Ontario, Wisconsin, and Missouri to Massachusetts, Maine, and Nova Scotia.

Did You Know?
⬂ COLDEST PLACE ON EARTH

On August 10, 2010, in the middle of the Southern Hemisphere winter, in the hollow of a high ridge on the East Antarctic Plateau, the temperature dropped to an unimaginable minus 136°F. It was the coldest temperature ever recorded on Earth.

The East Antarctic Plateau

Winter storms, which drop inches of snow, often bring cold waves with them.

And that was at the end of a brutal month of cold weather, with band after band of snow, ice, and freezing temperatures sweeping down from the Canadian Arctic, reaching the Deep South and moving on over the North Atlantic. Dozens of deaths were blamed on the cold during December, not to mention all of the nonlethal injuries, illnesses, challenges, and discomforts.

Some times, and in some places, the weather extremes coming at us are frigid cold. These days, we may know better if and when the cold is coming, but that raises the obligation for us to stay informed and prepared.

What Is a Cold Wave?
The National Weather Service describes a cold wave as "a rapid fall in temperature within 24 hours to temperatures requiring substantially increased protection to agriculture, industry, commerce, and social activities." NWS looks at two criteria: the rate that the temperature falls and the lowest temperature reached. In short, it's a cold wave when it stays colder than usual for a longer-than-usual period of time.

Winter Weather Terminology
One of the ways we know what's coming is through the National Weather Service winter

The wind blows in a snowy forest. Wind chill makes the air feel colder.

weather alerts, any one of which may accompany a cold wave. As in any extreme weather situation, a warning is serious and urgent; a watch indicates possibility; and an outlook or advisory suggests upcoming difficulties:

Winter Storm Warning: A winter storm—heavy snow, heavy freezing rain, or heavy sleet—is on its way or already occurring. Winter Storm Warnings are usually issued 12 to 24 hours beforehand.

Winter Storm Watch: A winter storm—blizzard, heavy snow, heavy freezing rain, or heavy sleet—is likely. Winter Storm Watches are usually issued 12 to 48 hours beforehand.

Winter Storm Outlook: Conditions suggest a winter storm is possible. Winter Storm Outlooks are usually issued three to five days ahead.

Blizzard Warning: A blizzard— with winds of 35+ mph, falling or blowing snow, visibility at or below ¼ mile—is predicted to persist for at least three hours.

Wind Chill Warning: The current wind chill index is so low that several minutes of exposure would be hazardous.

Wind Chill Advisory: The wind chill index will make exposure uncomfortable and, if caution is not exercised, could be hazardous.

Good Idea
↘ INSULATE WATER PIPES

There are many reasons to insulate water pipes, inside, outside, and in your attic, basement, or crawl space. Insulated water pipes save money on water heating bills and increase the temperature and speed at which hot water gets to the tap. During cold waves, they can save you from frozen pipes, which cause an immediate inconvenience and can cause major leaks and damage later on. If your home does not have insulated pipes already, you should do it yourself.

Try foam insulation on pipes.

Wind Chill

"Wind chill" has become a familiar term, used extensively by weather reporters to say how cold it feels when winds make low temperatures feel even colder. In fact, the wind chill index is a mathematical equation expressing the rate of heat loss from combined wind and cold: As the wind picks up, it carries heat away from your body much more quickly.

For example, at 0°F with wind of 5 miles an hour (which calculates to a wind chill of minus 11°F), frostbite can occur in 30 minutes; at 0°F with wind of 15 miles an hour (wind chill of minus 19°F), frostbite can occur in 15 minutes or less.

The very first wind chill formula was developed by Paul Allman Siple and Charles Passel, who worked together in the Antarctic before the Second World War. Their tables were adopted by the National Weather Service in the 1970s and have undergone revision, but the concept remains.

An important point about wind chill: A wind chill "temperature" does not mean that the temperature falls to that value. It indicates only that you chill quicker when wind is blowing and carrying away relatively warm air from around your body than you would in still air.

Did You Know?

10 LOWEST TEMPERATURES RECORDED IN THE UNITED STATES

1. Prospect Creek, Alaska	-80°F	January 23, 1971
2. Rogers Pass, Montana	-70°F	January 20, 1954
3. Yellowstone, Wyoming	-66°F	February 9, 1933
4. Maybell, Colorado	-61°F	February 1, 1985
5. Island Park, Idaho	-60°F	January 18, 1943
6. Tower, Minnesota	-60°F	February 2, 1996
7. Parshall, North Dakota	-60°F	February 15, 1936
8. McIntosh, South Dakota	-58°F	February 17, 1936
9. Couderay, Wisconsin	-55°F	February 2 & 4, 1996
10. Ukiah and Seneca, Oregon	-54°F	February 9 & 10, 1933 (Respectively)

A child is bundled up to protect against cold weather.

What's Going On?

During recent cold waves, many people have commented that frigid temperatures and blanketing snows do not seem to correlate with the science showing global-scale warming. But one cold wave, or even a month or season of unusual cold, does not necessarily contradict climate change findings. In a recent report, the Intergovernmental Panel on Climate Change noted that it is "virtually certain that there will be more frequent hot and fewer cold temperature extremes . . . as global mean temperatures increase," but also that "occasional cold winter extremes will continue to occur." The meteorology supports that analysis.

As Arctic sea ice continues to melt at an increasing rate, the Arctic Ocean warms, because the dark ocean absorbs sunlight whereas ice and snow reflect sunlight and heat away. Surface temperatures affect atmospheric pressures aloft, and some hypothesize that the change in winter water temperature in the Arctic Ocean could destabilize the polar vortex by raising the barometric pressure within it. Because wind speeds depend on differences between high and low pressure, ocean warming may be decreasing the staying force of the polar vortex over the Arctic and allowing more cold air to blast south.

These shifts in the vortex's strength are called the Arctic

Penguins in Antarctica enjoy a cold splash that could be fatal for humans.

Oscillation (AO). In its positive phase, lower air pressures hover over the Arctic and strong upper air winds around latitude 55° N (southern Alaska and southern Canada). This weather pattern blocks cold outbreaks from hitting the northeastern United States and Canada.

The AO's negative phase includes higher air pressure over the Arctic and weaker upper air winds around 55° N, which allows more cold outbreaks in the East and Northeast.

The AO can switch between positive and negative phases in a matter of days, but one phase can dominate for a long period. From the early 1960s until the mid-1990s, the AO was positive more often than negative. Now we may see a negative AO more frequently, such as during the winters of 2009–10, 2010–11, and 2013–14.

When the Arctic Oscillation is in negative mode, containment of the polar vortex by pressure differentials is compromised. Cold Arctic air breaks free and heads south. There it can meet up with warmer, moisture-laden air coming from the south, producing severe winter weather.

All this is to say that although the average global temperature may be rising, extreme winter conditions, while potentially less frequent, will still pack a punch.

The Threat of Hypothermia

Cold waves threaten our human need to stay warm. The human body's ideal core temperature is 98.6°F; when it drops just 4 degrees, to 95°F or less, the body enters into the state of hypothermia, and cold can then prove fatal.

In the cold, the body loses heat faster than it can produce it. Shivering is actually a natural defense against cold: Involuntary muscle shakes can increase body heat production, up to five times more than is necessary under normal conditions. But stay shivering in the cold too long, and that defense weakens. Your muscles tire out, your body's glucose levels drop. In just a few hours, shivering decreases and then stops. By that point, many more internal complications can develop

Continued on page 310

Gear and Gadgets
↘ LEARN HOW TO LAYER

The most effective way to dress for the cold is in layers: a base layer that manages moisture, a middle layer that keeps you warm, and an outer layer that protects you from the wind and rain. Old-style long johns don't work as well as today's moisture-wicking thermals. When you exert yourself in cold weather, you will sweat, but the worst thing you can do is expose wet skin or clothing to cold air. The trick is to wear a base layer made of fabric that lofts or wicks—that is, sends the moisture out to a middle layer of clothing, while keeping dry air in. Materials that wick are wool, silk, or synthetics designed for the purpose. The middle layer should be your insulating layer—think sweaters and fleece. Wool and natural down (goose feathers) insulate well, although natural down doesn't work when wet. Synthetic fleece has been designed to insulate and dry fast.

The outer layer of protection should be resilient against rain, snow, and harsh elements. Heavy outer fabrics are okay for stationary activities, whereas lighter (single-ply) fabrics are best for when you exert yourself and your body produces more heat.

Dress in layers to keep warm.

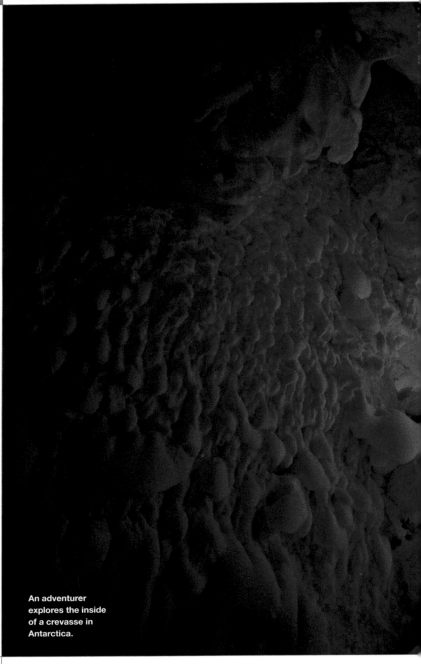

An adventurer explores the inside of a crevasse in Antarctica.

EXTREMES
RECORD LOWS

• A polar blast blew through the United States and Canada in January 2014, and sent temperatures to minus 60°F (with wind chill) in some areas.

• A cold snap blasted through Europe in 2012, claiming more than 650 lives. Many people, mostly in eastern Europe, froze to death.

• Russia holds the record for the lowest recorded temperatures in both Asia and Europe: minus 96.1°F in Oymyakon and minus 72.6°F in Ust'-Shchuger, respectively.

including hypoxia (insufficient oxygen in the tissues), inflammation of the pancreas, fluid in the lungs, and kidney and heart failure.

Brain function diminishes when a person gets too cold. People may seem drunk or display the "mumbles, stumbles, fumbles, and grumbles." The worst part is, with judgment impaired by hypothermia, a person can make decisions that are not in the best interest of survival. Left untreated, hypothermia can eventually lead to complete failure of the heart and respiratory system and to death.

Hypothermia can happen inside or outside, to the very young or the very old. It can even happen at temperatures above freezing, when a person is wet from rain, sweat, or submersion in cold water. Older people may even develop mild hypothermia in the summer, when air-conditioning makes their room too cold. In fact, the elderly are particularly susceptible to hypothermia. Their slower metabolisms and lack of physical exercise mean their bodies do not generate heat as well. Inside thermostats should be kept higher for those over 65 when a cold wave hits.

Beware of Frostbite

Hypothermia affects the body core while frostbite affects the extremities. It requires temperatures below freezing (not just wind chill below freezing), but add wind chill factors to a freezing outdoor temperature, and conditions can cause frostbite even faster. It can occur in 15 minutes or less in conditions with a wind chill of minus 18°F.

Frostbite happens when the skin and tissue right under the skin freezes. It most commonly affects smaller external body parts such as fingers, toes, nose, and ears. The frostbitten area of the body becomes numb, and so the sufferer may not realize what is happening. Frostbite can result in permanent damage. It can develop into gangrene. In severe cases, it may necessitate amputation. Although rare, frostbite can even lead to death, usually from a later complication such as gangrene.

Signs and symptoms of frostbite include:
→ A slightly painful, prickly, or itching sensation.
→ Red, white, pale, or grayish yellow skin.
→ Hard or waxy-looking skin.
→ A cold or burning feeling.
→ Numbness.
→ Clumsiness due to joint and muscle stiffness.

Frostbite advances through three stages: (1) Frostnip is mild and won't permanently damage the skin, which turns red and

When outside
in the cold,
be aware:
Hypothermia
can impair
judgment.

Always keep your hands and head covered to stay warm.

may feel numb or prickly. (2) Superficial frostbite turns the skin white or pale. At this point, ice crystals may be forming in the tissue, but the skin can feel warm. (3) Severe frostbite penetrates even deeper, and such numbness sets in that the person will not feel pain or discomfort.

If you or someone else shows any of these symptoms of frostbite, the best response is to seek professional medical attention. If that is impossible, here are steps recommended by the Centers for Disease Control:

→ Get inside and into warmth as soon as possible.

→ If toes or feet are frostbitten, don't walk on them.

→ Warm the affected area, either with warm water (not hot; about 100°F) or body heat. For example, the heat of an armpit can be used to warm frostbitten fingers.

→ Do not rub the frostbitten area with snow.

→ Do not massage the frostbitten area. This can cause more damage.

→ Do not overheat frostbitten areas. They are numb and easily burned.

→ Do not use a heating pad, heat lamp, stove, fireplace, or radiator to warm up frostbite.

Affected areas are numb and can be easily burned.

Staying Safe Indoors

It is possible to suffer from hypothermia even when you're inside, if your thermostats are set too low and your clothing and coverings aren't adequate. People who are ill or elderly are particularly vulnerable. They and their loved ones should beware and keep in touch during the coldest of times.

Here are a few pointers on staying warm inside. They all derive from common sense, but sometimes people who are not accustomed to bitter cold don't know to follow these rules:

→ Keep your thermostats at 68°F (or warmer), according to the National Institute on Aging.

CDC BEST PRACTICES CONSERVE HEAT

Keep heat inside the house during cold weather and especially during a power failure. Avoid opening any doors or windows. Close off extra rooms you can do without for the short run. Use towels or other pieces of fabric to plug cracks, particularly around doorjambs. Keep the curtains closed, especially at night. If using an alternative heat source, make sure the area is well ventilated.

A woman enjoys a hot drink to keep warm.

EXTREME WEATHER BASICS
Creating Cold Waves

The Earth's tilt in relation to its orbit around the sun causes cold waves to form. From the June solstice until the December solstice, the Northern Hemisphere tilts away from the sun. Days grow shorter, and the sun drops lower in the sky from then until the December solstice, when days start slowly growing longer and the sun moves higher in the sky until the June solstice—and the cycle begins again. At the North Pole, the sun sets on the September equinox, not to rise again until the March equinox.

With little or no winter sunlight, the air's warmth radiates away into space without being amply replenished, which creates masses of cold, dry, high-pressure air that can be hundreds of miles across. At times, upper air winds, including the jet stream, begin pushing a cold, high-pressure air mass such as this toward the south, causing a cold wave. The air begins losing its chill as it travels over warmer ground, but the strongest cold waves bring freezing temperatures as far south as the Gulf of Mexico states.

Some of the coldest air to hit the 48 contiguous states grows over eastern Siberia to slide southeast over Alaska and Canada and across the border. You often hear one of these air masses called a "Siberian express."

Recent warming trends in the North Pole have loosened the arctic grip on the so-called polar vortex, a cyclone of frigid winds that can dip farther south and bring extreme cold weather sweeping from southwest to northeast through North America, as occurred in 2013–14.

FORECASTING COLD WAVES

Established patterns of jet stream movement drive cold weather. Meteorologists can also successfully predict extremes in cold air masses and movement far enough in advance to give you a few days heads-up to prepare for a cold wave.

Jet stream tailwinds blow from the west.

→ Shut the doors on rooms you do not need to heat.

→ Use only space heaters with automatic shutoffs and protective grills.

→ Use no more than one space heater to a wall socket.

→ If you must use an extension cord, use one that is thicker than the appliance cord itself. Energy.gov says to use 14-gauge wire or larger extension cords.

→ Place space heaters in an area more than three feet from any combustibles, including drapery, clothing, and furniture.

→ Never use the oven to heat your house.

Good Idea
↘ PROTECT YOUR EXTREMITIES

When it gets cold, your body draws blood from the extremities to protect more vital organs such as the heart and lungs. Fingers and toes are the most susceptible to frostbite, so take special care of them.

Layer everywhere you can: socks, mittens, scarves, even hats. Don't neglect your eyes. Sunglasses or goggles are important for eye protection. Snow and ice reflect ultraviolet radiation and can seriously harm your eyes. So wear eye protection—sunglasses or goggles—if you plan on spending anytime outside.

Between gloves or mittens, choose mittens: Four fingers together produce more body heat. If you need dexterity, layer mittens on top and strip down to gloves when you need to.

Wear outer and inner garments made of waterproof and breathable materials.

Bandages help prevent frostnip from becoming frostbite.

→ Wear winter-protective clothing day and night.

→ Wear long underwear, tights, or other undergarments under your pajamas.

→ Keep your feet covered. Wear socks at night; wear socks and shoes or warm slippers during the day.

→ Pull a cap on over your head to sleep.

→ Never light a charcoal stove or run an internal combustion appliance such as a generator indoors for heat.

→ If you are using a kerosene heater, open a window slightly for circulation. Remember to check with your state for regulations on kerosene heaters.

Protect Your Pets

Just because pets have fur doesn't mean they're immune from the cold. In general, long-haired or thick-coated animals tend to be more cold tolerant, but they are still at risk in cold weather. Pets with short hair will feel the cold more quickly, and pets with short legs may come into direct contact with ice or snow. Younger and older pets, as well as those with chronic illnesses, may be more vulnerable to temperature extremes.

Dogs will want to walk, though, so during a cold wave:

→ Consider shorter walks for your dog to protect both of you during cold snaps.

→ Use sweaters, coats, and booties to help keep a pet warmer when outside.

→ Check dogs' paws during and after winter walks. The skin can crack or they can accumulate ice balls. Clipping hair between toe pads may help keep ice from accumulating there.

→ After a walk, wipe down paws and low bellies so your dog does not lick off the chemicals. Especially in city settings, a dog's feet, legs, and belly may come into contact with de-icers, antifreeze, or other winter chemicals that are potentially toxic.

→ Don't leave pets in cold cars.

Good Idea
↘ IF YOU FALL IN

You fall into cold water—through the ice, off a boat, from a dock. Your body responds by going into cold-water shock. You gasp, you hyperventilate, you cannot catch your breath, and your heart rate picks up.

Don't panic. Don't splash about. Curl up into a heat escape lessening position (HELP) to reduce heat loss from your body as you wait for rescue. Bring your knees up to your chest to protect the trunk of your body. If you're wearing a life jacket that turns your face down in this position, bring your legs tightly together, arms to your sides and head back. Crossing your ankles can help you raise your legs. Covering your chest with your arms helps, too.

Now remain as still as you can. Swimming can sap energy and shorten survival time. If you are with others, huddle in a tight circle facing each other. Don't remove your clothing. In fact, buckle, button, and zip up your clothes to retain heat. Put something on your head if possible, and keep your head above water.

Cold-water shock happens quickly.

According to the U.S. Search and Rescue Task Force, the body loses heat 32 times faster in cold water than cold air, so it's critical to get out of the water as fast as possible. Above all else, avoid letting this happen. Don't boat in cold water alone, and don't walk on thin ice.

→ Don't keep dogs and cats outside for long periods of below-freezing weather. If your dog ordinarily stays outside, it needs a warm shelter, off the ground, with a door that does not face the wind. Provide thick bedding and water, remembering that the water will turn to ice very quickly.

→ Do not use electric space heaters in doghouses. They present too great a risk of burning your pet or causing a fire.

→ During a cold wave, keep a watch for any signs of hypothermia, including whining, shivering, anxiety, lethargy, weakness, stillness, or burrowing. Frostbite is harder to recognize and may not be noticed until after the damage is done. If you think your pet may be suffering from hypothermia or frostbite, contact your vet immediately.

→ Many a dog loves to escape into the snow for a good frolic, but be careful. Do not let your dog off the leash after a heavy snowfall. Dogs can lose their scent during winter storms and easily become lost.

→ Keep a pet emergency kit and supplies handy with items such as medical records, water, pet food, and medications, as well pet first aid supplies.

→ Make sure your pets wear collars and tags with up-to-date identification. The ASPCA recommends microchipping your pet as a permanent form of identification.

Where There's Fire

Burning wood, in a woodstove or fireplace, can be an economical and often comforting way to heat or supplement heat in a home. Anyone choosing to burn wood must follow essential rules for health and safety:

Installation and quality: Check the soundness of a fireplace or woodstove before using. Install a laboratory-tested woodstove. Give it at least three feet from

---

Did You Know?
↘ NATURE'S SIGNAL

A cold front is likely on its way if you find more spider webs inside your home. Spiders head indoors to seek shelter when the weather is going to turn cold. Black widows especially disdain lower temperatures, so watch out for them in dark corners, basements, and closets.

A shipping
lane is cleared
of thick ice.

A pet's fur doesn't always protect it from the cold. Bring pets in during extreme cold weather.

any wall, furniture, or other household objects.

Daily maintenance: To prevent creosote buildup inside the stove and chimney, burn a fire hot twice a day. Damp down the woodstove at night. Let the fireplace cool completely down before closing the damper.

Annual maintenance: Have the chimney inspected and cleaned professionally before using.

Fuel and fire starters: Never use charcoal lighter or other volatile chemicals in a fireplace or woodstove. Do not overuse paper to boost a fire.

Safe operation: Keep a metal grill in front of the fireplace while burning. Keep flammable objects away from the fireplace, especially off the mantel.

There's an App for That
Lots of weather apps use the GPS of your smartphone to sense your location and read out current conditions and weather predictions. Available from iTunes and/or Google Play, these apps have features especially useful during cold waves:
→ **Wind Chill Widget** for Android gives the current wind chill conditions for your locale.
→ **Thermometer Widget** for Android can show wind chill along with temperature.

→ The **Wind Speed Meter App** turns your phone into an anemometer, estimating wind speed based on the sound it makes as it whistles by your phone.

→ **Wind Chill and Wind Speed** for iPhone shows you both and does the calculation for you. This is a good way to get a sense for how the two are related and what their impact on you may be.

→ The **Winter Wake-Up** for iPhone and Android is an alarm clock that employs local weather forecasts and wakes you earlier if there is frost or snow, so that you have extra time to prepare. It may seem like a cute gimmick, but being prepared and having the time to travel cautiously might actually keep you from harming yourself. ■

CDC BEST PRACTICES WARMING UP WISELY

CDC
CENTERS FOR DISEASE
CONTROL AND PREVENTION

If your body temperature drops and you are having difficulty warming up, seek shelter immediately and remove all wet clothing. Warm the center of your body first—chest, neck, head, and groin—using an electric blanket or loose layers of blankets, towels, or sheets. Drink warm fluids to help increase the body's temperature, but abstain from alcohol. Get medical attention as soon as possible.

Warm fluids can lift your body temperature.

Sub-Zero for Days

A polar expedition requires special preparations.

SEBASTIAN COPELAND is an award-winning photographer and adventurer who has trekked to the North and South Pole, and has often dealt with the wrath of bitter cold. "I have not felt more insignificant than during the six consecutive days and nights I spent pinned down inside a tent on the Greenland ice sheet, waiting out a storm that hurled 80-mile-per-hour winds at our thin nylon walls," Copeland says.

Knowing that a storm was upon them, Copeland and his partner took special precautions. "We took extra care in securing the guylines and gathered up our sledges close to the tent," he says. "The skis were planted vertically into the ice for visibility. The tent's profile, as always, faced the wind."

By early morning the storm was on them. "I woke up to the severe flapping of the tent's fabric," Copeland says. "Winds had built to a respectable 40 miles per hour. Erring on the side of caution, we chose to wait and see where this was headed. Good thing: Within hours, conditions had grown to 70 miles per hours with violent gusts blasting past 80."

Wind and cold can be a deadly combination. "Greenland is, for the most part, one giant deserted ice mass, reaching two miles in depth at its thickest, and hugged by mountains along its coasts. With an average elevation of around 6,300 feet, the interior is barren and inhospitable, perhaps best described as a frozen sea. In other words, you are very alone," Copeland explains. "And in such a storm, with no possibility of rescue, should a tent be lost to the wind, a human might have a few hours—perhaps a day—before succumbing to exposure."

The right gear is key to survival—no matter if in the Arctic or Albany. Copeland, of course, knows this all too well. "Frost builds out sideways on the lines of the tent, and the wind chill temperatures drop to minus 50. But inside the tent, when the sun is out, the greenhouse effect can raise temperatures to moderate, even balmy conditions. You have to admire the design ingenuity of the sum of nylon cloth, four poles, and a few lines to anchor them, which together amount to an oasis of relative tranquility amidst such chaos. It says a lot about humans' ability to survive in the most hostile environments."

Old-school know-how plays an equally important part. "Aside from tearing fabric, I had a growing concern," says Copeland. "We were slowly being entombed by rising walls of snowdrift, threatening to collapse the tent! By day two, they had reached almost three feet to the leeward side. If someone should have happened upon our campsite, they might have thought that we had dug a hole to pitch our tent in! We took turns every

> **The right gear is key to survival—no matter if in the Arctic or Albany.**

few hours to dig ourselves out before the drift solidified into hard ice, making excavation hazardous on the thin fabric. The tent shook incessantly like a rag doll, and the flapping fabric blasted a decibel level akin to a turbo jet!"

But every storm comes to an end. "On the morning of the seventh day, I woke this time to the piercing weight of silence," Copeland recalls. "It was 4 a.m. and, stirred out of my dreams, it took a moment before I realized that the tent was dead still. That was reinforced when a gentle gust fluttered the walls. And then nothing. The storm had passed. We went on to complete our mission, setting a world record in the process."

Clearly it takes a lot to brave the elements. Knowing how to prepare, survive, and recover all play equal parts in living through extreme weather.

EXPERT WITNESS: Alasdair Turner

How to Dress for the Very Cold

In environments such as this, proper dressing is critical to survive.

Alasdair Turner, *a mountain guide with the U.S. Antarctic Program at McMurdo Station*

→ What are the biggest hazards of working in extreme cold?
The biggest hazard is frostbite. In very cold temperatures skin can freeze very quickly. Touching cold objects without gloves or spilling fuel can cause frostbite instantly. Here in Antarctica we do a lot of our work using snowmobiles, so it is very important to keep skin completely covered when riding them. One mistake can mean frostbite.

→ What's the best way to dress under those conditions?
I always dress in layers. Layers allow you to adjust for temperature much more easily. When I am hiking or climbing, I do not want to get too warm and start sweating, so I am careful to remove a layer or two. As soon as I stop, I put clothes back on before I get cold. The colder it is, the more layers I wear. I tend to avoid big, warm layers and use thinner layers instead. For example I never use expedition-weight long underwear: I use two lightweight layers. Also I tend to use two lighter-weight insulated jackets rather than one very large, very warm layer. Wet feet

are cold feet. I use antiperspirant on my feet to stop them from sweating, which keeps them a lot warmer.

To avoid frostbite, it is important to be able to completely cover every inch of exposed skin. For me this means using more than one type of face covering together, as I have not found one that works well on its own. I also tend to cut larger holes in these at the mouth so that I can breath more easily when working hard without fogging up my goggles.

→ What's the most common mistake people make?

The most common mistake I see is with glove systems. Many people go out into the cold with a single pair of giant mittens and then realize they can't do anything with them on. They then try to do simple tasks with bare hands, which often leads to frostbite. If you're going to be outside in extreme conditions, always bring a pair of lightweight gloves that fit under a pair of big mittens. I often travel with five sets of gloves, which I rotate throughout the day depending on what I am doing.

→ Based on your experience in Antarctica, what tips would you give readers about surviving extreme cold back home in the United States?

My biggest tip is to be prepared, and make sure to carry the right equipment. When you get cold, eat something, drink something, and move around a bit. Always remember to account for wind when you are dressing for the weather. Zero degrees and 30-mph wind is a lot more difficult to deal with than minus 30 and no wind.

In Antarctica, it's important to keep skin covered with more than one face covering.

HOW TO: **PREPARE**

→ **WHAT TO DO**

Indoors

☑ Have space heaters ready and store extra heating fuel (in a safe, ventilated space), or additional wood for your fireplace or stove.

☑ Ensure you have enough winter clothing and blankets to keep you warm.

☑ Keep tabs on the temperature by listening to a news reports, such as the National Weather Service advisories on NOAA Weather Radio.

☑ Insulate your walls and attics, and use caulking and weather stripping for doors and windows in your home. Also, consider installing storm windows (or use covering material).

☑ Clean your gutters and make roof repairs. Clear tree branches that could become hazardous by falling. (Cold often brings with it ice that can weigh down branches.)

☑ Keep your heating equipment and chimneys well maintained and clean.

☑ Insulate your water pipes where they are exposed and easily reachable.

☑ Know where your fire extinguishers are stored. Show other household members where they are and how to use them.

☑ Locate your water valves, and learn how to shut them off.

☑ Consider having a roofing contractor examine your roof to make sure it can stand the weight of heavy snow and/or ice.

Outdoors

☑ Before you go out into cold weather, dress in layers.

☑ Be prepared for even colder temperatures than predicted. You can always remove clothing.

☑ Ensure mittens or gloves are fitted snug at the wrist.

☑ Have water-repellent clothing ready as an outside layer.

☑ Eat higher-protein and well-balanced meals before going out in the cold. Your body uses more energy to digest protein, and therefore your body heat will rise.

☑ Pack a ski mask in case the wind whips up and extreme cold makes skin exposure unsafe or uncomfortable.

☑ Pack water. When your body is dehydrated, it is more susceptible to cold weather.

☑ Carry matches with you to make a fire for warmth.

Cleaning your gutters prevents ice buildup.

→ WHAT *NOT* TO DO

Indoors

☒ Do not leave pets unattended, and make sure to herd livestock to sheltered areas where there is a fresh supply of water that won't freeze in cold weather.

☒ Never store fuel-burning equipment in an unvented area. Keep it outside and clear of any flammable or hazardous liquids or materials.

☒ Do not let your pipes freeze. If you know subfreezing cold is coming and your pipes are vulnerable, allow a steady drip to keep from freezing.

☒ Do not ignore your animals' shelter needs. Winterize your barns and doghouses. These can even provide additional shelter for you and your family in an emergency.

Outdoors

☒ Do not rely on temperature readings alone. Factor in wind chill to understand the cold you are preparing for.

☒ Do not plan on talking (or singing) at length if the temperature dips below freezing. Extreme cold can affect your lungs and throat.

☒ Do not risk traveling long distances. Ensure there are shelters along the way for any planned travel.

HOW TO: SURVIVE

→ WHAT TO DO

Indoors

- ☑ Keep your thermostat at 68°F. This habit helps conserve fuel in case the cold weather lasts longer than expected.

- ☑ Follow all necessary precautions in using home space heaters. Make sure they are clear of all furniture, fabric, and combustibles.

- ☑ With kerosene-burning heaters, open a window slightly to provide ventilation. Refuel outside.

- ☑ Do not ignore the hazards of carbon monoxide poisoning; install carbon monoxide alarms.

- ☑ If your water pipes have frozen, remove any existing insulation. Wrap them in rags and pour on hot water. Begin where they are most exposed to the cold. Open all the faucets in your house to establish flow.

- ☑ Watch for signs of frostbite or hypothermia, even though you are inside and it may not seem all that cold; individual reactions to cold differ.

- ☑ Keep your garage doors closed to act as insulation, especially if the garage houses a water supply.

- ☑ If you are inside your house for a long period without heat, engage in moderate physical activity, such as walking, to warm your body.

- ☑ Regulate your body temperature with warm nonalcoholic beverages and well-balanced meals.

- ☑ Dress in layers, even indoors as you need to. Cover your extremities with mittens, socks or slippers, hats, and scarves.

Outdoors

- ☑ Seek shelter.
- ☑ Wear warm clothing, and cover exposed body parts.
- ☑ Choose multiple thin layers of clothing over one thick layer.
- ☑ Remain active to keep body temperature up, but take care not to overexert and sweat.
- ☑ Hydrate. Dehydration makes your body more susceptible to hypothermic illness.

2000W

Try to conserve fuel in case the cold persists.

→ WHAT *NOT* TO DO

Indoors

☒ If you vacate your house for any length of time, leave your thermostat set no lower than 55°F.

☒ Never operate a generator inside.

☒ Do not bring outdoor fuel-burning equipment inside to use as heaters. Grills, camp stoves, and other devices that burn gasoline, propane, natural gas, or charcoal must not be used inside your home.

Outdoors

☒ Do not drive or travel alone or at night. Stick to main roads.

☒ Do not drink alcohol. Despite the myth, it constricts blood vessels and minimizes blood flow to your skin.

☒ Do not overexert yourself. Heart attacks are frequent in extreme cold weather.

☒ Do not stay wet. Sweat buildup lowers your core body temperatures. Wet clothing causes your body's temperature to fall fast.

☒ Do not eat snow. It will sap core body heat. If you must use snow to hydrate, melt it first and then drink the water.

☒ Do not walk far. It is more strenuous to walk in the cold. Snow on the ground can make it difficult to judge distances.

HOW TO: **RECOVER**

→ **WHAT TO DO**

Indoors

☑ Examine your water pipes for cracks or leaks due to freezing. Reinsulate if necessary.

☑ Check and repair your foundation, walls, and ceilings for cracks that may have occurred due to sudden temperature fluctuations.

☑ Open up your kitchen and bathroom cabinet doors so warmer air can circulate around plumbing. Remove harmful chemicals and cleaners from the reach of children.

Outdoors

☑ Seek shelter even if the cold spell has passed so your body adjusts and you can examine yourself and others for possible frostbite.

☑ If you got wet, find a warm, dry place and remove all wet clothes.

☑ Adjust slowly to warm conditions by gradually increasing the heat your body is exposed to.

→ **WHAT *NOT* TO DO**

Indoors

☒ Do not get immediately into a hot tub, sauna, steam room, or other hot area. This can cause dizziness and even, in some situations, unconsciousness.

☒ Do not keep wet clothing on your body, even if the cold spell has passed.

☒ Do not pour boiling water directly on frozen water pipes or valves. It can shock and harm them. First, open all faucets. Wrap pipes in cloth and pour hot water over them, starting where the system is most exposed to the cold.

☒ Do not jump into the car and go driving. Ice and snow, even when temperatures rise above freezing, make for treacherous driving. Check with local authorities to learn when and where it is safe.

Good Idea
↘ CAR AND TRAVEL CARE IN THE COLD

Extreme cold weather can freeze your engine, slow down your battery, and leave you stuck on the side of the road. Prepare ahead of time.

As winter months approach, check your:
- antifreeze
- battery and ignition system
- brakes and brake fluids
- exhaust system
- heaters and defrosters
- lights and flashers
- oil
- thermostat
- tires
- windshield fluid
- windshield wipers

Be sure you have winter road-side emergency equipment with you, including:
- booster cables or a jump starter
- emergency flares or distress flags
- flashlight and extra batteries
- road salt or sand
- small broom
- tow chains or rope
- windshield scraper

Always be aware of weather conditions, present and predicted, as you set out to travel. If you must travel during or into a cold wave, take special precautions for your own safety.

Keep a personal winter safety kit inside your car including:
- battery-powered radio and extra batteries
- blanket
- extra outer gear
- first aid kit
- matches
- snack food
- water
- cell phone charger for the car

Designate friends or family as contact points, and keep them informed of your progress and safe arrival.

A car overturned on a slick road. Ice and snow can be a deadly combination.

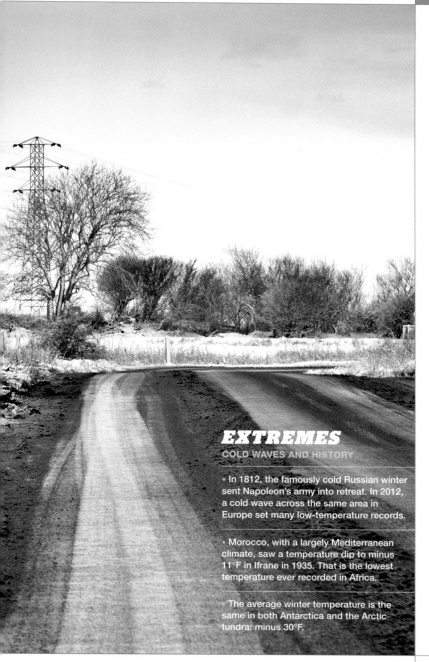

EXTREMES

COLD WAVES AND HISTORY

• In 1812, the famously cold Russian winter sent Napoleon's army into retreat. In 2012, a cold wave across the same area in Europe set many low-temperature records.

• Morocco, with a largely Mediterranean climate, saw a temperature dip to minus 11°F in Ifrane in 1935. That is the lowest temperature ever recorded in Africa.

• The average winter temperature is the same in both Antarctica and the Arctic tundra: minus 30°F.

Blizzards
bring not only
snow but also
winds that
block vision.

CHAPTER 10

BLIZZARDS

It had rained in New York City on March 11, and the *Tribune* predicted "clearing and colder, preceded by light snow." That night a low-pressure center off North Carolina rapidly developed, pulling in frigid northwest air on top of warmer humid Atlantic air, supplying the conditions for heavy snow. By noon on March 12, snowdrifts piled up as high as second-floor windows, winds gusted to 75 miles an hour, and temperatures dropped to 1°F. The snow didn't stop for 36 hours.

Known as the Great Blizzard of 1888, the storm swept from the Chesapeake Bay to Maine, costing more than $20 million in New York City alone. More than 400 died, including some 100 people who perished at sea. Most of the 200 New

Yorkers who lost their lives were found buried in snowdrifts on the sidewalks.

Today's blizzards can be just as forceful, but with weather predictions and preparedness savvy, the cost in lives has gone way down. Snowstorms swept through North America in February 2011, beginning February 1 with a storm that blanketed most of the continent east of the Rockies. Chicago took it hard, with more than 20 inches of snow and winds gusting to 70 miles an hour. Airports, highways, train routes had to close. All in all, ten people died.

Two more snowstorms pelted the country in the next week. Dallas, Texas, got as much as six inches on February 4. Then again, on February 8 and 9, the U.S. Midwest and Southeast

FEMA BEST PRACTICES STAY HOME

During a blizzard, the safest place is your home or shelter. If you run out of supplies and have to drive, do so in the daylight, always bring a companion, and stay on central, cleared roads. Make sure others are aware of your plan, so if you get stuck, you can be found on your scheduled course.

got snowed in. Twenty-six inches of total accumulation made 2011 the snowiest year ever for Tulsa, Oklahoma, and on February 10, the town of Nowata, also in Oklahoma, registered the lowest temperature ever in the state's history: minus 31°F.

Paradoxically, meteorologists and climatologists link these record storms with the trend of global warming. We may see fewer snowstorms and shorter winters, but many predict the blizzards that do occur will be stronger than ever. That's why understanding blizzards and taking steps to prepare for them is vital.

What Is a Blizzard?

We all know a snowstorm when we see one, but for the National Weather Service to consider a storm a blizzard, it has to deliver large amounts of falling or blowing snow in combination with winds 35 miles an hour or stronger, visibility of less than a quarter mile, and duration of three hours of more. Ramp that up to winds more than 45 miles an hour, temperatures near or below 10°F, and visibility near zero, and NWS considers it a "severe blizzard." Snowstorms that fulfill one or two blizzard conditions warrant a "winter storm" or a "heavy snow" warning.

Gear and Gadgets
↘ PUBLIC ALERT RADIOS

NOAA Weather Radio All Hazards transmitters broadcast on seven VHF frequencies from 162.400 MHz to 162.550 MHz, but they cannot be heard on a simple AM/FM radio. Standalone weather radio receivers, or multiband/multifunction receivers, can provide weather band service. Look for receivers that carry the Public Alert and/or the NOAA Weather Radio (NWR) All Hazards logo.

Also, in case the electricity goes out, get a rechargeable battery–operated receiver, or one that also features a hand crank or solar power option. Some have all three—with flashlight capabilities, too. Many smartphones can tune in weather reports, as well.

A mother shovels out after a winter storm. The East Coast is a target for blizzards.

A blizzard can last hours or days. During the Midwest Snowstorm of 1951, snow fell for as long as 100 hours in parts of Iowa and Missouri. Snowstorms operate in a narrow range on the thermometer; the temperature has to be below 32°F, but the air has to be warm enough to hold water, generally in the 20s. If the temperature is much colder, large snowstorms are less likely because there's not enough moisture in the air to create snow. Thus, a small uptick in temperature can turn a dry cold front into a snowstorm.

Blizzards most often blanket the U.S. Midwest and Great Plains. Flat land, fewer trees, and minimal barriers for wind

and blowing snow make this part of the country especially susceptible as low-pressure systems swoop down from the Rocky Mountains. The jet stream dips south, and a polar air mass from the northwest meets a warm, moisture-laden air mass from the south.

Lake-effect blizzards pummel Salt Lake City; South Bend, Indiana; Rochester, New York; and other areas near large bodies of water. When frigid air flows across warmer water, it pulls moisture up into clouds, which then dump the moisture as snow once they move over land. The relatively warm Atlantic Ocean can provide the water vapor needed for snow as well,

Plowing early and often is paramount during a blizzard.

hence the blizzards that hit the East Coast, too.

Blizzards are also common on mountaintops—like Mount Washington in New Hampshire and Mount Rainier in Washington. Mountain slopes push warm, moist air masses up into colder reaches of the atmosphere; mountain peaks rake that moisture out of the clouds in the form of ice and snow. A mountain slope to windward—that is, the side of the mountain that gets the windy blast—will see more snow by far than the slope on the other side of the same mountain.

That said, any region that has snowfall can experience a blizzard. Even Arizona can experience blizzards when a strong low-pressure system moves across the southern part of the state and high pressure pushes into the Great Basin.

Many Words for Winter Weather

There is a good reason why languages spoken by peoples of the Arctic have so many words for snow—and why we love to perpetuate that story. It's because winter weather sends a lot of different storms our way, whether or not we have the words for them. Not all are blizzards, but many can be as inconveniencing, some dangerous:

Snow flurries occur when light snow falls briefly, resulting in a

---

Did You Know?
↘ AVERAGE ANNUAL SNOWFALL

These are annual totals for places in the United States that averaged more than 300 inches a year:

Location:	Inches:
Mount Rainier, Paradise Station, Washington	671
Alta, Utah	546
Crater Lake National Park Headquarters, Oregon	483
Brighton, Utah	411
Echo Summit, California	407
Wolf Creek Ski Area, Colorado	392
Caples Lake, California	375
Brian Head, Utah	368
Valdez, Alaska	326
Mount Evans Field Station, Colorado	301

light dusting or no accumulation at all.

Sleet occurs when raindrops freeze into ice pellets before reaching the ground. Usually it bounces off surfaces and does not stick, but sleet can accumulate and cause hazards.

Snow showers bring snowfall that varies in intensity

Good Idea
↘ SHOVELING SNOW

Pick a shovel with a curved handle or adjustable handle length. This minimizes bending and arching your back. Try using a shovel that has a smaller, more lightweight blade, which can help reduce the amount of weight you pick up.

Warm up either by stretching or moving about to limber your body, and wear shoes with good treads. Pace yourself by removing smaller amounts over time. Take a break every 10 to 15 minutes.

Use proper lifting techniques:
• Keep your hips and shoulders squarely facing the snow you are shoveling.
• Bend at the knees, not the lower back, and push your chest out, pointing forward.
• Grip the shovel as close to the blade as comfortably possible with the other hand on the handle.
• Avoid twisting and extending your arms to toss the snow.
• Keep both feet on the ground.

It's important to learn the dos and don'ts of proper shoveling.

Heavy snowfall in Colorado buries a street sign and much of a house.

for short spans of time, with some accumulation.

Snow squalls are intense, short-lived periods of snow with reduced visibility and strong, gusty winds. A squall can bring significant accumulation.

Freezing rain occurs when rain falls on frozen surfaces, such as tree limbs, cars, and roads, and freezes, forming a coating or glaze of ice. Even small accumulations of ice can cause a significant hazard.

Blowing snow can create or intensify a serious storm, occurring either as the snow falls or after, as the wind drives loose snow on the ground. It reduces visibility and causes significant drifting.

That's Heavy Snow

Meteorologists define "heavy snowfall" by the amount that comes down out of the sky: Four inches in 12 hours or six inches in 24 constitutes heavy snow for them. But for anyone who has a driveway, sidewalks, or porch to shovel, heavy snow means something else entirely.

Falling snow seems almost weightless. But remember: That snow is made of water. Fluffy snow 12 inches deep is estimated to equal 1 inch of melt (or water), and water weighs five

Ice storms can down trees and power lines, knocking out electricity.

pounds per square foot. Snow can compact dramatically, even just upon falling, so a square foot—a hefty snow shovelful—will often weigh much more than five pounds.

A study in *The American Journal of Emergency Medicine* found that between 1990 and 2006 in the United States, some 11,500 people were treated for injuries related to shoveling snow. Most of the injuries were from musculoskeletal exertion, along with lower-back injuries and injuries related to slipping and falling. Nearly 100 deaths a year were the result of the cardiac demands of snow shoveling.

Here are a few pointers for safe snow shoveling, no matter if you've got a couple of inches or a couple of feet to move out of the way:

→ Warm up before, during, and after. Stretch your muscles before you start shoveling. Wear loose, layered clothing including gloves and hat. Stretch and rest indoors afterward, and allow yourself the occasional break if you have a lot of snow to move.

→ Have a strategy. Decide where you will bank the snow, move it there, and never move it twice. Remember that a pile of snow you make could last a lot longer than the blanket of snow you are moving.

→ Square up and use your body wisely. Let your legs and lower torso carry the weight of the snow. Avoid twists. Spread your hands out as you hold the shovel, one near the handle and the other near the blade.

→ Pace yourself. Beat the snow if you can by shoveling several times during the course of a major snowstorm. Newly fallen snow is lighter in weight, and establishing a path will make it easier to shovel later.

→ Shovel early in the day and make use of sunshine. If the storm has passed and you have blue skies ahead, you can use the sun to your advantage. Any dark surface you expose, such as a concrete sidewalk or an asphalt driveway, will absorb the heat and melt the surrounding snow for you.

→ Take it easy. Don't overexert. Keep drinking water. Keep a few layers on, even if you get sweaty. Rest occasionally. Share the task with family members or neighbors if you can.

The weight of snow concerns homeowners as inches accumulate on the roof as well. Roof pitch, heat transfer through the roof, roof design, and roofing materials all factor into a house's snow-worthiness. If you're buying or building, be sure to assess your roof according to your region's snow predictions.

Trees and tree branches, power lines, clotheslines, decks, porches—snow and ice can bear down, bend, and even break many things in the daily landscape. All the more reason to dedicate some warm-weather time to observe, clean up, trim, and prune with blizzard potential in mind.

Continued on page 346

Good Idea
↘ SIGNALING FOR HELP

If you are in a car, hang a rag, plastic bag, or piece of cloth from a window or antennae as a distress signal. If you are on foot, stomp out the word HELP or SOS in the snow, and place rocks or tree limbs in the impressions. They will contrast with the snow and allow rescuers surveying the area from above to better spot you.

EXTREMES
CRIPPLING BLIZZARDS

The worst blizzard witnessed was in Iran in 1972. Twenty-six feet of snow fell over the course of a week and covered 200 towns. Some 4,000 people died.

The Great Blizzard of 1888 in the United States dropped five feet of snow in some places in the Northeast. Four hundred people were killed.

In 1993, "The Storm of the Century" dropped so much snow on the country that nearly half the people in the United States were caught in it. More than 200 people died.

A homeowner in Washington State digs out after a major snowstorm.

Ice Storms

Some winter storms will bring ice instead of snow—or ice before, or ice after, or ice mixed with snow. Ice storms present risks and dangers all their own.

Precipitation begins as snow high aloft but melts into rain while falling through warmer air. If it travels through another layer of freezing cold air, the precipitation refreezes and comes down as sleet: tiny pellets that bounce and accumulate. If instead it travels through a narrow band of cold air right above the ground, it falls as rain that freezes on contact. In many ways, this freezing rain is slicker, harder to recognize, and more treacherous than sleet.

Sleet and freezing rain can fall together. And the same winter storm can bring snow, sleet, freezing rain, and ordinary rain as it travels and evolves, depending on changes in atmospheric and ground temperatures. The most devastating storms can result in an inch of accumulated ice on road surfaces, a very dangerous driving situation best avoided if at all possible.

Whiteouts

Whiteouts occur when visibility lowers to zero, or near zero, and the horizon line becomes indistinguishable. Overcast cloud cover appears to merge with the surface of snow, creating uniform whiteness; contrast largely disappears.

A whiteout can take four nominal forms:
→ During a blizzard, ground snow stirs and produces the light effect.
→ During heavy snowfall, the sheer volume of snow obscures visibility.
→ During complete snow cover on the ground, light is near totally reflected.

U.S. SEARCH AND RESCUE TASK FORCE
BEST PRACTICES KEEP AN EYE ON HEALTH

Stay hydrated. Watch for signs of hypothermia: uncontrollable shivering, memory loss, disorientation, incoherence, slurred speech, drowsiness, and apparent exhaustion. Also, watch for signs of frostbite: loss of feeling and white or pale appearance in your extremities. Get medical help immediately if any of these symptoms is detected.

Cars navigate
a snowy road.
Whiteouts can
lower visibility.

EXTREME WEATHER BASICS
Inside Blizzards

When cold waves arrive with little snow and light winds, few events are canceled, few routines disrupted.

But when the cold and snow arrive in combination with an extratropical cyclone—a large storm system that forms over cold air or cold water, far away from the tropics, with winds more than 35 miles an hour—a blizzard forms, and wintry weather becomes disruptive and potentially life-threatening. Such a storm draws in very cold, dry air, and also humid air that not only supplies more raw material (water vapor) for snow but also increases the chances of freezing rain and sleet as well as ordinary—but cold—rain. Blizzards often feature intense bands of heavy snow that move across a region. These can be 10 to 50 miles wide and dump three inches of snow or more each hour.

FORECASTING BLIZZARDS

Meteorological computer models have become quite good at giving an alert that a blizzard is possible almost a week ahead of time, which is a signal that you should begin preparing for the storm, but you shouldn't change plans for an event or trip yet; just be ready to do this a day or two before the storm arrives.

This is especially true along the U.S. East Coast where many winter storms that are blizzards inland bring only windy rain closer to the coast. Forecasting the location of the rain-snow line is tricky and sometimes cannot be done until the blizzard is arriving. An upgrade of all NWS radars completed in April 2013 gives forecasters a better picture of what's happening inside blizzards, which helps them forecast for the next few hours of a storm.

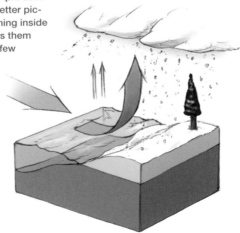

Lake-effect blizzards occur when bitter cold air flows over warmer water, causing heavy snow when air meets land.

Snow blankets a bus station in Finland. Apps can inform you about travel schedules.

→ During ground-level fog when there is snow, visibility is impaired.

Whiteouts pose a number of threats, especially to drivers and airplane pilots who lose a sense of perspective. Pedestrians, too, are at risk; people have reportedly gotten lost in their own front yards.

Thundersnow

When thunder and lighting occur during a snowstorm, we get thundersnow. This weather phenomenon usually happens in late winter or early spring, because that's when the specific components required for thundersnow—a mass of cold air on top of warm air, plus moist air closer to the ground—come together.

But as entertaining as it may sound—it's thunder, it's snow, it's thundersnow!—it has the potential to be quite dangerous if you're outside when it happens. It can bring lightning strikes and ice pellets larger than hail; and thundersnow can turn into a circular and prolonged storm when the conditions are aligned, resulting in long spates of lightning. Thundersnow can also signal

Remember that dogs can lose their scent during a storm.

a heavy snowfall. One study found that when lightning strikes during a snowstorm, there is a likely chance that at least six inches of snow will fall.

Caught in a Blizzard

Your best safety plan is to stay inside during a blizzard, but if you must drive, keep these important safety rules in mind:
→ Travel in daylight.
→ Don't travel alone.
→ Use main roads and avoid back road shortcuts.
→ Let someone know your planned route, destination, and expected time of arrival.

→ Clear off all snow and ice from windows, lights, hood, and roof before driving.
→ Keep your headlights on.
→ Leave room for stopping between you and other vehicles.
→ Brake early and carefully, not abruptly.
→ Keep alert and look farther out than usual in all directions.

If you have to stop your vehicle and stay in it en route, here are pointers on how to keep safe:
→ Stay in your vehicle.
→ Turn off your engine. Snow and drifts can clog the tailpipe, causing carbon monoxide poisoning. If you must use your

heater, be sure the tailpipe is clear. Run your engine for no more than ten minutes at a time.

→ Tie a colorful piece of fabric to your antenna or door handle to signal rescue crews.

→ Loosen your clothing, move around, rub your hands together, and rub your feet occasionally.

There's an App for That

A cell phone is so helpful in emergency weather situations, because you can call 911 for help or use it to determine your exact location. Available from iTunes and/or Google Play, the following apps can make your smartphone even more helpful during blizzards and heavy snow conditions:

→ The **Dark Sky** app taps into radar data to predict rainfall and snow for your exact location by the hour.

→ The **Winter Survival Kit** app has some safety features in case you get caught in your car. It can send your location to emergency services, calculate how long you can run your engine before running out of gas, and alert you every 30 minutes to remind you to turn off your engine and check your exhaust pipe for snow buildup.

→ The **Winter Storm Warnings** app provides winter storm news updates, forecasts, facts, and coverage, and shows you what impending winter weather may be headed for your location. ■

Did You Know?
↘ DRESS FOR THE COLD

It's best not to drive when a winter storm threatens, but if you must, be sure to dress for survival in case you're caught in your car. Dress to be outdoors, maybe even to walk to safety if your vehicle becomes stuck in snow. Wear long underwear, a parka instead of a dressy topcoat, boots and thick socks instead of dress shoes, and a stocking cap. A ski mask is a good idea in really cold weather.

Scarves and hats protect your face and head.

FIRST PERSON: Mike O'Brien, former city manager,
Worcester, Massachusetts

Preparing for a Brave New Blizzard

A resident pushes his snowblower through deep snow in Massachusetts.

GUT INSTINCT. That's what Mike O'Brien, former city manager of Worcester, Massachusetts—one of the snowiest cities in the United States—says is key to blizzard safety and readiness. He's been a city employee for more than 20 years and relies on his own understanding of the local climate as well as that of other veterans of storms in the Northeast.

In February 2013, when a gargantuan storm covered Worcester in 28 inches of snow, the city was ready. Planning meetings began almost a week in advance of the storm. The Department of Public Works—along with police, fire, emergency management, and utilities—all participated, assessing what vehicles were available and what resources were needed. Worcester spends about $5 million annually on snow removal alone. The city's average snowfall is 68 inches a year, and in the winter of 2012–13, it saw 109 inches.

Worcester is known as the

"city of seven hills," and because of its high terrain, equipment has to be deployed early to high ground. "You don't want to plow uphill," O'Brien notes. At the same time, schools, large employers, and city employees have to be notified of closures. Congestion is a concern. Storm planning is very different for a Wednesday afternoon than a Saturday morning, says Worcester's emergency communications director, David Clemons. To that end, the city works with businesses to stagger closures. Traffic gridlock means sanders, salters, and plows cannot do their job.

Once the storm hits and the roads are being cleared and people are for the most part indoors, the next big wave of consideration arises: electricity. "Whether we want to believe it or not, our entire society is based on the supply of electricity," O'Brien says. A day or two without power is manageable, but more than that and serious concerns kick in; shelters are warranted.

During the 2013 storm, for example, the Red Cross announced it would not be opening shelters in the Worcester area out of safety concerns for its staff. The National Guard had to be called in to help plow the roads, and their Humvees were used as ambulances. A baby was born in one.

Roads cleared, electricity restored, constant messaging of conditions sent through the local and social media, and safety concerns largely abated, the hardest part comes next, according to O'Brien: when to say the storm has passed. "You don't want to make the call, and then see another snow cover," he says.

Compounding this dilemma is the change in weather patterns. "There's no question in my mind: The severity, the frequency, the volumes of precipitation that we are seeing have changed—so much so, we have looked out ahead from an infrastructure standpoint on how we can prepare for the brave new world."

> "The severity, the frequency, the volumes of precipitation that we are seeing have changed."

A dump truck spreads salt and sand.

EXPERT WITNESS: Paul Kocin

Knockout Blizzards on the Rise

Snow strands cars
on Chicago's Lake
Shore Drive during
a 2011 blizzard.

Paul Kocin, *an analyst for the National Weather Service and co-author of* Northeast Snowstorms

→ What causes a blizzard?

Well, "blizzard" is a sort of made-up word for severe snow-storms with heavy falling snow, reduced visibility, very strong winds, and, in some definitions, low temperatures. All of those combined indicate a potential for more life-threatening conditions than heavy snow by itself.

→ Can you describe the atmospheric forces that cause those knockout blizzards that hit every five or ten years?

In the United States, it's usually when we get really strong dips in the jet stream, in combination with some source of unusually cold air. The Chicago blizzard in 2011 was a combination of heavy snows—up to 10 to 30 inches—and winds of 70 miles an hour or more.

→ Was that the storm where so many cars and trucks were stranded on interstates?

Yes, it was a bad one, extremely widespread, in places that really hadn't seen much snow, from Oklahoma to Missouri and Illinois into Michigan, with winds that were gusting near hurricane force. A widespread whiteout. Chicago really got blasted.

→ Has there been an increase in severe snowstorms during the past few decades?

There is some indication that they may be increasing. Some of my research has shown that storms are trending a little larger, with heavier snow. It's not a real strong relationship yet, but it's sort of adding up.

→ So it's a question of storms getting bigger and stronger, rather than more of them?

Correct. In some cases, there may be fewer blizzards as the atmosphere is getting warmer, depending on where you are—especially in areas where you don't get many storms in the first place, like Washington, D.C.

→ We've had some weird winters lately. One year we'll be buried in snow and another year winter never really shows up. Does it seem like there's been more variability in winter weather?

There may be more variability as well. It seems that way, but again the statistics don't necessarily show that. There has been a trend in some of the larger cities of the Northeast where snowfall seems to be diminishing over the past few decades as the climate has been getting a little warmer. But this is offset by the fact that we've had a few bigger storms, so the average snowfall might actually increase. That's happened in New York, where for most of the winter they might get absolutely nothing, but when they do get a storm, it's been huge. In Washington in 2009–10, we had three winter storms that were about as big as they could possibly be.

→ Europe's been hammered recently by heavy winters. But we've also seen headlines about the past decade being the warmest on record. Does that seem crazy?

Sometimes, even though the planet is warming overall, some areas will see unusual weather patterns that might even look like the opposite is occurring, such as heavier snow.

School can sometimes be closed for days.

HOW TO: **PREPARE**

→ **WHAT TO DO**

Indoors

- ✓ During winter months, keep up to date on coming weather.

- ✓ Be sure you have working flashlights and backup batteries.

- ✓ Know how to find weather information on the radio, and have a battery-powered or hand-crank radio on hand.

- ✓ Plan ahead for backup power and heat in case electricity is disconnected in a storm.

- ✓ Keep at least three days of food, water (a gallon/day/person), and medications on hand all winter long.

- ✓ Tighten up weather stripping, and caulk leaks around windows, doors, and vent openings throughout your house or apartment.

- ✓ Be sure you have a manual backup for your can opener, toothbrush, or any other kitchen or bathroom tool you usually power with electricity.

- ✓ Store extra blankets and several layers of warm clothing for each family member in a designated closet in case the power goes out at night.

Outdoors

- ✓ Check older roofs that may have been underbuilt or may have weakened over time, and consider repair or renovation to withstand heavy snow accumulation.

- ✓ Look for signs or problems typical of older roofs: reroofing (three or more layers of shingles) or insulation installed without proper ventilation.

- ✓ Build with metal roofs. They shed snow more easily than shingled roofs.

- ✓ Pitch your roof to reflect snow risk in your area. Snow won't slide off a flat roof.

- ✓ Turn off the water to your outside hoses. Snow, ice, and freezing cold can split them.

- ✓ Winterize your car. Check antifreeze level. Be sure the battery is strong and the battery terminals are clean. Switch to lighterweight oil for cold weather. Check the windshield wipers and top off windshield fluid. Be sure your tires are roadworthy for the sort of winter driving your area will require.

Melting the ice
with blue ice
melt, or salt

→ WHAT *NOT* TO DO

Indoors

✗ Do not store fire extinguishers near heat sources.

✗ Do not let your pipes freeze. When extremely cold temperatures are expected, leave taps open slightly so they drip. Keep indoor temperatures warm. Open kitchen cabinet doors beneath the sink.

✗ Do not your cell phone charge drop too low. There may come a time when you cannot charge it at the wall for a while.

Outdoors

✗ Do not leave tree limbs unpruned if they could fall on your house, your car, or your power lines.

✗ Do not let your car's gas tank go under half full. Keep your car fueled up as a rule, so you don't get caught at home needing to fill up during a blizzard.

✗ Do not ignore warnings when you hear them. Remember that a Winter Storm Watch means storm conditions are predicted within the next two to three days, while a Winter Storm Warning or Blizzard Warning means storm conditions have been observed and are imminent.

HOW TO: **SURVIVE**

→ **WHAT TO DO**

Indoors

- ☑ Conserve fuel. Consider turning down or turning off the heat in little-used rooms.

- ☑ If your water pipes freeze, remove their insulation and wrap the pipes in rags. After you open all the faucets in your house, pour hot water over the rags and pipes.

- ☑ When you are using portable heaters such as those that use kerosene, ensure there is adequate ventilation to avoid any buildup of toxic fumes.

- ☑ When you refuel kerosene heaters, make sure that you are outside and at least three feet from flammable objects.

- ☑ Set your home temperature to no lower than 55°F if you decide to leave your home. This will keep pipes from freezing.

Outdoors

- ☑ Walk carefully on snowy, icy walkways.

- ☑ If you are caught on foot during a whiteout or blizzard and cannot find your way indoors, staying put should be your first directive.

- ☑ When caught in a storm, toss an object such as a dirty and darker-colored snowball, a piece of clothing, or a dark or brightly colored item ahead of you to determine if the terrain is safe, and then walk to it.

- ☑ If you are driving, stay alert and reduce distractions such as changing the radio channel or drinking a beverage.

- ☑ To take a driving break, exit the roadway. Stopping on a side shoulder can be dangerous.

- ☑ If forced to pull off the road, put on your hazard lights, but conserve the car's battery by turning the lights off periodically.

- ☑ Start your engine and let it run with the heater on for ten minutes every hour. Charge your phone during that period as well.

- ☑ Before you turn on the engine, make sure the exhaust pipe is clear of snow and debris.

- ☑ Open one window a crack when the engine is running.

- ☑ At night, turn the inside light on so rescuers can see you.

- ☑ Take turns staying awake if you are with others, and huddle for warmth.

- ☑ Move your body as much as you can to maintain body heat.

If you have to be out, stay on main roads during a storm.

→ WHAT *NOT* TO DO

Indoors

☒ It may seem obvious, but do not go outdoors and explore during a blizzard. Stay indoors.

☒ Do not use a generator, camp stove, or other gas- or charcoal-burning heating device inside. Carbon monoxide from these sources can be deadly. Even using them in an attached garage area can be harmful as toxic fumes can find their way inside.

Outdoors

☒ If you must travel, do so during the daytime and stay on main roads. Avoid back road short-cuts. Public forms of transportation may be safer options.

☒ Do not slam on your brakes. Slow down to a stop instead.

☒ Do not change lanes or try to pass other drivers.

☒ Do not keep your engine running with the windows closed; carbon monoxide poisoning can result.

☒ If you are caught in a snowstorm while out walking, don't continue forward. Rather, retrace your steps.

☒ Do not leave pets outside, even if they usually sleep outside.

HOW TO: **RECOVER**

→ **WHAT TO DO**

Indoors

☑ Stay on the alert for coming weather.

☑ Stretch and hydrate thoroughly before heading out to shovel snow.

☑ Use a broom or brush to remove loose snow from your car to begin with.

☑ Check windows and doors for any breaks in seals. Use weather-stripping to reseal them.

☑ Check pipes for any leaks created by freezing. Repair or replace them.

☑ Be aware of the direction snow and ice will take as they melt. Icicles sometimes fall off in one piece.

☑ If you find yourself without power or heat, consider moving temporarily to a designated public shelter. To find the nearest one, text SHELTER followed by your zip code (for example, *shelter 12345*) to 43362 (4FEMA). Infants and elderly family members will be much more susceptible to cold than youths and adults.

☑ As you are able, be in touch with others nearby who have elderly or very young family members who may need more help than you do.

☑ If you are lighting a fire in the fireplace for the first time after a blizzard, pay close attention to how the smoke travels, to be sure the chimney has not been damaged or clogged with snow or ice.

Outdoors

☑ Shovel walkways and driveways as soon as possible to expose the ground and capture sunlight. The warmth will melt remaining snow and keep ice from forming.

☑ Use salt and sand to melt snow and ice.

☑ Sprinkle sand or nonclumping cat litter to create traction on surfaces still covered with snow or ice.

☑ Watch out for downed power lines, and call your local electric company if you spot one.

☑ Use a match or lighter to heat your car key in case you find the lock frozen.

☑ Dress appropriately for any work outside. If you drive anywhere, be sure to have the right gear in case road conditions force you to stay in your car or walk somewhere.

Try to clear the snow as soon as possible.

→ WHAT *NOT* TO DO

Indoors

✗ Do not use a diesel- or gas-powered generator indoors.

✗ Do not use a kerosene-burning heater without first opening a window for ventilation.

✗ Do not stop worrying about staying warm, even if your heat is working. Keep wearing layers of clothing for best warmth.

Outdoors

✗ Do not mistake black ice for pavement. Black ice is a thin, almost transparent layer of ice that can cause numerous hazards and accidents. Bridges and overpasses are particularly susceptible to black ice forming because air circulates both above and below the roadway's surface.

✗ Do not drive with snow still piled on the hood or roof of your car.

✗ Do not overexert when shoveling snow. Overexertion can cause a heart attack and is a major cause of death in the winter.

✗ Do not use warm water to thaw snow or ice on your windshield. It could cause it to crack.

✗ Do not overapply de-icing compounds as these can corrode your driveway and walkways.

A person walks near utility poles during a blizzard whiteout.

EXTREMES
SNOWFALL AMOUNTS

· The Groundhog Day blizzard of 2011 was one of the worst snowstorms to hit the United States. Record snow amounts fell in Boston and Baltimore—27.5 inches and 28.2 inches, respectively.

· The most amount of snowfall officially recorded was in 1921 in Silver Lake, Colorado, when 75.8 inches of snow accumulated in 24 hours.

· A blizzard in December 2013 pushed sea ice around a passenger ship headed for Antarctica and froze it in place, stranding 52 passengers for more than a week.

DOING YOUR PART

The most important message you can take from this book involves three actions: Prepare. Survive. Recover. Each of these actions leads to the next. In fact, the most effective way to express their interaction would be: Prepare = Survive = Recover. Understanding underscores it all.

Being prepared for extreme weather needs to be as second nature as making sure that your children get annual physical exams or your business has liability insurance. The cost of not being prepared is rising. As Hurricane Sandy showed, an unexpected monster storm can disrupt travel, interrupt trade, flatten communities, and flood even the wealthiest cities. By 2025, experts predict the economic risks to the global economy from severe storms, floods, droughts, and other weather hazards linked to climate change could climb by 50 percent.

Climate change isn't the only thing at work here. Many of the forces that shape weather disasters are natural and often unpredictable. But the long-term trend is clear: As our atmosphere and oceans continue to warm, the tragic weather events that follow are likely to increase.

For that reason, it makes sense to take steps now to mitigate the impacts of both. Small steps by individuals may not seem like strong preventative measures. But en masse, small steps can produce big change. If every home in the United States switched out five traditional incandescent lightbulbs for more energy-efficient compact fluorescent types, more than one trillion pounds of greenhouse gases could be kept out of the atmosphere. Greenhouse gases can affect the weather in all sorts of ways. Most notably, an increase in greenhouse gas emissions helps to boost warmer temperatures; pull back on greenhouse gases, and we might make a difference for generations to come.

The primary mission of this book is to relay tactical information that can be put to use on the spot during a storm or other extreme weather event. But it's equally important to suggest actions that could address the macro-environment and the longer-term effects produced by climate change. Here's a short list of simple activities you can do to take action:

→ **Pledge to prepare.** By joining the National Preparedness Community *(community.fema.gov),* you can connect with others, collaborate on best practices to prepare for storms, and share experiences. There is no cost to join the community and take the pledge, and you get access to exclusive resources, workshops, meetings, and receive updates from emergency management professionals. For those who want to become more active and engaged in storm preparedness, there is even a tool kit you can download that includes newsletter articles, blog posts, posters, and other educational materials to assist in community outreach efforts. Teaching others how to stay safe can often mean a safer environment for you, too.

→ **Strengthen your home.** Where you live and build your home is just as important as how you affect the environment by the things you do. Good siting and

A man uses snowshoes to navigate Milwaukee streets in February 2011.

strong building practices can influence not only tornado damage to you but also to others. If you are in a tornado zone, take steps to build or reinforce your house so it can better withstand a tornado's force. The extra protection can provide more safety for you and your family, as well as lessen the chance that flying debris from your yard will hurt neighbors.

→ **Buy local foods and products.** A major source of land degradation is large farming operations. Industrial-scale farms often practice monoculture, which deprives soil of nutrients and makes it more susceptible to flooding. Large farms use synthetic fertilizers and pesticides that when washed downstream can contaminate waterways and coastal ecosystems, and in turn, riverbanks. That exacerbates floods because the soil that strengthens natural levees becomes degraded and water is more easily washed over banks. We lose approximately one percent of our topsoil every year due to erosion, and farming is a major factor in this erosion. In fact, nearly half of all the soil we use for agriculture has been degraded.

→ **Recycle and compost.** Consider making a compost pile from organic matter such as cut grass and dead leaves, as well as certain food leftovers. In addition, recycle glass, plastic, tin, and metals, and any other solid materials.

→ **Turn off the lights when not in use.** The burning of fossil fuels to create electricity is the biggest source of our global contribution to greenhouse gases. Burning fossil fuels puts carbon dioxide in the atmosphere. Carbon dioxide, one of the main ingredients for increasing temperatures, naturally exists. In fact, carbon dioxide is constantly being exchanged in huge amounts between plants, oceans, soil, and other elements. So why not flip off a switch?

→ **Try not to leave your car idling.** Letting your car idle may seem like a convenient way to stay warm when it's cold, or cool when it's hot, but the extra fuel and exhaust you waste aren't worth the expense—both in economic and environmental terms. Moreover, you are more likely to breathe harmful emissions when your car is idling than when it's moving. Modern engines do not need to "warm up" before you drive. For older models and/or if you live in a cold climate, consider engine block heaters. There are even interior "car warmers" available online or at most auto parts stores.

→ **Stay on marked paths when you tour or hike.** Also, consider not going four-wheeling or riding ATVs in the desert. When you go off trail, delicate habitats and vegetation can be destroyed. This weakens soil and makes particles on the ground more susceptible to being swept up by the wind. Moreover, *Coccidioides immitis,* a pathogenic fungus, can accompany the airborne debris and spread valley fever, resulting in respiratory and even nervous system complications.

→ **Unplug your appliances** that use standby power—that is, electric power consumed by appliances while they are switched off, or in standby mode. This not only saves electricity demand during peak hours, but it also helps prevent power surges after a blackout, many of which occur during heat waves.

To be sure, these are just a few of the many steps you can take to make the world we live in a better and safer place. Too often we shrug off environmental friendliness. We ignore the science of climate change. We refute the logic that links climate and weather. Natural elements may produce weather events, but we can tip the balance. So by mitigating our role in the bigger picture of climate change, we can help thwart the worsening effect of weather on our lives.

And it's important to prepare now. Haiyan, which hit Southeast Asia in 2013, was one of the most powerful typhoons ever recorded. Sandy, which hit the Atlantic coast of the United States in 2012, was one of the most expensive ever. In recent years, severe tornadoes, floods, wildfires, and blizzards have rocked the world.

Thousands of people are killed every year because of weather and weather-related events. And although this book goes a long way toward prevention, it is only a step in the direction of safety and preparedness.

The month of September has been designated national preparedness month in the United States. This is a good time to take stock and make notes on what to do to prepare for the extreme weather Mother Nature continues to throw our way. September is but a reminder, however. Every day should be a preparedness day. And if you haven't begun to prepare yet, today is a good day to start.

RESOURCES AND ORGANIZATIONS

This book collects information and advice from a number of organizations, national and international, from which readers can find further insight by visiting their websites.

American Red Cross

A humanitarian organization that provides emergency assistance, disaster relief, and education in the United States.
www.redcross.org

American Society of Prevention of Cruelty to Animals (ASPCA)

A nonprofit organization dedicated to preventing cruelty towards animals by providing education, shelter, and other resources for animals and pet-owners.
www.aspca.org

Centers for Disease Control and Prevention (CDC)

The national public health institute of the United States, the CDC aims to protect public health and safety through control and prevention of disease, injury, and disability. The CDC focuses its efforts on education about infectious disease, environmental health, and health promotion.
www.cdc.gov

Environmental Protection Agency (EPA)

An agency of the U.S. federal government created for the purpose of protecting human health and the environment. The EPA conducts environmental assessment, research,

and education along with maintaining environmental standards.
www.epa.gov

Federal Emergency Management Agency (FEMA)

As part of the U.S. Department of Homeland Security, FEMA's primary purpose is to coordinate disaster recovery efforts within the United States.
www.fema.gov

Insurance Institute for Business & Home Safety (IBHS)

A U.S. organization that helps make buildings more resistant to hurricane damage by using scientific research to create resilient buildings and disaster safety plans.
www.disastersafety.org

Intergovernmental Panel on Climate Change (IPCC)

A scientific body established by members of the United Nations and the international authority on climate change.
www.ipcc.ch

National Interagency Fire Center (NIFC)

An arm of the National Fire and Aviation Executive Board, the NIFC coordinates wildland firefighting resources along with support in

response to floods, hurricanes, and earthquakes.
www.nifc.gov

National Aeronautics and Space Administration (NASA)

An agency of the U.S. government responsible for aeronautics, aerospace research, the space program, and better understanding Earth through satellite monitoring and other programs.
www.nasa.gov

National Climatic Data Center (NCDC)

Managed by the National Oceanic and Atmospheric Administration, the NCDC is the world's largest active archive of weather data.
www.ncdc.noaa.gov

National Drought Mitigation Center (NDMC)

Established in 1995 at the University of Nebraska-Lincoln, the NDMC helps people and institutions develop and implement measure to reduce vulnerability to drought by stressing preparedness and risk management.
www.drought.unl.edu

National Drought Policy Commission (NDPC)

Created in 1998 to conduct a study of current federal, state, local and tribal drought preparedness, and review laws and programs to determine if deficiencies exist in current relief policies and resources.
govinfo.library.unt.edu/drought/

National Oceanic and Atmospheric Association (NOAA)

A scientific agency within the U.S. Department of Commerce, NOAA studies and monitors the conditions of the ocean and atmosphere. They provide daily weather forecasts, severe storm warnings and climate monitoring services.
www.noaa.gov

National Storm Damage Center

The National Storm Damage Center is a consumer advocacy organization that assists homeowners before and after violent storms. The NSDC offers free information and technology to monitor and protect your home.
stormdamagecenter.org

National Weather Service (NWS)

As a part of NOAA, the NWS provides forecasts, public warnings, and general information about weather patterns in the United States.
www.weather.gov

National Wildlife Federation (NWF)

The largest private, nonprofit conservation organization in the United States, the NWF seeks to find balanced, commonsense solutions to environmental issues and to educate Americans about wildlife protection.
www.nwf.org

U.S. Army Corps of Engineers (USACE)

One of the world's largest public engineering, design, and construction management agencies, the USACE builds dams, canals, and flood protection services along with hydropower and outdoor recreation opportunities.
www.usace.army.mil

U.S. Department of Agriculture (USDA)

The government department responsible for developing and executing federal policy on farming, agriculture, forestry, and food.
www.usda.gov

EMERGENCY WEBSITES

Keep these websites bookmarked on your computer for easy access in an emergency.

Stay Ready

An informative site designed by FEMA to educate and empower Americans to prepare for and respond to emergencies including natural and man-made disasters. Available in Spanish and English.
www.ready.gov

Regional Extreme Weather Information Sheets

For states and regions most vulnerable to hurricanes—East Coast, Gulf Coast, and Hawaii—phone numbers and websites are updated annually.
www.ncddc.noaa.gov/activities/weather-ready-nation/newis/

Responding to Natural Disasters

Fourteen types of disasters are described, including dangers and how to face them, based on the experience of FEMA officials.
www.ready.gov/natural-disasters

Finding Shelter During Disaster

Maps out Red Cross shelters within your vicinity, updated every 30 minutes in response to urgent local needs.
www.redcross.org/find-help/shelter

Safe and Well Message Board

The Red Cross operates a website designed as a central communication method for people during disaster to communicate with loved ones. You must register ahead to use it. It operates 24 hours a day, 365 days a year, in English and Spanish.
www.redcross.org/find-help/contact-family/register-safe-listing

ABOUT THE CONTRIBUTORS

Eric Williams

Thomas M. Kostigen is a *New York Times* best-selling author who has written numerous books on the environment, including the National Geographic children's book *Extreme Weather*. His journalism is regularly featured in publications worldwide, and he appears frequently as a public speaker, as well as television host and guest expert.

Peter Miller is a contributing writer for *National Geographic* magazine and author of *The Smart Swarm: How to Work Efficiently, Communicate Effectively, and Make Better Decisions Using the Secrets of Flocks, Schools, and Colonies*. He specializes in science and adventure topics, and was formerly a senior editor on the magazine staff.

Melissa Breyer is a writer and editor specializing in science, health, and culture. She is the co-author of National Geographic's *True Food: 8 Simple Steps a Healthier You* and

Build Your Running Body. Her work appears across the web, as well as in magazines and newspapers, including the *New York Times*.

Jared Travnicek, a scientific and medical illustrator, received his M.A. in biological and medical illustration from the Johns Hopkins University School of Medicine in Baltimore. Travnicek is a certified medical illustrator and professional member of the Association of Medical Illustrators. His illustrations are featured in the *National Geographic Illustrated Guide to Nature*.

Darlene Shields

Jack Williams was founding editor for the *USA Today* weather page in 1982. After retiring from *USA Today* in 2005, he was director of public outreach for the American Meteorological Society until 2009. Since then, he has been a freelance writer, contributing to several books, including the *National Geographic Illustrated Guide to Nature*.

ILLUSTRATIONS CREDITS

All agency logos were supplied directly from the agency.

INDEX

Boldface indicates illustrations.

DON'T BE CAUGHT UNPREPARED!

Described by National Geographic as "one of the best traveled and fastest hikers on the planet," author Andrew Skurka shares his hard-earned knowledge in this essential guide to backpacking gear and skills.

▼

▲

With 200 color photographs and maps, and a durable, waterproof cover, this vital reference is a necessity for families, outdoor enthusiasts, and anyone who needs to know what to do in a real emergency situation.

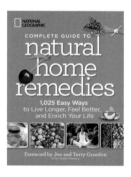

Edgy, young, authoritative, and amusingly illustrated, this title features the perfect advice to conquer any obstacle, whether it threatens life or social status or both. A great book for young teens and gift-buyers alike.

▼

▲

This book features practical cures, medicinal herbs, healing foods, green housecleaning, sustainable cosmetics, alternative therapies, and lifestyle changes.

 Like us on Facebook: Nat Geo Books
Follow us on Twitter: @NatGeoBooks

AVAILABLE WHEREVER BOOKS ARE SOLD
nationalgeographic.com/books

Extreme Weather Survival Guide

Published by the National Geographic Society
Gary E. Knell, *President and Chief Executive Officer*
John M. Fahey, *Chairman of the Board*
Declan Moore, *Executive Vice President; President, Publishing and Travel*
Melina Gerosa Bellows, *Executive Vice President; Publisher and Chief Creative Officer, Books, Kids, and Family*

Prepared by the Book Division
Hector Sierra, *Senior Vice President and General Manager*
Janet Goldstein, *Senior Vice President and Editorial Director*
Jonathan Halling, *Creative Director, Books and Children's Publishing*
Marianne Koszorus, *Design Director, Books*
Susan Tyler Hitchcock, *Senior Editor*
R. Gary Colbert, *Production Director*
Jennifer A. Thornton, *Director of Managing Editorial*
Susan S. Blair, *Director of Photography*
Meredith C. Wilcox, *Director, Administration and Rights Clearance*

Staff for This Book
Barbara Payne, *Editor*
Peter Miller, *Developmental Editor*
Michelle R. Harris, *Editorial Researcher*
Elisa Gibson, *Art Director*
Kristin Sladen, *Illustrations Editor*
Linda Makarov, Ruthie Thompson, *Designers*
Marshall Kiker, *Associate Managing Editor*
Judith Klein, *Production Editor*
Lisa A. Walker, *Production Manager*
Galen Young, *Illustrations Specialist*
Katie Olsen, *Production Design Assistant*
Michelle Cassidy, *Editorial Assistant*

Production Services
Phillip L. Schlosser, *Senior Vice President*
Chris Brown, *Vice President, NG Book Manufacturing*
Nicole Elliott, Director of Production
George Bounelis, *Senior Production Manager*
Rachel Faulise, *Manager*
Robert L. Barr, *Manager*

The National Geographic Society is one of the world's largest nonprofit scientific and educational organizations. Founded in 1888 to "increase and diffuse geographic knowledge," the member-supported Society works to inspire people to care about the planet. Through its online community, members can get closer to explorers and photographers, connect with other members around the world, and help make a difference. National Geographic reflects the world through its magazines, television programs, films, music and radio, books, DVDs, maps, exhibitions, live events, school publishing programs, interactive media, and merchandise. *National Geographic* magazine, the Society's official journal, published in English and 38 local-language editions, is read by more than 60 million people each month. The National Geographic Channel reaches 440 million households in 171 countries in 38 languages. National Geographic Digital Media receives more than 25 million visitors a month. National Geographic has funded more than 10,000 scientific research, conservation, and exploration projects and supports an education program promoting geography literacy. For more information, visit nationalgeographic.com.

For more information, please call 1-800-NGS LINE (647-5463) or write to the following address:

National Geographic Society
1145 17th Street N.W.
Washington, D.C. 20036-4688 U.S.A.

For information about special discounts for bulk purchases, please contact National Geographic Books Special Sales: ngspecsales@ngs.org

For rights or permissions inquiries, please contact National Geographic Books Subsidiary Rights: ngbookrights@ngs.org

ISBN: 978-1-4262-1376-2
ISBN: 978-1-4262-1486-8 (deluxe hardcover)
ISBN: 978-1-4262-1682-4 (special sale edition)

Library of Congress Cataloging-in-Publication Data

Kostigen, Thomas.
  National Geographic extreme weather survival guide : understand, prepare, survive, recover / by Thomas M. Kostigen.
    pages cm
  Includes bibliographical references and index.
  ISBN 978-1-4262-1376-2 (pbk. : alk. paper)
  1. Severe storms. 2. Natural disasters. 3. Weather. 4. Emergency management--Handbooks, manuals, etc. I. National Geographic Society (U.S.) II. Title. III. Title: Extreme weather survival guide.
  QC941.K67 2014
  613.6'9--dc23

                                        2014005362

Printed in Hong Kong

15/THK/1